Rapid Prototyping Technology - Principles and Functional Requirements

Rapid Prototyping Technology - Principles and Functional Requirements

Editor

Renard Nowak

scitus academics

Rapid Prototyping Technology - Principles and Functional Requirements
Edited by **Renard Nowak**

ISBN: 978-1-68117-537-9
Library of Congress Control Number: 2016942937

www.scitusacademics.com
Box No. 4766, 616 Corporate Way,
Suite 2, Valley Cottage,
NY 10989

Printed in United States of America on Acid Free Paper

Preface

Modern engineering often addresses custom design that requires fast, cost-effective and easy manufacturing. Rapid prototyping (RP) is a popular technology that allows for the easy and fast manufacture of customized computer-aided design forms/objects (CAD). The requirements for rapid product development, reduced time on the market and highly customized and low-quantity parts drive the RP technology requirements. Rapid prototyping is a set of techniques used to quickly manufacture a scale version associated with an actual part or assembly using computer-assisted three-dimensional design data. The construction of the part or possibly the assembly is often carried out using the technology "additive layer or 3D printing production." Until recently, prototypes had been built by qualified 2D engineering designers. This is a time-consuming and costly process. With the arrival of new layer production and CAD/CAM technologies, prototypes from 3D computer models can now be produced quickly.

This compendium provides up-to-date information on RP technology with an overview of principles, functional requirements, design limitations, etc. of particular technology.

Table of Contents

Chapter 1

Rapid Prototyping — A Tool for Presenting 3-Dimensional Digital Models Produced by Terrestrial Laser Scanning

Juho-Pekka Virtanen [1,*], Hannu Hyyppä [1,2,4], Matti Kurkela [1], Matti Vaaja [1], Petteri Alho [1,3] and Juha Hyyppä [1,4]

[1] School of Engineering, Aalto University, P.O. Box 15800, FI-00076 Aalto, Finland

[2] Department of Construction and Real Estate, Helsinki Metropolia University of Applied Sciences, FI-00079 Metropolia, Finland

[3] Department of Geography and Geology, University of Turku, FI-20014 Turun yliopisto, Finland

[4] Finnish Geodetic Institute, P.O. Box 15, FI-02431 Masala, Finland

ABSTRACT

Rapid prototyping has received considerable interest with the introduction of affordable rapid prototyping machines. These machines can be used to manufacture physical models from three-dimensional digital mesh models. In this paper, we compare the results obtained with a new, affordable, rapid prototyping machine, and a traditional professional machine. Two separate data sets are used for this, both of which were acquired using terrestrial laser scanning. Both of the machines were able to produce complex and highly detailed geometries in plastic material from models based on terrestrial laser scanning. The dimensional accuracies and detail levels of the machines were comparable, and the physical artifacts caused by the fused deposition modeling (FDM) technique used in the rapid prototyping machines could be found in both models. The accuracy of terrestrial laser scanning exceeded the requirements for manufacturing physical models of large statues and building segments at a 1:40 scale.

KEYWORDS

rapid prototyping; TLS; 3D printing; FDM; 3D modeling; terrestrial laser scanning; point cloud, laser scanner

1. INTRODUCTION

Several applications in the fields of urban planning, construction, and cultural heritage require models that are at the same time accurate, visually pleasing, and easy to study, especially if the models are used for presentation and exhibition purposes.

Rapid prototyping (RP) techniques make it possible to easily manufacture physical models based on digital 3D models, meaning that model building is no longer a time-consuming, manual process. With RP, model making becomes an interesting and accessible tool for illustration [1,2]. RP techniques can be divided into additive and subtractive techniques, even though some authors only include additive techniques in RP [3]. With additive manufacturing techniques, such as stereolithography (SLA), the model is manufactured by adding material in layers [4]. Machining techniques, like milling, are subtractive techniques: The manufactured object is made by removing material from a block with a tool [5]. RP is widely used in industrial design, usually for making physical models [3]. In engineering, RP techniques have been used, e.g., in manufacturing tooling for sheet metal forming [6]. In addition, models made with RP have been used to validate simulation results [7] and visualize data obtained from Geographic Information Systems (GIS) [8]. To utilize RP, a triangle mesh model of the object is required [9]. This mesh model has to unambiguously define the internal volume of the object, so its surface has to be free of any holes. In design applications, this is created by tessellation from a CAD model. The resulting mesh model is sliced to determine the parallel horizontal cross sections of the model [9]. Based on these cross sections, the path that the machine is using in fabrication is calculated, typically this is referred to as a toolpath.

Additive manufacturing techniques used for RP include, for example, SLA, selective laser sintering (SLS), laminated object manufacturing (LOM), 3D printing and fused deposition modeling (FDM) [4,9,10]. In SLA, a directed laser beam is used to cure photo-curable resin, manufacturing the object in layers [4,9]. In LOM, the object is made by cutting and gluing layers of sheet material [4,9]. In 3D printing, a powder material is selectively bound with glue by an inkjet, forming the object in layers [4,9]. Fused deposition modeling (FDM) is one of the most common additive manufacturing techniques used in RP. With FDM, a heated thermoplastic material is extruded and used to build the model in layers (Figure 1) (e.g., see [4,9]). One of the advantages of FDM technology is that the machines can be used in a regular office environment, unlike for example SLA machines, where hazardous resins are used [10]. A disadvantage of FDM technology is that models require support structures during the manufacturing process, which have to be removed afterwards [10], in addition it cannot be used for manufacturing objects from metal materials. Typical build layer thicknesses for FDM range from 0.05 mm to 0.25 mm, producing a surface roughness of 56.6 µm Ra to 17.9 µm Ra, depending on the angle of the surface built [10]. The dimensional accuracy of a FDM print was found to be low compared to other RP methods, resulting in average linear dimensional accuracy of 95.3 percent [10].

In recent years, there has been a major change in the market of FDM machines. There are currently several, quite affordable, FDM machines available. Many of them are based on open-source projects. This has made RP equipment more accessible than ever before. The performance of one of these affordable RP machines has been studied by Pei *et al.* [11], who refer to these machines as Entry Level Rapid Prototyping (ELRP) machines.

Typically, these machines use acrylonitrile butadiene styrene (ABS) or polylactic acid (PLA) as printing materials [12,13,14,15,16], ABS requiring a higher extrusion temperature [12]. Some of the models are capable of using two materials in the same print, to produce multi-colored models [12,13], while many only use one material at a time [14,15,16]. The build envelope of ELRP machines is dependent on the specific model, but typical values range from 100 mm by 100 mm by 125 mm [17] to 230 mm by 270 mm by 200 mm [12]. In addition to these ELRP machines being sold, there are also numerous service providers in the market offering RP as a service over the Internet (e.g., see [18,19]). When discussing RP by additive manufacturing, it has to be noted that occasionally the term "3D printing" is used to refer to all additive RP technologies. In a similar way, most RP machines are sometimes called "3D printers", even if they are based on a different technology, such as FDM.

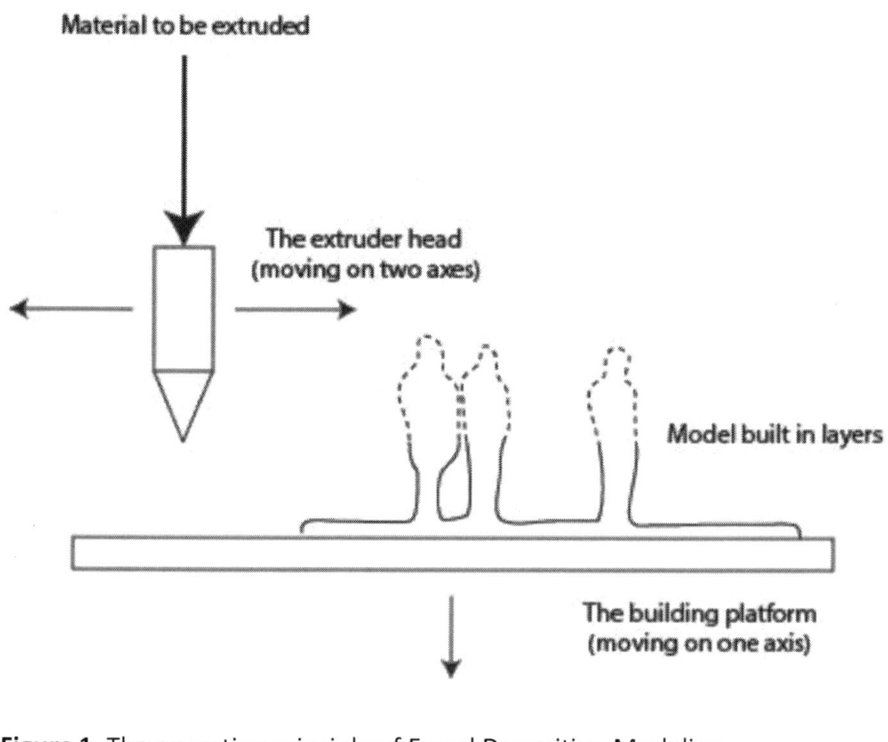

Figure 1. The operating principle of Fused Deposition Modeling.

There are several different techniques for acquiring three-dimensional virtual models of the physical environment, for example photogrammetry and laser scanning (LS). Both of these are used extensively in the field of geo-information. Other methods also exist: A digital model can be created by measuring the key points of the original using, for example, a tachymeter if the geometry is simple enough. Existing drawings or plans can also be used in modeling, if they are available.

Photogrammetry is the technology of deriving 3D data, characteristics, and attributes from 2D images. Fraser [20], and Grün *et al.* [21], for example, have studied 3D modeling based on terrestrial images. Studies related to 3D modeling based on image sequences have been done, e.g., Bethmann *et al.* [22], and Cornelis *et al.* [23].

Static terrestrial laser scanning (TLS) can produce dense point clouds (up to hundreds of thousands of pts/m^2 from a range of 10 m). A specific TLS instrument has been demonstrated to reach an accuracy of 8 mm (in 92% of tests, 4 mm) or better in ranges of 10 m to 50 m [24]. By combining several scans, a larger point cloud can be created for the target [25]. TLS makes it possible to survey built environments with great accuracy, great precision, and high spatial data intensity [26]. Studies by, for example, Arayici [26], Buckley *et al.* [27], Pu [28], and Pu and Vosselman [29], present approaches on how to use 3D modeling with TLS.

Mobile laser scanning (MLS) is an emerging technique, in which a laser scanning system is mounted on a vehicle. The vehicle might be, for example, a car or a boat and the measurements are made while the platform is moving. Global Navigation Satellite System (GNSS) and Inertia Measurement Units (IMU) are used for positioning and orienting the scanner. There have been several recent studies on MLS systems and their accuracy, as well as on environmental modeling done with MLS [30,31]. A relative accuracy of 10 mm or less has been reached with the Lynx Mobile Mapper system [32], making it possible to survey large areas with a very high detail level.

Point clouds obtained using laser scanning techniques are typically very large in size and contain up to hundreds of millions of points. Processing them requires computational resources and can also be rather time consuming [33]. Typical problems encountered when working with point clouds include gaps in the data caused by obstructions in the target and environment and varying point density in the data set (Figure 2).

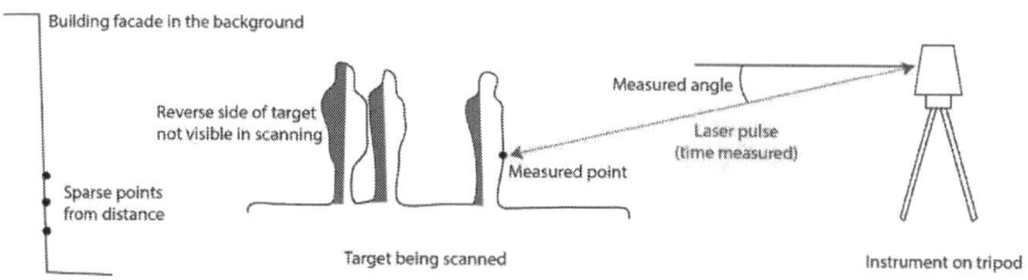

Figure 2. The operating principle of Terrestrial Laser Scanning.

By combining 3D digitizing techniques with RP, physical models of the environment and artifacts can easily be made. The use of RP techniques also has the benefit that copies of the same model can easily be made [34]. These models have been used, for example, as demonstration and reconstruction models in archaeology [4,35,36], for making replicas of objects for museum purposes or preserving original artifacts [4,37], and as tactile models that make it possible for visually impaired users to study various targets [4,34,38]. These models can be made in either real size or to scale [4]. RP techniques can also be used to produce more sophisticated presentation models. With the use of color, more data can be included in the physical models. In a similar manner, three-dimensional legends can be added to help interpret the model [39]. The physical model can also be made from other data than just the three-dimensional geometry of a physical original; this approach has been presented by Rase [8,39] for visualizing data from geo-information systems.

Mesh models created by triangulating point clouds can also be used for RP. Some editing of the models is usually required to achieve a hole-free mesh model from 3D digitizing. The editing process can include stitching the scanned surfaces together, fixing of individual triangulation errors, filling holes in surface, and possibly splitting the model to be manufactured in pieces [4,5]. This editing can be performed with the Geomagic Studio software, for example [5]. This strategy was employed by Tucci *et al.* [5] to create sculpture replicas. In their case, the mesh model generation and editing processes were performed using Geomagic Studio software. Models created with this method [5] reflect the original, 3D digitized targets quite closely, and they also include any possible surface errors, like dents, scratches, or other geometric defects from them if no additional mesh editing is performed.

ELRP machines have generated a certain amount of interest, and they increase the utilization of RP. In this study, we will test whether one of these ELRP machines based on FDM technology can be used to visualize the complex models produced by TLS. Based on the existing research, we can assume that this is possible with professional hardware [4,35,36], but not much research exists on the use of ELRP machines. Using the point clouds acquired with TLS, we will create the three-dimensional mesh models by triangulation. After this, we edit the mesh models to attain hole free models that can be used in RP. In addition, we aim to gain practical experience with using an ELRP machine. To compare the workflow and the quality of the results, we present two cases. In the first case, we utilize an older, professional-quality RP machine and in the second case we use a new ELRP machine. In both cases, TLS is used to acquire the models to be manufactured.

2. CASES

2.1. Segment of Façade from Grönqvist's Building

The façade of the Grönqvist's building, which is in the Neo-Renaissance style (Figure 3), is said to be one of the most complex façade in the city of Helsinki, Finland. We used a Leica HDS6100 terrestrial laser scanner to measure the façade. The HDS6100 is a 690 nm, phase-based, continuous-wave laser scanner with a 360° × 310° field of view. The distance measurement accuracy for it is ±2 mm at a distance of 25 m. The circular beam diameter at the exit and the beam divergence are 3 mm and 0.22 mrad, respectively. In the “High” resolution setting, the HDS6100 produces a point spacing of 6 mm on an orthogonal target at 10 m distance from the scanner. With the “Super high” setting, the corresponding spacing is 3 mm. In total, the façade was measured from four separate TLS scanning positions. Three of the measurements were done using the “High” resolution setting, and one with the “Super high” setting, producing a higher point density. All measurements were taken with the instrument mounted on a tripod, from the street level. TLS measurements were collected in the multiscan mode and the objective of the measurements was to obtain the best possible point coverage for the target. The reference targets were placed around the study area for point cloud registration. The TLS point clouds were co-registered using sphere reference targets, with the Leica Cyclone software. The resulting average overlap errors for the four scans were: 0.012 m, 0.007 m, and 0.011 m. In total, 364 million points were measured from the area. The façade was separated from the data set; it contained 46 million points.

For creating a mesh model from the point cloud Geomagic Studio 11 was used. The selected area of the façade was segmented using the combined point clouds of the façade (shown in Figure 3). The excess points were removed by manual selection, including the surface of the sidewalk along the lower edge of the façade, which was also visible during the scanning. In total, 2,119,631 points were used for the triangulation. The triangulation was performed with the ”Wrap” function, during which noise reduction was performed with the “Medium” setting. The density of the polygon mesh was reduced with the “Decimate” function. After this, the gaps remaining in the mesh were filled using the “Fill holes” tool (Figure 4). The filling was performed manually, hole by hole, using the “Curvature” type fill. This was the most laborious part of the process. Finally, the model was edited to a solid mesh model by extruding the mesh edges and adding a straight back surface to the model (Figure 3.). A similar procedure was carried out for the visible windows in the doors in the data set.

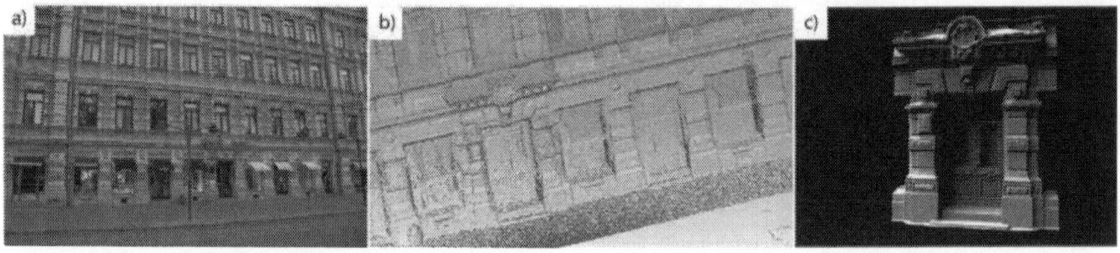

Figure 3. (**a**) The façade of the building; (**b**) the obtained point cloud; (**c**) the completed mesh model.

Figure 4. A segment of the mesh before and after decimation and filling holes.

2.2. Statue at the University of Turku Campus

The "Three Witty Men" statue was made by the sculptor Harry Kivijärvi in 1968. It is located at the University of Turku. The statue was digitized (Figure 5a) as a part of a larger survey project, which covered most of the main buildings on campus. We scanned the statue using the same instrument as in the first case. A larger number of terrestrial laser scans were taken from the area, two of which were used to model the statue (Figure 5b). They were taken with the same "High" resolution setting as in the first case. In total, they consisted of 57 million points. Three spherical reference targets were placed around the statue for point cloud registration. The point clouds were co-registered with the Z + F software, with the resulting average error being 0.012 m. The Figure 5b provides an overview of the measured area from a top projection in the vicinity of the statue.

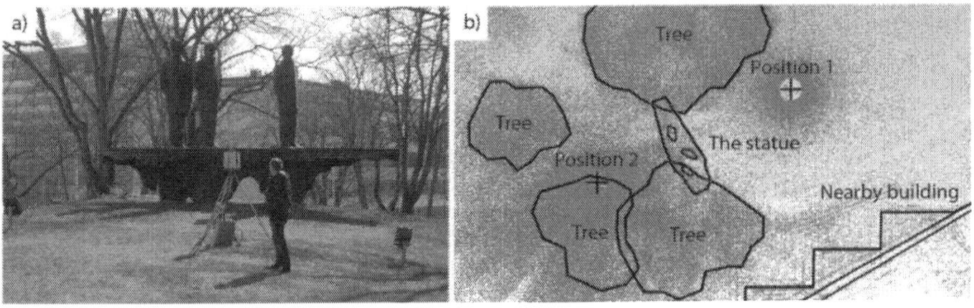

Figure 5. (**a**) Laser scanning the statue; (**b**) top view of the area showing the scanning positions.

The 3D mesh model of the statue was built from two TLS point clouds, using again Geomagic Studio 11 software. A total of 1.3 million points were used for the modeling. Points not belonging to the target were removed manually and the point clouds were filtered to remove the outlying points, using the "Select outliers" tool. After further segmentation, 1,040,824 points were used for triangulation. Noise reduction was applied during the triangulation process, as in the first case. The resulting triangle meshes were combined, and surface editing tools were used to fill holes remaining in the mesh (Figure 6). During this process, the upper surface of the pedestal of the statue had to be modeled based on the edges of the pedestal as it was not visible in the terrestrial laser scans. This was done with the "Fill holes" tool, using the "Flat" fill type and selecting the edges of the mesh in segments. The gaps in the sides of the figures also had to be filled this way, using the "Curvature" fill type of the "Fill holes" tool. This editing process was, again, the most laborious part of the process.

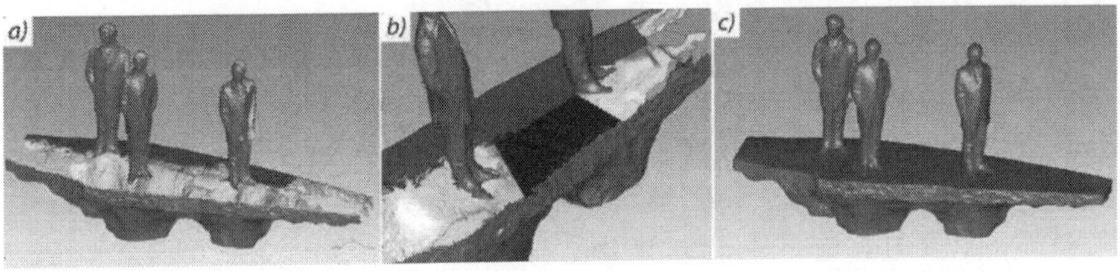

Figure 6. (**a**) The triangulated point clouds colored according to normal direction, with outside facing normals marked in blue; (**b**) Constructing a surface to the top of the pedestal. Segments of mesh edges have been selected, and the new surface to be created is marked in red; (**c**) The mesh after editing.

3. EVALUATION METHODS

Since we will discuss both our experiences with two different RP machines, and the quality of the results achieved with them, we have chosen to evaluate the original data sets, the manufacturing process, and the completed models (Figure 7).

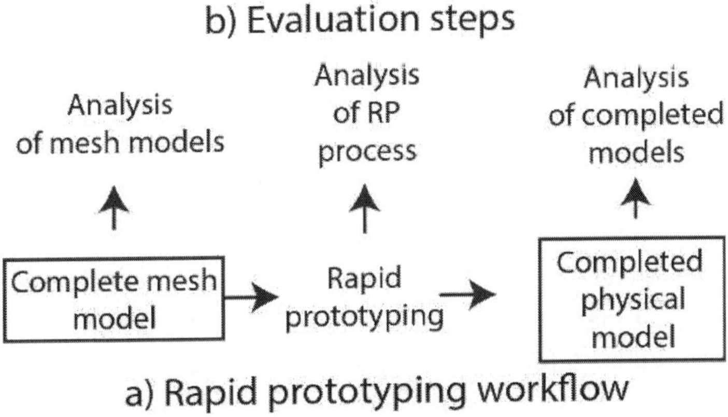

Figure 7. Workflow (**a**); and evaluation steps (**b**).

3.1. Evaluating the Mesh Models

We chose to perform a set of comparisons since we had used two different data sets. We did this to identify potential differences in the mesh models that could affect our comparison of the two machines. For the algorithmic evaluation of the complexity of the 3D mesh models, we used methods introduced by Valentan *et al.* [40]. These methods are extremely simple, and, therefore, they may not always produce accurate results [40]. We began by making an extremely simple estimation, where complexity (C_1) is described by the amount of triangle facets (n) in the model:

$$C_1 = n \tag{1}$$

For the second method, we calculated the ratio between the model volume (v) and number of triangle facets in the mesh (n):

$$C_2 = \frac{v}{n} \tag{2}$$

Third, we calculated the ratio between the volume of the model and the surface area (a) of the model:

$$C_3 = \frac{v}{a} \tag{3}$$

3.2. Evaluating the Rapid Prototyping Process

To evaluate the two different RP machines, we mapped the process steps in both cases. By identifying any possible extra steps in the manufacturing process caused by differences in the equipment, we were able to compare the usability and utility of these machines in practice. In an optimal situation, the RP should be a one-step process, where the model is made without any preliminary steps and no modification of the model is required after manufacturing. In practice, there are typically some finishing steps after RP with FDM technology, for example removing support material from the model [4].

3.3. Evaluation the Completed Models

To evaluate the visual quality of the physical models, we identified possible surface errors and other three-dimensional artifacts caused by the RP machines. These artifacts may have included visible steps, extra shapes, or gaps in the model. To document the artifacts, we used digital macro photography with a Nikon D800E DSLR camera, which had a sensor resolution of 7360 × 4912 pixels, a physical sensor size of 35.9 × 24 mm, and a macro-lens with a focal length of 105 mm and an aperture value of F 4.92 when producing a maximum reproduction ratio of 1:1. We photographed the physical models in artificial lighting, using an exposure time of 1/100 s and an aperture of F 10.0. In an optimal case, the model should be as close to the original mesh model as possible, and, therefore, it should not be possible to observe the artifacts.

To evaluate the accuracy of the models when compared to the original mesh models used for calculating the toolpaths, we 3D-digitized the models and compared the original mesh model to the scanned surface of the model made with the RP machine. We used a Konica Minolta Vivid 9i 3D laser scanner to 3D digitize the physical models. The scanner is based on laser triangulation. It projects a moving stripe of monochromatic light on the object being scanned, via a galvano mirror. The deformation of the projected stripe is captured by the devices' internal camera, having an 8.46 mm CCD sensor with 340,000 pixels. The cameras image can also be used to capture the texture of the object being scanned. Lenses of different focal lengths can be used with the devices' camera to change the size of the measured area. The accuracy of digitizing is ± 0.05 mm when using a f = 25 mm lens at a distance of 0.6 m, the measuring area being 111 mm by 83 mm. Before scanning, the device is calibrated using the field calibration system. To facilitate scanning, a rotating stage platform can be used to automatically rotate the object being scanned.

4. RESULTS

4.1. Segment of Façade from Grönqvist's Building

We manufactured the model of the façade segment out of white ABS plastic using an older, professional-quality RP machine (Table 1). We calculated the toolpaths using the manufacturer's software suite. We built the model using support structures, which were removed via an ultra-sonic cleaner afterwards. After this, the model was painted since the white color of the material made it difficult to study the surface geometry in detail.

The same mesh model was also used to manufacture the model with an Ultimaker ELRP machine from white PLA material. Netfabb Studio for Ultimaker 4.9 was used to calculate the toolpaths. The model was built with the backside down, resulting in a relief-like geometry that did not require support structures. After the manufacturing, extra threads of the plastic material, and a platform shape left by the machine were removed manually (Figure 8). No further finishing of the model was performed.

4.2. Statue at the University of Turku Campus

We made the model out of PLA plastic material using an ELRP machine (Table 1). We created toolpaths using open-source software. Since the ELRP machine being used only supported manufacturing with one material at the time, meaning that it was not possible to make dissolvable support structures, we decided to split the 3D model into two components before manufacturing. By splitting the model along the pedestal of the statue, both of the pieces were relatively relief like and possible to manufacture without support structures. Figure 9a shows the segmentation of the model. We made the upper part and the lower part of the model separately, with the lower part (in blue color) being manufactured upside down (Figure 9). After RP, both parts of the model were finished manually with a knife, removing all material not belonging to the model, such as extra threads of plastic left by the ELRP machine. Once completed, the pieces were joined with glue. No further finishing was applied to the model's surface.

Table 1. Specifications of the rapid prototyping machines used.

Case	Gröngvist's Building	Gröngvist's Building	Statue
Manufacturer	Stratasys	Ultimaker	Ultimaker
Model	Prodigy Plus	Ultimaker Kit (BETA)	Ultimaker Kit (BETA)
Build envelope size	203 × 203 × 305 mm	210 × 210 × 220 mm	210 × 210 × 220 mm
Build material used	ABS plastic	PLA plastic (white)	PLA plastic (metallic gray)
Software used to generate toolpaths	Stratasys Insight	Netfabb Studio Basic for Ultimaker 4.9	Cura 12.08
Layer thickness used in manufacturing	0.245 mm	0.150 mm	0.200 mm
Software used in mesh modeling	Geomagic Studio 11, 64 Bit Edition	Geomagic Studio 11, 64 Bit Edition	Geomagic Studio 11, 64 Bit Edition
Total amount of facets in mesh model	1,322,068	1,322,068	2,224,986

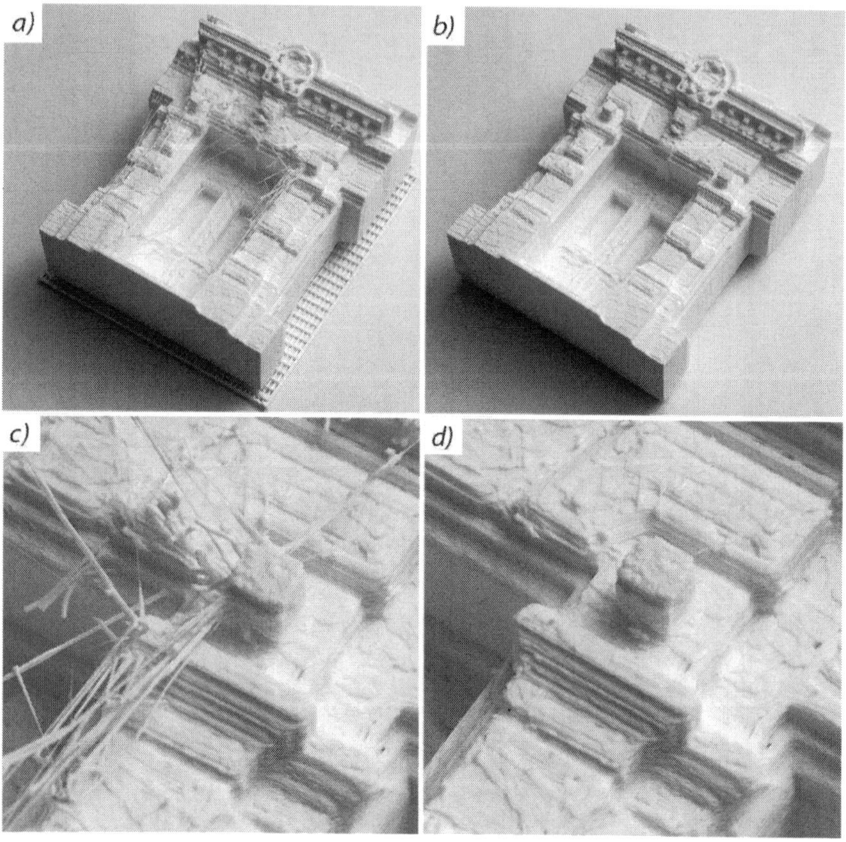

Figure 8. The model before (**a**) and after (**b**) manual cleaning, with detail images (**c**,**d**).

Figure 9. (**a**) Both parts of the completed mesh model, with the lower part shown in blue, (**b**) the top part of the model in the ELRP machine; (**c**) and the completed physical model.

4.3. Analyzing the Data Sets Used

Since both models were made to scale, we calculated the ratios mentioned in the scales at which they were made. The results (Table 2) are difficult to interpret, but not conflicting. Both the C_1 andC_2 are lower in the statue data set, indicating a higher level of complexity for both calculation methods. This reflects the shape of the models, where the façade segment is more a single body volume and the statue model consists of more separate, but connected, volumes.

The number of triangles in the mesh is independent of the scale of the model. Valentan *et al.* [40] considered a model with roughly 500,000 facets complex, where simple meshes only contained several hundred triangles. Compared to this, both of our models were extremely complex, even though they were considerably different in terms of the number of triangles. This reflects the complexity of the mesh models obtained with TLS.

Table 2. Dimensions, scales and calculated complexity indexes of the created models.

Parameter	Statue Mesh Model	Façade Segment Mesh Model
Bounding box (mm)	54 × 188 × 107	99 × 119 × 55
Scale (to real measured target)	1:40	1:40
Amount of triangles in mesh	2,224,986	1,322,068
Mesh surface area (mm^2)	30,157.2	47,762.6
Mesh volume (mm^3)	145,749.0	355,536.2
$C_2 = v/n$	0.066	0.437
$C_3 = v/a$	4.833	7.444

4.4. Analyzing the RP Process

As we studied the processes for making the physical models (Figure 10), it became apparent that the process was most complex in the case of the statue model. The steps used for data acquisition and mesh modeling were similar. In all cases, the models were edited to fill holes in the mesh. After the mesh model had been completed, the processes were different. Since we had decided to manufacture the statue model in two segments, we needed to include an extra modeling step, in which the model was segmented and solid mesh models were created from each segment. After this, we made the model in two pieces, which were finished manually and then joined. This would not have been necessary with the professional machine that supported the creation of support material removable by ultra-sonic cleaner. The differences in geometry therefore placed some restrictions on the way in which the model was manufactured when using the ELRP machine. As the geometry of the façade segment model was different, and permitted the manufacturing without support structures, it was possible to manufacture the model with the ELRP machine without segmentation. With the façade segment model manufactured with the professional machine, we decided to paint the model to achieve a better definition of shape via light and shadow in the final model.

4.5. Analyzing the Completed Models

When looking at the machine-induced artifacts, the models are quite similar. Layers, a step pattern, and over extrusion, and holes can be seen in all models (Table 3). These perhaps characterize the FDM as a technique. The lack of supporting material and the less controllable extrusion of the ELRP machine are visible as gaps in the layers, and some hanging layers are visible in the statue model (Figure 11). The gluing seam is clearly visible in the statue model because of slight warping of the models. In terms of accuracy and surface quality, the differences were not significant. A modern ELRP machine based on FDM could, in our experiments, reach the same degree of visually evaluated surface quality as an older, professional-quality machine. The smaller layer height used in the ELRP machine in these tests rendered the ELRP machines' layers less visible.

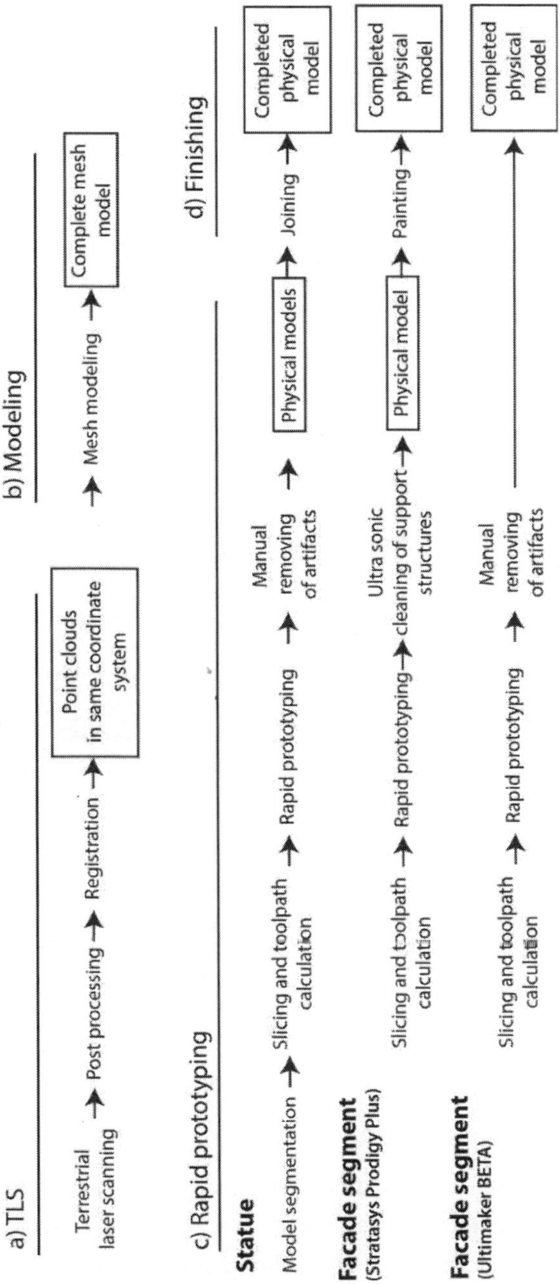

Figure 10. Comparison of rapid prototyping processes at different stages: (**a**) TLS stage; (**b**) Modeling stage; (**c**) Rapid prototyping stage; and (**d**) Finishing stage.

Table 3. Visible artifacts caused by rapid prototyping (RP) machines found in the models.

Type of Artifact	Façade Segment Model (Stratasys Prodigy Plus)	Façade Segment Model (Ultimaker BETA)	Statue Model
Visible layers	X	X	X
Step pattern	X	X	X
Hanging layers			X
Gaps in layers		X	X
Over/under extrusion	X	X	X
Seam			X

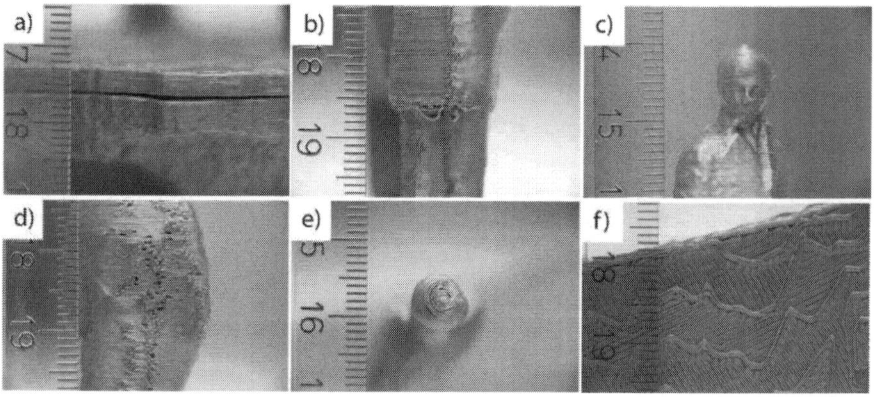

Figure 11. Different artifacts caused by RP machines: (**a**) Seam; (**b**) Hanging layers; (**c**) Visible layers; (**d**) Gaps in layers; (**e**) Over/under extrusion; (**f**) Step pattern.

To verify the dimensional accuracy of the manufactured models, we 3D digitized all models using the specified Konica-Minolta Vivid i9, non-contact digitizer. In all cases, we digitized the models in 12 segments, with the object rotated 30 degrees between scan positions around the Z-axis (height). All models were digitized using the f = 14 mm lens. The scanning was performed using the Konica Minolta Polygon Editing Tools software, which triangulates the scans directly after scanning. The individual scanned mesh surfaces were then exported in stl format. The scans were registered in Geomagic Qualify 11 software using the “Global Registration” tool. The average distances between scans were 0.11 mm with the standard deviation of 0.17 mm in the façade model case manufactured with the Stratasys Prodigy machine, 0.08 mm and 0.14 mm for the same model manufactured with the Ultimaker, and 0.12 mm and 0.25 mm for the statue model. The scans were combined with the "Merge" tool, after which the resulting mesh models were used in the deviation analysis.

The models were co-registered with the original mesh model that was used in toolpath calculation using the "Global Registration" tool. In the façade segment model manufactured with the Prodigy Plus machine, the average distance was 0.43 mm and standard deviation 0.31 mm. In the façade segment model manufactured with the Ultimaker the corresponding values were 0.25 mm and 0.26 mm. In the Statue model case, the average distance was 0.33 mm and the standard deviation 0.28 mm. The calculated 3D deviations are in Table 4.

Table 4. 3D Deviations.

Model	Statue	Façade Segment (Prodigy Plus)	Façade Segment (Ultimaker BETA)
Standard deviation	0.35 mm	0.42 mm	0.36 mm
Average deviation (+/−)	+0.19/−0.36 mm	+0.51/−0.28 mm	+0.25/−0.23 mm

Looking at the results of deviation analysis (Table 4), the standard deviation was largest in the Façade segment model manufactured with the older, professional FDM machine. The visualized results (Figure 12), and the high positive average deviation confirm this. The model is too large. This is most likely caused by the manufacturer's toolpath calculation software scaling the model slightly to make it possible to sand the FDM layer steps away without causing a considerable error in the final measurement. We did not perform this sanding, and it is visible in the results. The scattering of deviations is less even, and observed deviations are larger in the façade segment model manufactured with the ELRP machine (Figure 13). This indicates more variation in model details, caused by FDM surface errors, such as over- and under extrusion. Looking at the positive and negative average deviations, and the scattering of deviations, the scale of the model is more correct in this model, than in the one manufactured with the older professional machine.

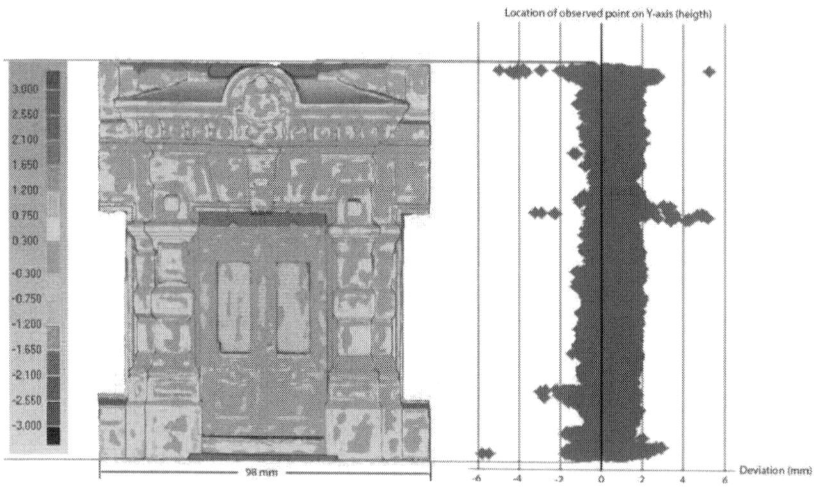

Figure 12. Deviation analysis and scatter of the Façade segment model (Stratasys Prodigy Plus).

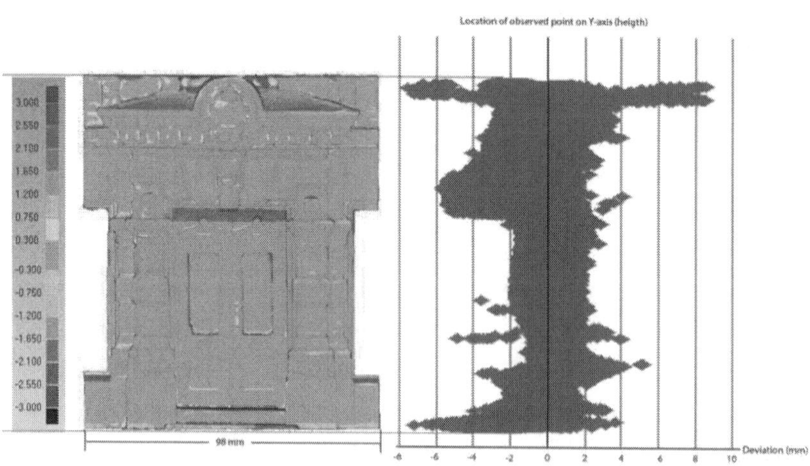

Figure 13. Deviation analysis and scatter of the Façade segment model (Ultimaker).

The deviation scatter of the statue reveals, first, a slight misalignment of the two glued components. In Figure 14, we can see how the top part of the pedestal is just a bit too much on the left. The seam is also visible. The higher deviations in the left-most figure in the statue were caused by the model being damaged during storage and transport. The figure is not completely attached to the pedestal. This can also be observed in the deviation scatter, the deviations of the figure increasing with height. The average deviations may indicate the model being slightly too small, this can also be observed in the deviation scatter.

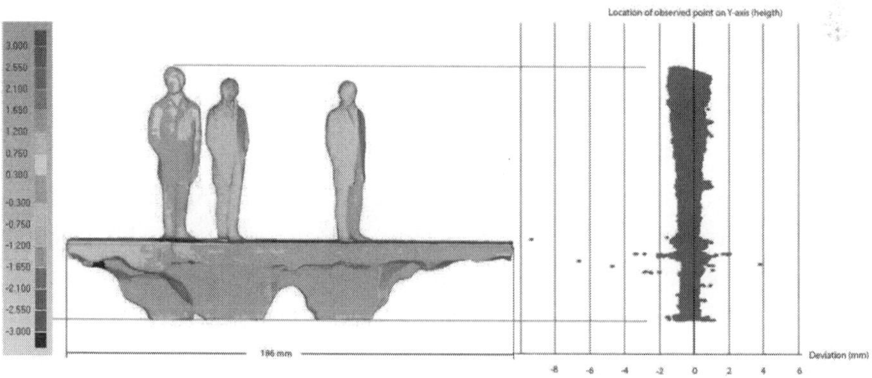

Figure 14. Deviation analysis and scatter of the Statue model.

5. DISCUSSION AND CONCLUSIONS

Recent developments in terms of the affordability of FDM machines have changed the field of RP. With the emergence of ELRP machines, RP has become more available to users than ever before. In this paper, we looked at how RP technology is currently being used, namely FDM, to manufacture physical models from three-dimensional data sets obtained with TLS.

We tested RP with two different laser-scanned data sets and two different RP machines, both based on FDM technology. A traditional, professional-quality RP machine was used in the first case. In the second case, the model was manufactured with an ELRP machine.

The data sets were different in terms of their algorithmic and perceived complexity. The complexity of the statue data set was significantly greater with all of the estimation methods used: It had a 68% higher triangle count and its complexity indexes were only 15% and 64% of the complexity indexes for the façade segment data set, indicating a higher degree of complexity.

It was possible to manufacture the models in both cases, but in the statue model case the model had to be made in two parts. This was because the ELRP machine was unable to create removable support structures for the object during the manufacturing process, and unsupported shapes could therefore not be made. The process of splitting the model of the statue before manufacturing illustrated the trade-offs that become necessary when utilizing ELRP machines. The other alternative method would have involved making manually removable support structures from the same material as the model. In this case, the professional-quality RP machine offered a higher degree of geometric freedom during manufacturing. Evaluating the manufacturability of solid mesh models is clearly dependent on the chosen RP technology and its characteristics as well as the model's geometry. The complexity of the model does not necessarily affect the ability to manufacture it with an RP machine. More attention had to be paid to the orientation and geometric properties of the model when manufacturing it with the ELRP machine. This highlights the need for obtaining more experience in using ELRP machines. Because it was possible to remove the support material with an ultra-sonic cleaner used in the professional-quality machine, there was less manual work in finishing the model manufactured with it. All models have visible artifacts caused by the RP manufacturing technology. More of these artifacts can be found in the models made with the ELRP machine. However, the results that we obtained with a single ELRP machine cannot be generalized to all ELRP machines, since there are several different models available. Some of them, for example, have a dual extrusion system, enabling the extrusion of removable support structures.

Looking at the accuracy of models, the data acquisition can be performed by TLS with the accuracy of a few mm. With the Leica HDS6100 the ranging accuracy is reported by manufacture to be ±2 mm. In addition to the instruments accuracy, the co-registering of point clouds affects the accuracy of the data set obtained. In our cases, the largest co-registration average overlap error of two scans was found to be 12.46 mm. In a model made to scale of 1:40, this creates an error of roughly 14 mm/40 = 0.35 mm in the final model. The deviations caused to the models by the manufacturing were similar or larger, ranging from 0.35 mm to 0.42 mm. The accuracy of the 3D digitizing instrument used in measuring models was ±0.05 mm, as reported by the manufacturer. In the 1:40 scale used, the errors caused by the TLS are comparable or smaller than the observed errors of FDM manufacturing, making TLS a well-suited method for acquiring virtual models that can be used to manufacture physical representations. The FDM machines could be used to create illustrative models, with a few centimeters accuracy in targets' real world size.

Since a single material RP machine was used in both cases, the physical models produced were mono-colored. Colored physical models could have been made by using a different RP technique [34], such as powder-based devices (e.g., [41]). However, it would have been necessary to acquire texture images from the digitized targets to obtain color information. In our case, only the laser intensities were recorded.

One alternative to buying and operating ELRP machines is to subcontract. There are service providers offering RP over the Internet that use different additive manufacturing technologies [18,19]. The choice between using subcontractors *versus* owning and operating the machines is a difficult one. When using a service provider, all of the setup work and machine maintenance work are also subcontracted. Neither, does the client have to spend time manufacturing the model. On the other hand, the delivery times need to be taken into the account and price of the models is higher. In "one-off" models, using service providers is an interesting option. If RP becomes more commonly used as an illustration tool in the projects, the decision will be more difficult. In both of our cases, the file size of the models was too large to be easily ordered from these services.

Successfully using RP technologies to visualize complex, three-dimensional models have been studied by many authors. The technologies have been used to visualize geometrically complicated objects [4,34]. In some cases, the original targets have been documented using TLS [4]. Clearly, RP machines can be used to visualize three-dimensional models produced with TLS. However, the process of using RP machines is often not documented, making it impossible to estimate how easy it actually is to use the techniques [4,34]. In addition, there is very little research on using ELRP machines in this manner; in most reported cases, professional-quality machines have been used. It was fascinating to see that a modern, affordable RP machine could achieve the same surface quality and level of detail as a traditional professional machine. New 3D-digitizing methods, such as backpack-based MLS [42], make it possible to efficiently survey large and geometrically complicated outdoor and indoor environments. New presentation methods are needed to communicate the measured results in a simple manner. ELRP machines offer an interesting possibility for doing so in this particular field. With the price of machinery such as this being quite low already, we expect to see an increase in the use of RP-made models in a variety of purposes, including the visualization of 3D models obtained via 3D-digitizing methods.

ACKNOWLEDGMENTS

This research project was supported by the Academy of Finland (CoE-LaSR), the Centre of Excellence in Laser Scanning Research (project number 272195), the Academy of Finland RivCHANGE project (project number 272711), The Finnish Funding Agency for Innovation (Tekes) ÄRY project, the Aalto Energy Efficiency Research Programme (Light Energy—Efficient and Safe Traffic Environments project), Research on Resident-Driven Infill Development Possibilities—Case Study in Urban Areas in Finland (REPSU), Aalto University doctoral program and the EUE project (project number 2141226). The authors wish to thank the Aalto University School of Arts, Design and Architecture's Department of Design for the 3D print of the Grönqvist building.

AUTHOR CONTRIBUTIONS

Juho-Pekka Virtanen was the main author of the article and made the analyses. Hannu Hyyppä, Matti Kurkela and Matti Vaaja were responsible for the TLS measuring campaigns. The article was improved by the contributions of all the co-authors at various stages of the analysis and writing process.

REFERENCES

1. Sass, L. Rapid Prototyping Techniques for Building Program Study. In Proceedings of the 9th International Conference on Computer Aided Architectural Design Research in Asia (CAADRIA '04), Seoul, Korea, 28–30 April 2004; Lee, H.S., Choi, J., Eds.; Institute of Millennium Environmental Design and Research, Yonsei University and the Korean Housing Association: Seoul, Korea, 2004; pp. 655–670.
2. Celani, G.; Piccoli, V. The roles of a model. *Arquiteturarevista* **2010**, *6*, 50–62.
3. Chua, C.K.; Chou, S.M.; Wong, T.S. A study of the state-of-the-art rapid prototyping technologies. *Int. J. Adv. Manuf. Technol.* **1998**, *14*, 146–152.
4. Tucci, G.; Bonora, V. From Real to... "Real". A Review of Geomatic and Rapid Prototyping Techniques for Solid Modelling in Cultural Heritage Field. In Proceedings of the ISPRS Trento 2011 Workshop, Trento, Italy, 2–4 March 2011; Remondino, F., El-Hakim, S., Eds.; Copernicus GmbH: Göttingen, Germany, 2010; Volume XXXVIII-5/W16.
5. Tucci, G.; Bonora, V. Application of High Resolution Scanning Systems for Virtual Moulds and Replicas of Sculptural Works. In Proceedings of the Twenty-First CIPA Symposium, Athens, Greece, 1–6 October 2007; Copernicus GmbH: Göttingen, Germany, 2007; Volume XXXVI-5/C53, pp. 721–726.

6. Mueller, D.H.; Mueller, H. Experiences Using Rapid Prototyping Techniques to Manufacture Sheet Metal Forming Tools. In Proceedings of the ISATA Conference, Dublin, Ireland, 25–27 September 2000.

7. Yang, T.; Buswell, R.A.; Cook, M.J. Exploring Rapid Prototyping Techniques for Validating Numerical Models of Naturally Ventilated Buildings. In Proceedings of the 12th International IBPSA Conference, International Building Performance Simulation Association, Sydney, Australia, 14–16 November 2011; pp. 965–971.

8. Rase, W.-D. Physical Models of GIS Objects by Rapid Prototyping. In Proceedings of the ISPRS Commission IVSymposium 2002, Ottawa, ON, Canada, 9–12 July 2002; Armenakis, C., Lee, Y.C., Eds.; Volume XXXIV. Part 4.

9. Yan, X.; Gu, P. A review of rapid prototyping technologies and systems. *Comput. Aided Des.* **1996**, *28*, 307–318.

10. Upcraft, S.; Fletcher, R. The rapid prototyping technologies. *Assem. Autom.* **2003**, *23*, 318–330.

11. Pei, E.; Campbell, R.I.; de Beer, D. Entry-level RP machines: How well can they cope with geometric complexity? *Assem. Autom.* **2011**, *31*, 153–160.

12. Creatr. Available online: https://www.lpfrg.com/product/creatr/ (accessed on 12 May 2014).

13. Cube 3D Printer. Available online: http://cubify.com/en/Cube/TechSpecs (accessed on 12 May 2014).

14. Ultimaker 2 Our Latest 3D Printer. Available online: https://www.ultimaker.com/pages/our-printers/ultimaker-2 (accessed on 12 May 2014).

15. Solidoodle 3D Printer, 3rd Generation. Available online: http://store.solidoodle.com/index.php?route=product/product&product_id=79 (accessed on 12 May 2014).

16. R1 "ABS + PLA Model" 3D Printer. Available online: http://www.robo3dprinter.com/collections/3d-printers/products/robo-3d-abs-model-fully-assembled (accessed on 12 May 2014).

17. Makerbot Replicator Mini. Available online: http://store.makerbot.com/replicator-mini(accessed on 12 May 2014).

18. 3D Printing Service i.materialise. Available online: http:// i.materialise.com/ (accessed on 3 December 2013).

19. Shapeways—Make, Buy, and Sell Products with 3D Printing. Available online: http://www.shapeways.com/ (accessed on 3 December 2013).

20. Fraser, C.S. Network Design. In *Close-Range Photogrammetry and Machine Vision*; Atkinson, K.B., Ed.; Whittles Publishing: Caithness, UK, 1996; pp. 256–282.

21. Grün, A.; Remondino, F.; Zhang, L. 3D Modeling and Visualization of Large Cultural Heritage Sites at Very High Resolution: The Bamiyan Valley and Its Standing Buddhas. In Proceedings of the XXth ISPRS Congress Technical Commission V, Istanbul, Turkey, 12–23 July 2004; Altan, O., Ed.; Volume XXXV, Part B5. pp. 603–608.

22. Bethmann, F.; Herd, B.; Luhmann, T.; Ohm, J. Free-Form Surface Measurement with Image Sequences Under Consideration of Disturbing Objects. In *Optical 3D Measurement Techniques*; Technical University Vienna: Vienna, Austria, 2009; pp. 51–61.

23. Cornelis, N.; Leibe, B.; Cornelis, K.; van Gool, L. 3D urban scene modeling integrating recognition and reconstruction. *Int. J. Comput. Vis.* **2008**, *78*, 121–141.

24. González-Jorge, H.; Riveiro, B.; Armesto, J.; Arias, P. Standard artifact for the geometric verification of terrestrial laser scanning systems. *Opt. Laser Technol.* **2011**, *43*, 1249–1256.

25. Vaaja, M.; Hyyppä, J.; Kukko, A.; Kaartinen, H.; Hyyppä, H.; Alho, P. Mapping topography changes and elevation accuracies using a mobile laser scanner. *Remote Sens.* **2011**, *3*, 587–600.

26. Arayici, Y. An approach for real world data modelling with the 3D terrestrial laser. *Autom. Constr.* **2007**, *16*, 816–829.

27. Buckley, S.J.; Howell, J.A.; Enge, H.D.; Kurz, T. Terrestrial laser scanning in geology: Data acquisition, processing and accuracy considerations. *J. Geol. Soc.* **2008**, *165*, 625–638.

28. Pu, S. Automatic Building Modelling from Terrestrial Laser Scanning. In *Advances in 3D Geoinformation Systems*; Springer: Berlin/Heidelberg, Germany, 2008; pp. 147–160.

29. Pu, S.; Vosselman, G. Knowledge based reconstruction of building models from terrestrial laser scanning data. *ISPRS J. Photogramm. Remote Sens.* **2009**, *64*, 575–584.

30. Hyyppa, J.; Jaakkola, A.; Hyyppa, H.; Kaartinen, H.; Kukko, A.; Holopainen, M.; Zhu, L.; Vastaranta, M.; Kaasalainen, S.; Krooks, A.; *et al.* Map Updating and Change Detection Using Vehicle-Based Laser Scanning. In Proceedings of the Urban Remote Sensing Event, 2009 Joint, Shanghai, China, 20–22 May 2009.

31. Barber, D.; Mills, J.; Smith-Voysey, S. Geometric validation of a ground-based mobile laser scanning system. *ISPRS J. Photogramm. Remote Sens.* **2008**, *63*, 128–141.

32. Puente, I.; Gonzales-Jorge, H.; Riveiro, B.; Arias, P. Accuracy verification of the Lynx Mobile Mapper system. *Opt. Laser Technol.* **2013**, *45*, 578–586.

33. Beraldin, J.-A.; Picard, M.; El-Hakim, S.F.; Godin, G.; Valzano, V.; Bandiera, A.; Latouche, C. Virtualizing a Byzantine Crypt by Combining High-Resolution Textures with Laser Scanner 3D Data. In Proceedings of the VSMM 2002, Gyeongju, Korea, 25–27 September 2002.

34. Voigt, A.; Martens, B. Development of 3D Tactile Models for the Partially Sighted to Facilitate Spatial Orientation. In Proceedings of the 24th eCAADe Conference, Volos, Greece, 6–9 September 2006.

35. Balzani, M.; Santopuoli, N.; Grieco, A.; Zaltron, N. Laser Scanner 3D Survey in Archaeological Field: The Forum of Pompeii. In Proceedings of International Conference on Remote Sensing Archaeology, Beijing, China, 18–21 October 2004.

36. Reznicek, J.; Pavelka, K. Culture Heritage Preservation with Optical Correlation Scanner. In Proceedings of the 22nd CIPA Symposium, Kyoto, Japan, 11–15 October 2009.

37. Sansoni, G.; Trebeschi, M.; Docchio, F. State-of-the-art and applications of 3D imaging sensors in industry, cultural heritage, medicine, and criminal investigation. *Sensors* **2009**, *9*, 568–601.

38. Schwarzbach, F.; Sarjakoski, T.; Oksanen, J.; Sarjakoski, L.T.; Weckman, S. Physical 3D Models from LIDAR Data as Tactile Maps for Visually Impaired Persons. In *True-3D in Cartography*; Springer: Berlin/Heidelberg, Germany, 2012; pp. 169–183.

39. Rase, W.-D. Visualization of Cartographic Surfaces Using 3D Printing and Subsurface Engraving. Available online: http://www.bbsr.bund.de/cln_016 /nn_340582/BBSR/DE/Raumbeobachtung/DE/Raumbeobachtug/Werkzeuge/Visualisierung/Veroeffentlichungen__Artikel/Veroeffentlichungen__Downloads.html (accessed on 12 December 2013).

40. Valentan, B.; Brajlih, T.; Drstvensek, I.; Balic, J. Basic solutions on shape complexity evaluation of STL data. *J. Achiev. Mater. Manuf. Eng.* **2008**, *26*, 73–80.

41. ZPrinter® 450. Available online: http://www.zcorp.com/en /Products/3D-Printers/ZPrinter-450/spage.aspx (accessed on 3 December 2013).

42. Kukko, A.; Kaartinen, H.; Hyyppä, J.; Chen, Y. Multiplatform mobile laser scanning: Usability and performance. *Sensors* **2012**, *12*, 11712–11733.

Chapter 2

A Compact and Low Cost Electronic Nose for Aroma Detection

Miguel Macías Macías [1,*], J. Enrique Agudo [1], Antonio García Manso [2], Carlos Javier García Orellana [3], Horacio Manuel González Velasco [2] and Ramón Gallardo Caballero [2]

[1]University Center of Merida, University of Extremadura, Sta. Teresa de Jornet, 38, Mérida 06800, Spain

[2]Polytechnic School, University of Extremadura, Cáceres 10003, Spain

[3]Faculty of Science, University of Extremadura, Avda. Elvas s/n, Badajoz 06006, Spain

ABSTRACT

This article explains the development of a prototype of a portable and a very low-cost electronic nose based on an mbed microcontroller. Mbeds are a series of ARM microcontroller development boards designed fo fast, flexible and rapid prototyping. The electronic nose is comprised of an mbed, an LCD display, two small pumps, two electro-valves and a sensor chamber with four TGS Figaro gas sensors. The performance of the electronic nose has been tested by measuring the ethanol content of wine synthetic matrices and special attention has been paid to the reproducibility and repeatability of the measurements taken on different days. Results show that the electronic nose with a neural network classifier is able to discriminate wine samples with 10, 12 and 14% V/V alcohol content with a classification error of less than 1%.

KEYWORDS

electronic nose; microcontroller; neural network

1. INTRODUCTION

During the last four decades a lot of research has been directed towards developing olfactory electronic systems or electronic noses. During this time, automatic odour detection systems have been applied in many industrial applications in agriculture [1], indoor air quality [2], environmental monitoring [3], quality control of food products [4,5], medical diagnosis [6], as well as many others.

Some developments have been directed towards the construction of low cost and compact electronic noses [7], which have led to a number of commercial e-nose products [8]. However, they are still too expensive for widespread use and are usually closed systems that do not allow the user to change the hardware. This means that, for example, the sensors in the commercial electronic noses may not be changed for specific applications.

Current microcontrollers allow products and devices to be controlled easily and quickly. The mbed NXP LPC1768 Microcontroller [9] is a single-based board 32-bit microcontroller that is designed for prototyping all sorts of devices as well as a teaching tool somewhat along the lines of Arduino [10,11]. This platform is also the first commercially available solution to fully implement the cloud-based model for embedded systems programming on real hardware [12] and permits many types of applications, such as use in the control of residential electricity [13], in educational CANSAT's rocket for aerospace education [14], to develop a behavioural-based robot platform [15] or in a self-balanced personal transporter robot platform [16].

Microcontrollers cover a high range of applications like automotive control systems, implantable medical devices, remote controls and toys. The use of microcontrollers for E-Nose systems is not new [7,17–19], microcontrollers allow portability, connection with the different sensors and prototyping possibilities. However in some cases [7,20,21] you need an external PC or PDA with a data acquisition card to collect or process the data and complete the system. In addition, if you want to use a microcontroller you need to understand the microcontroller architecture and the specific instruction set and assembler code in order to start to work. In the case of the mbed microcontroller you have a powerful ARM-based tool that allows you to create autonomous applications with lots of interfaces to connect with and an easy to learn architecture programmable in C++, which means a project can be developed with limited knowledge of electronics and programming.

In this paper, we report on the development of a portable e-nose system prototype using an mbed microcontroller that allows, in a very simple way, control of the operation of the electronic nose, data storage and communication with the user during the measurement process. This design allows the research community to have a very low cost electronic nose (around $US 200) that can be configured and used with a very basic knowledge of electronics. Finally, the performance of our electronic nose has been tested by choosing between synthetic wine samples (aqueous ethanol solutions) with different ethanol content 10, 12 and 14% V/V.

Section 2 describes the electronic nose hardware and the general characteristics of the mbed microcontroller. In Section 3 we test the viability of our olfactory system in the detection of the ethanol content of synthetic wine matrices and, finally, in Section 4 the results and conclusions of the project are presented.

2. THE HARDWARE

2.1. The MBED Microcontroller

The setup and development of a microcontroller platform is often difficult, especially more powerful controllers. Even expensive tools require a lot of time and training to operate correctly. NXP helps those who need to work with ARM controllers: the mbed module comes with online development tools. The module, 44 mm × 26 mm, contains an LPC1768 ARM7 microcontroller and a USB port. It can also include an Ethernet connection, the flexibility of lots of peripheral interfaces and FLASH memory. It is packaged as a dual in-line package for prototyping with through-hole PCBs and includes a built-in USB FLASH programmer. This last characteristic is one of the most important because it means neither an external programmer nor removal of the mbed is necessary to program or update an application, it can be done through the USB port. The NXP LPC1768 includes an ARM Cortex-M3 core running at 96 MHz. It includes 512 KB FLASH, 32 KB RAM and lots of interfaces: built-in Ethernet, USB Host, USB Device, CAN, SPI, I2C, ADC, DAC, PWM among others. In Figure 1, the pinout and the commonly used interfaces and their locations can be seen.

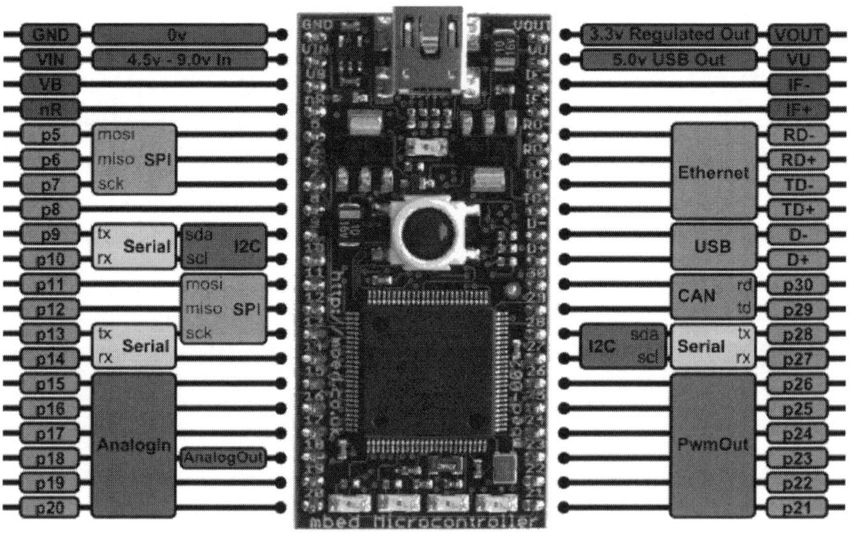

Figure 1. Mbed pinout [9].

The FAT filesystem feature is one of the keys to easy use. Creating a new program for the device is simply a matter of copying the binary file to this drive. Once copied, only the reset button needs to be pressed and the new program is copied to the internal flash and run. Neither a special programming hardware dongle nor special bootloader software are needed, just drag and drop.

The programming philosophy of mbed is based on the cloud computing concept. The mbed microcontroller's programs are hosted by the *mbed.org* developer website, including a lightweight online compiler for instant access to your working environment through a web browser and therefore possible on any OS. One can move between home and office and resume editing code on any system. There is no need to check for software updates, as the server will always be current. Mbed programs are written in C++ and the environment includes a C/C++ SDK for productive high-level programming of peripherals. Combined with a complete set of libraries and code examples published by the mbed community, the platform provides a productive environment for achieving results.

2.2. The Proposed Electronic Nose System

Measurements with our e-nose are taken using the dynamic headspace technique [22]. In dynamic headspace sampling, the headspace of the vials is continuously swept into the detector by a clean purge flow for analysis. This way, the gaseous analyte concentration immediately above the liquid phase is kept as low as possible to increase the evaporation rate. This evaporation rate depends on the surface area, the analyte surface concentration, the analyte volatility and the sample temperature.

To do this, the electronic nose hardware is composed of two small pumps, two electro-valves and a sensor chamber which are connected and controlled by the mbed. A view of the mbed electronic nose can be observed in Figure 2.

Figure 2. View of the mbed electronic nose.

Each measurement with our electronic nose is divided into two stages, *injection* and *cleaning*. In the injection phase the volatiles of the sample (carried by pump 1) mixed with fresh air (carried by pump 2) are transported to the sensor chamber to be analyzed by the array of sensors. In the cleaning phase all traces of volatiles must be removed from the electronic nose to avoid interference with the next measurement. The voltage applied to the pumps controls the amount of gas flow and the electro valves control the path of the gases. In addition, to ensure the cleaning of the entire system, the cleaning stage is divided in two substages *cleaning1* and *cleaning2*. The flow of gases in the injection and cleaning stages can be observed in Figures 3, 4 and 5 respectively.

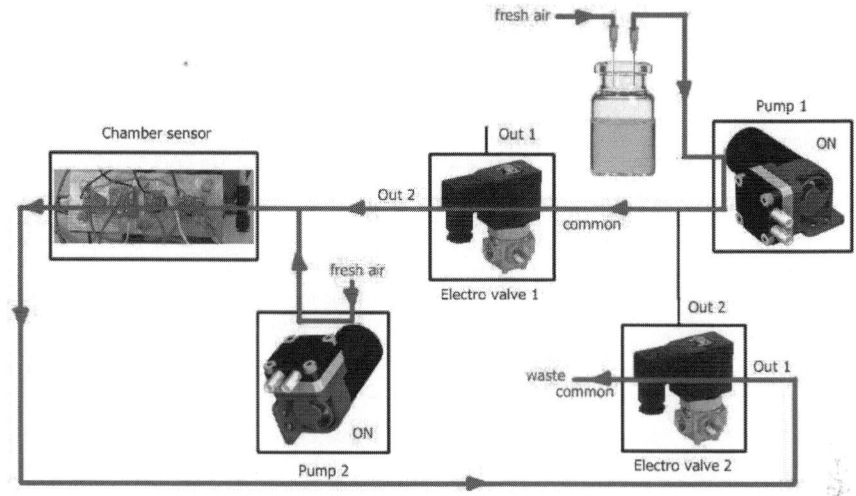

Figure 3. Flow of gases at the injection stage.

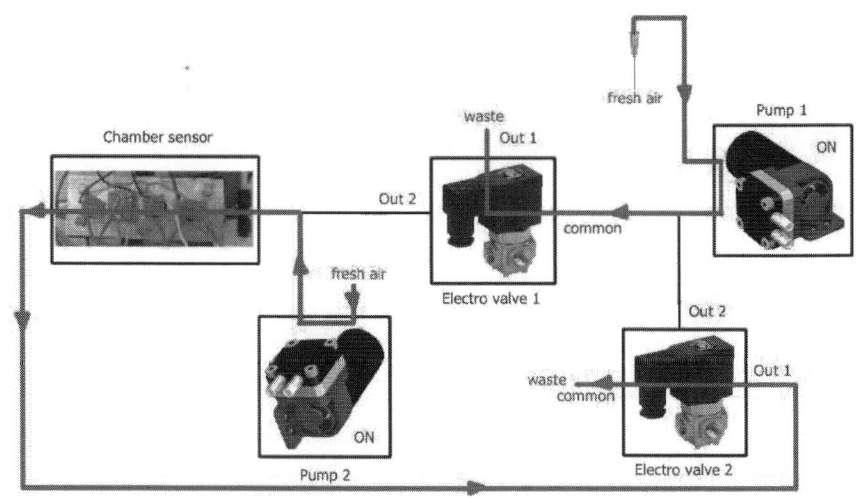

Figure 4. Gases flow at the cleaning1 stage.

This project uses four TGS Figaro gas sensors, TGS26XX (with XX = 02,11,00,20) obtained from Figaro Engineering, Inc. (Osaka, Japan). These sensors show a certain degree of affinity towards a specific gas but are sensitive towards a wide spectrum of gas types with overlapping sensitivities. These sensors have been mounted in a stainless steel sensor chamber. A load resistor is connected in series with each sensor and a common power supply of 5 V is used for both the heater voltage of the sensors and the voltage applied to the voltage divider formed by the sensors and the load resistances. Finally, the response of the sensor is the voltage measured at the output of the voltage divider.

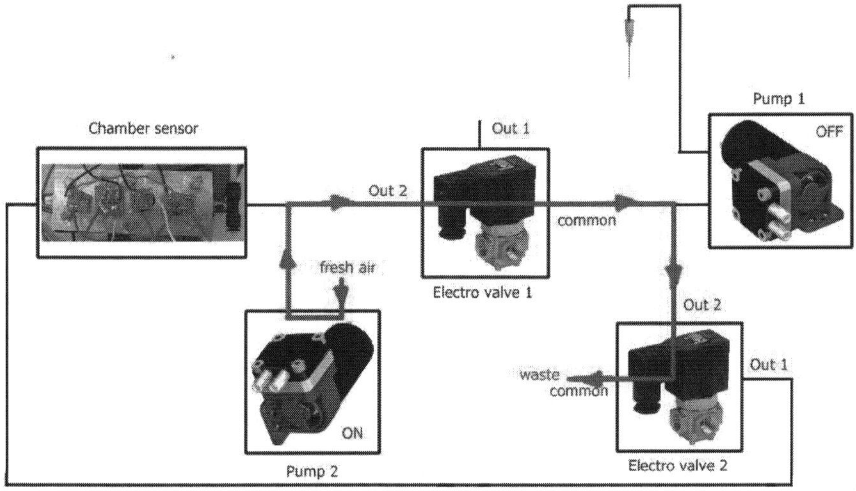

Figure 5. Flow of gases at the cleaning2 stage.

Additionally, a SHt71 temperature and humidity sensor has been installed in the sensor chamber. This sensor has a relative humidity accuracy of ±3.0%RH and a temperature accuracy of 0.4 °C. It operates from a voltage supply in the range of 2.4 V and 5.5 V and is connected to an I^2C bus on the mbed microcontroller.

Fresh air is used as carrier gas and measures start when the sensor resistances in the presence of the carrier gas are stabilized. Before a new measurement the value of the initial voltage output (V_o) is calculated as the mean value of the measurements made during an interval of time called the *set time*. Then, in the cleaning and injection stages, measures are taken at intervals of time, the*measurement interval*, and the value of the output voltage of the sensor divided by the initial voltage (V/V_o) is saved in a *measurement file*.

2.3. Working Modes

The electronic nose can operate in two different ways, the measurement mode and the analysis mode. In the measurement mode a *measurement configuration file* is read from the USB o SD card and a *measurement file* with the measurements of the sensors is written in the USB. These measurement files can be used in a PC to train a neural network that can be used in a subsequent analysis phase. In the analysis mode a neural network previously trained is used to make the analysis of the new measurements. In this case two configuration files must be read a *measurement configuration file* and another file containing information about the parameters of the PC's previously trained neural network in the *neural network configuration file*.

Regardless of the operation mode, a new measurement always starts reading the *measurement configuration file* that contains the following parameters defined in the previous section:

- Number of sensors
- Cleaning1 stage time
- Cleaning2 stage time
- Injection stage time
- Set time
- Pump 1 voltage
- Pump 2 voltage
- Measurement interval

2.4. The MBED Configuration

The pins of the mbed are configured as follows:

- p15–p20: Analog inputs to read the voltage of the sensors.
- p5–p14: Control the LCD display.
- p27–p28: Control the sh71 temperature and humidity sensor that communicates with the microcontroller by the bus I^2C.
- p21–p22: PWM out to control the gas flow of pumps 1 and 2. The amount of gas flow is controlled by the duty cycle of the PWM signal.
- P23: PWM out to control the sound alarm that warns the user of the beginning of a new injection stage.
- P24–p25: Digital outs that control the two electro valves
- P31–p32: Control the USB mass storage device to save the measurement files and the configuration files of the electronic nose.

The mbed also includes a network environment and a remote procedure calls over web sockets that allow the user to control the electronic nose via the internet, which can be very useful in high risk applications.

3. THE ELECTRONIC NOSE TEST

The alcohol content of some synthetic wine samples was quantified in order to test the electronic nose. To do this three synthetic wine samples were prepared, aqueous ethanol solutions at 10, 12 and 14% V/V and twenty measures of each one were taken, so 60 prototypes were classified in three different classes and labeled as *alc10*, *alc12* and *alc14*. Each prototype is contained within a file with the measurements of the four sensors during the injection and cleaning phases.

Moreover, given that the big problems faced while working with electronic noses are reproducibility and repeatability, measures were taken on different days and, especially, prototypes measurements of the different classes were taken alternatively. If the measurements are not taken in this way, the ability to separate classes could be due to sensor drift or instability, among other causes, rather than the alcohol content of the sample.

After numerous tests, measurements were taken with the following values of the adjustable parameters of the electronic nose:

- Number of sensors: 4
- Cleaning1 stage time: 400 seconds
- Cleaning2 stage time: 50 seconds
- Set time: 10 seconds
- Injection stage time: 2 seconds.
- Pump 1 voltage: 100% duty cycle (200 mL/min).
- Pump 2 voltage: 10% duty cycle (20 mL/min).
- Measurement interval: 0.25 seconds.

In Figure 6 we can observe the sensor response curves of sensor 1 for the 60 prototypes in the 12–30 seconds interval of time.

3.1. Feature Extraction

During the measurement time of the electronic nose and depending on the sampling period, each response curve is composed of N points. A lot of features have been proposed for the characterization of sensor response curves: maximum, minimum, slope, average, etc. In this project, the use of principal component analysis (PCA) [23] is proposed to reduce the dimensionality of the N-dimensional vector that initially characterizes the sensor response.

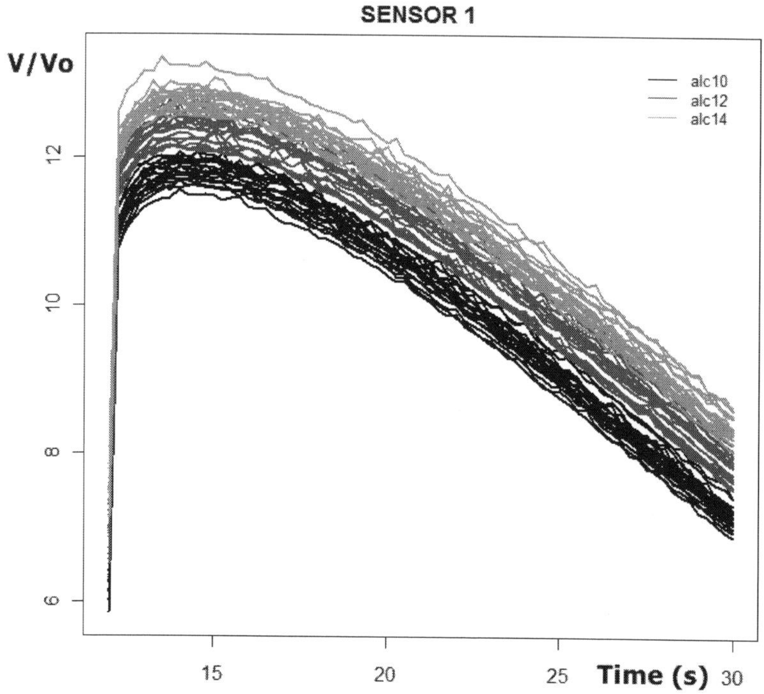

Figure 6. Sensor 1 response curves for the 60 prototypes.

The original purpose of PCA was to reduce a large number of variables to a much smaller number of new ones, the principal components (PCs), whilst retaining the variation in the original variables as much as possible. If we consider the sensor's response curves in figure one there are 60 curves of 56 points each (28 seconds and a sampling interval of 0.5 seconds) therefore there is a data matrix of 60 rows and 56 columns. Applying PCA to the data matrix the principal components were obtained. The first three autovectors of the covariance matrix can be observed in Figure 7, and according to PCA, each initial response curve of Figure 6 can be approximated by a linear combination of these auto vectors or basis functions. The coefficients of this linear combination (the first principal components) form the new variables representative of each response curve.

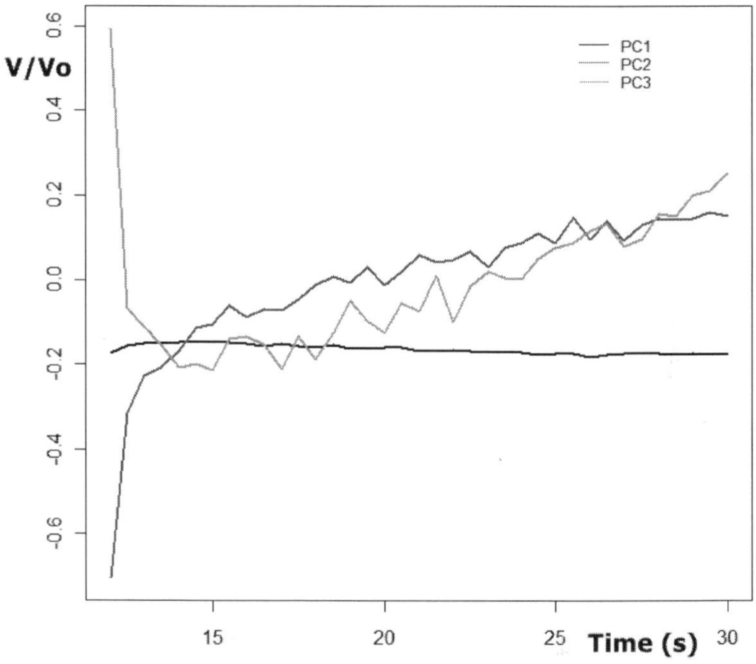

Figure 7. First three principal components of the PCA.

In Table 1, the proportion of the variance of the first three principal components can be observed. In this case, only the first PC accumulates the 98.1% of the initial variance, and therefore this component was only used to characterize each response curve. This allows us, hereinafter, to represent each sensor response curve with a one-dimensional characteristic vector, the first principal component.

Through using PCA as we have described above and by inspecting the four sensors response curves we have extracted six features that form the initial characteristic vector representative of each measurement of the electronic nose. These parameters can be observed in Table 2.

Table 1. Importance of the first three components.

	Standard deviation	Proportion of Variance
PC1	2.90	0.981
PC2	0.28	0.008
PC3	0.19	0.004

Table 2. Definition of the characteristic vector representative of the measurements.

Feature	Description of the feature
1	Projection of the sensor 1 response curve at the interval 10–40 seconds onto the first PC
2	Projection of the sensor 1 response curve at the interval 40–70 seconds onto the first PC
3	Projection of the sensor 2 response curve at the interval 10–20 seconds onto the first PC
4	Projection of the sensor 3 response curve at the interval 10–40 seconds onto the first PC
5	Projection of the sensor 3 response curve at the interval 40–70 seconds onto the first PC
6	Projection of the sensor 4 response curve at the interval 10–30 seconds onto the first PC

In addition, as will be described in Section 3, the best classification results are obtained with a subset of this initial characteristic vector.

3.2. The Classification Systems

Hidden layer perceptrons (MLP) and support vector machines (SVM) were used to resolve the classification problem. Neural networks were trained with the package *amore* and SVM with the package *e1071*, both from the free software environment for statistical computing and graphics R (The R project for statistical computing) [24].

The k-fold cross-validation method [25] was used in order to assess the performance of our classification systems in practice. One round of k-fold cross-validation involves partitioning our sample of data into k complementary subsets, from which k-1 subsamples are used to fit our predictive model, and the other subsample (the test set) is used to test its performance. In addition, to achieve a good generalization capability, the set used for adjusting the neural models is divided into a training set and a validation set. The training set is used to train the systems and the validation set is used to choose the best model when a minimum of the error over this set is reached.

In the neural network case, for each experiment one hidden layer perceptron was used where the number of neurons of the hidden layer varied from five to 30 neurons in steps of 5. To avoid local minimum each training process was repeated 10 times randomizing the initial weights. Finally, from all these experiments, the neural network model with the minimum error over the validation set was returned and its performance was measured calculating the error over the test set.

In the SVM case a radial basis is used as a kernel function and the validation set is used to adjust the smoothing parameters of the model, C and γ. These parameters took values of 2^x with $x$varying from −5 to 10. Finally, to reduce variability, multiple rounds of cross-validation were performed using different partitions, and the test results were averaged over the rounds.

4. RESULTS

Finally, we had 60 prototypes and three classes with each prototype characterized by an initial six dimensional vector. Appling the classification systems as described previously, the best classification results were obtained by using a subset of the initial characteristic vector formed by Features 1 and 6. In Figures 8 and 9 the plot of Feature 6 *versus* Feature 1 and the plot of these features versus the temperature and humidity respectively can be observed. In Figure 9 the data shows that there is not a clear dependency of Features 1 and 6 on the temperature and humidity, so no correction of the initial data has been made.

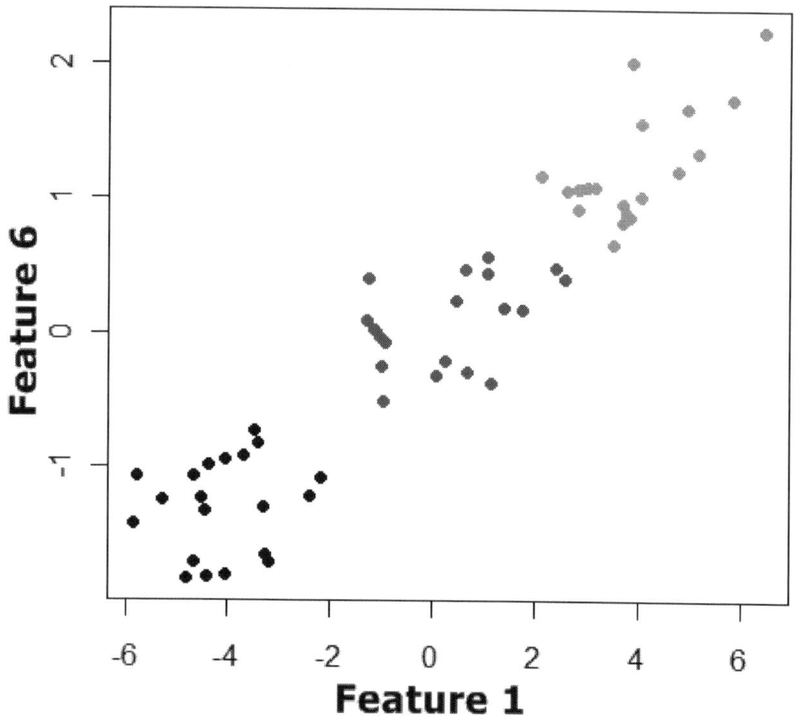

Figure 8. Two dimensional representation of the classification problem.

The classification results were estimated using a 10-fold cross validation method and performing 10 rounds of cross-validation, and 100 neural network models and 100 SVMs were tested. The box plot of the errors over the test sets of the 100 simulations previously mentioned can be summarized in Figure 10. In Table 3, the confusion matrix of the 100 neural networks and SVMs generated applying 10 rounds of 10-fold cross-validation is shown. Each one of the 100 networks and 100 SVM was tested over one test set of six prototypes, so 600 individual classifications were made in each case. It can be observed that correct classifications were over 93.5% in the SVM case and 99% in the SVM case. On the other hand, the whole process of training and testing the 100 models lasted over three hours in the SVM case and four days in the NN case.

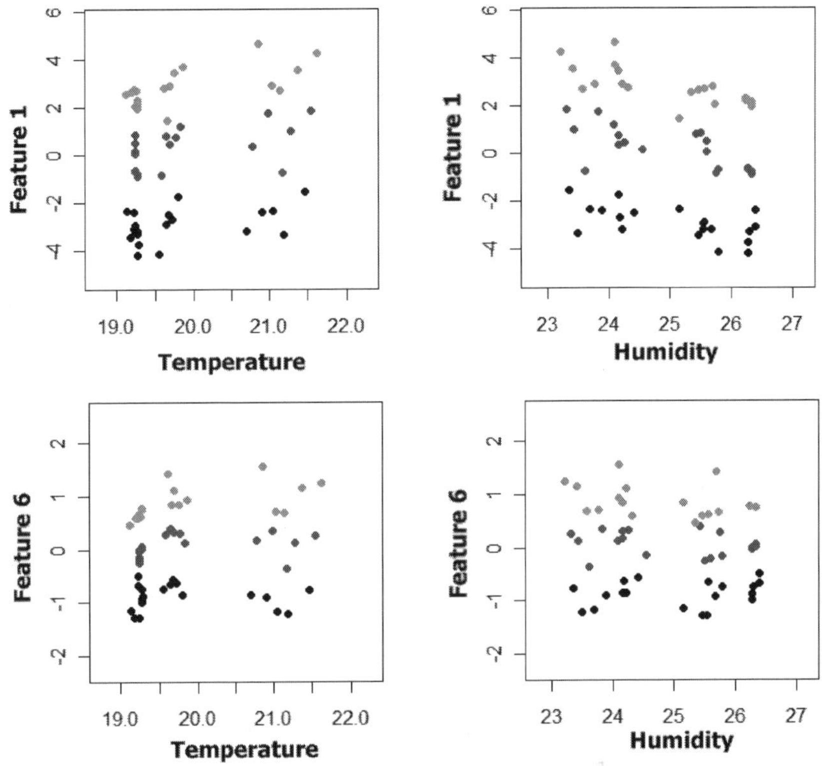

Figure 9. Features 1 and 6 versus temperature and humidity.

4. CONCLUSIONS

We have built a versatile and low cost system that allows an e-nose prototype to be created for a cost of only around $US 200. An mbed microcontroller, two micro pumps, two electro-valves and a chamber sensor (apart from connectors) are all that is needed to start research in the e-nose system field. In addition, the sensors can be easily interchanged or new ones added and it is easy to program and configure the complete system thanks to the mbed microcontroller. The mbed microcontroller has been shown to be a powerful tool for prototyping thanks to its different interface capabilities, easy to use and the need for only limited knowledge of electronics and programming as well as high extensibility.

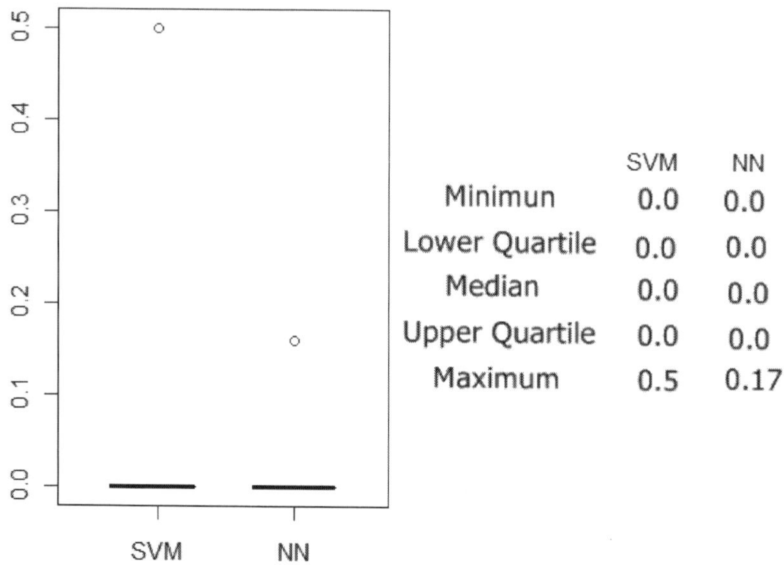

Figure 10. Boxplot of the error calculated over the test sets.

Table 3. Confusion matrix for the neural network (NN) and the SVM.

NN/SVM	Alc10	Alc12	Alc14
Alc10	100%/96%	0%/2.5%	0%/1.5%
Alc12	0%/2%	99.5%/95%	0.5%/3%
Alc14	0%/4%	0%/2.5%	100%/93.5%

The results show that this e-nose is comparable with other commercial ones and that it is a valid tool for research requiring a low cost e-nose. The prototype has been tested with three synthetic wine samples, aqueous ethanol solutions at 10, 12 and 14% V/V. NN and SVM classification algorithms were used with good classification results for both, but better for NN. In the NN case correct classifications are 100% for the alc10 and alc14 classes and 99.5% for the alc12 class.

ACKNOWLEDGMENTS

This work has been partly supported by "Junta de Extremadura" and FEDER through the projects PDT09A005 and GR10018.

REFERENCES

1. Jansen, R.; Hofstee, J.W.; Bouwmeester, H.; Henten, E.V. Automated Signal Processing Applied to Volatile-Based Inspection of Greenhouse Crops. *Sensors* **2010**, *10*, 7122–7133.

2. Zampolli, S.; Elmi, I.; Ahmed, F.; Passini, M.; Cardinali, G.C.; Nicoletti, S.; Dori, L. An Electronic Nose Based on Solid State Sensor Arrays for Low-Cost Indoor Air Quality Monitoring Applications. *Sens. Actuators B Chem.* **2004**, *101*, 39–46.

3. Cai, C.-J.; Geng, F.-H.; Tie, X.-X.; Yu, Q.; Peng, L.; Zhou, G.-Q. Characteristics of Ambient Volatile Organic Compounds (Vocs) Measured in Shanghai, China. *Sensors* **2010**, *10*, 7843–7862.

4. Peris, M.; Escuder-Gilabert, L. A 21st Century Technique for Food Control: Electronic Noses.*Anal. Chim. Acta* **2009**, *638*, 1–15.

5. Zhang, H.; Chang, M.; Wang, J.; Ye, S. Evaluation of Peach Quality Indices Using an Electronic Nose by MLR, QPST and BP Network. *Sens. Actuators B Chem.* **2008**, *134*, 332–338.

6. Kateb, B.; Ryan, M.A.; Homer, M.L.; Lara, L.M.; Yin, Y.; Higa, K.; Chen, M.Y. Sniffing out Cancer Using the JPL Electronic Nose: A Pilot Study of a Novel Approach to Detection and Differentiation of Brain Cancer. *NeuroImage* **2009**, *47*, T5–T9.

7. Tang, K.; Chiu, S.; Pan, C.; Hsieh, H.; Liang, Y.; Liu, S. Development of a Portable Electronic Nose System for the Detection and Classification of Fruity Odors. *Sensors* **2010**, *10*, 9179–9193.

8. Röck, F.; Barsan, N.; Weimar, U. Electronic Nose: Current Status and Future Trends. *Chem. Rev.* **2008**, *108*, 705–725.

9. Rapid Prototyping for Microcontrollers. mbed. Available online: http://mbed.org/ (accessed on 23 June 2013).

10. Burgess, P. Review: mbed NXP LPC1768 microcontroller. Available online: http://hackaday.com/2009/11/21/review-mbed-nxp-lpc1768-microcontroller/ (accessed on 23 June 2013).

11. Mellis, D.A.; Banzi, M.; Cuartielles, D.; Igoe, T. Arduino: An Open Electronic Prototyping Platform. Proceedings of the 2007 Conference on Human Factors in Computing Systems, San Jose, CA, USA, 28 April–3 May 2007.

12. Bungo, J. Embedded Systems Programming in the Cloud: A Novel Approach for Academia.*IEEE Potent.* **2011**, *30*, 17–23.

13. Bin Abdullah, N.; Yaacob, S. S.; Handaga, B.; Yaacob, Y. Automation of Residential Electricity Cut off Using Network Based Embedded Controller. Proceedings of International Conference on Computer Information Science (ICCIS), Kuala Lumpur, Malaysia, 12–14 June 2012; pp. 689–693.

14. Aydemir, M.E.; Vivas, E.V.; Celebi, M.; Bustinza, F.C.; Ay, S.; Phan, D. Design and Implementation of a Rover-Back CANSAT. Proceedings of 5th International Conference on Recent Advances in Space Technologies, Istanbul, Turkey, 9–11 June 2011; pp. 800–803.

15. Putra, B. P.; Mutijarsa, K.; Adiprawita, W. Design and Implementation of Software Architecture Behavioral-Based Robot Control System Using Active Object Computing Model. Proceedings of International Conference on Electrical Engineering and Informatics, Bandung, Indonesia, 17–19 July 2011; pp. 1–6.

16. Cardozo, G.S.S.; Vera, L.M.S. Prototype for a Self-Balanced Personal Transporter. Proceedings of 2012 IEEE Workshop on Engineering Applications, Bogota, Colombia, 2–4 May 2012; pp. 1–6.

17. Hong, H.-K.; Kwon, C.H.; Kim, S.-R.; Yun, D.H.; Lee, K.; Sung, Y.K. Portable Electronic Nose System with Gas Sensor Array and Artificial Neural Network. *Sens. Actuators B Chem.* **2000**,*66*, 49–52.

18. Fuchs, S.; Strobel, P.; Siadat, M.; Lumbreras, M. Evaluation of Unpleasant Odor with a Portable Electronic Nose. *Mater. Sci. Eng.* **2008**, *28*, 949–953.

19. Che Harun, F.K.; Covington, J.A.; Gardner, J.W. Portable e-Mucosa System: Mimicking the Biological Olfactory. *Procedia Chem.* **2009**, *1*, 991–994.

20. El Barbri, N.; Llobet, E.; El Bari, N.; Correig, X.; Bouchikhi, B. Application of a Portable Electronic Nose System to Assess the Freshness of Moroccan Sardines. *Mater. Sci. Eng.* **2008**,*28*, 666–670.

21. Chueh, H.-T.; Hatfield, J.V. A Real-Time Data Acquisition System for a Hand-Held Electronic Nose (H2EN). *Sens. Actuators B Chem.* **2002**, *83*, 262–269.

22. Swinnerton, J.W.; Linnenbom, V.J.; Cheek, C.H. Determination of Dissolved gases in Aquous Solutions by Gas Chromatography. *Anal. Chem.* **1962**, *34*, 483–485.

23. Jolliffe, I.T. *Principal Component Analysis*, 2nd ed.; Springer-Verlag: New York, NY, USA, 2002.

24. R Development Core Team. *A Language and Environment for Statistical Computing*; R Foundation for Statistical Computing: Vienna, Austria, 2008.

25. Devijver, P.A.; Kittler, J. *Pattern Recognition: A Statistical Approach*; Prentice-Hall: London, UK, 1982.

Chapter 3

A frame-based domain-specific language for rapid prototyping of FPGA-based software-defined radios

Ganda Stephane Ouedraogo,Matthieu Gautier and Olivier Sentieys

University of Rennes 1, IRISA, INRIA, 6 Rue de Kerampont, Lannion 22300, France

ABSTRACT

The field-programmable gate array (FPGA) technology is expected to play a key role in the development of software-defined radio (SDR) platforms. As this technology evolves, low-level designing methods for prototyping FPGA-based applications did not change throughout the decades. In the outstanding context of SDR, it is important to rapidly implement new waveforms to fulfill such a stringent flexibility paradigm. At the current time, different proposals have defined, through software-based approaches, some efficient methods to prototype SDR waveforms in a processor-based running environment. This paper describes a novel design flow for FPGA-based SDR applications. This flow relies upon high-level synthesis (HLS) principles and leverages the nascent HLS tools. Its entry point is a domain-specific language (DSL) which handles the complexity of programming an FPGA and integrates some SDR features so as to enable automatic waveform control generation from a data frame model. Two waveforms (IEEE 802.15.4 and IEEE 802.11a) have been designed and explored via this new methodology, and the results are highlighted in this paper.

KEYWORDS

Software-defined radio (SDR), Field-programmable gate array (FPGA), Domain-specific language (DSL), High-level synthesis (HLS)

1 INTRODUCTION

Software-defined radio (SDR) is a flexible signal processing architecture with very high reconfiguration capabilities to adapt itself to various air interfaces. It was first introduced by Joseph Mitola and turned out to be a sustainable underlying structure for cognitive radio (CR) [1]. An important research and development work has been done to release SDR solutions, and a survey of SDR platforms is given in [2,3].

The mainstream approach to specify an SDR application has consisted in implementing the signal processing blocks on digital signal processors (DSP) coupled with hardware accelerators such as field-programmable gate array (FPGA) or application-specific integrated circuit (ASIC) fabrics [4]. As a matter of fact, the reason why such heterogeneous DSP-centric SDR platforms have been popularized is mainly due to the fact that current DSPs offer some important reconfiguration capabilities while being programmed with software design flows. However, DSPs suffer from high power consumption as compared to hardware fabrics. Thus, FPGA turned out to be an interesting alternative by trading-off between energy consumption and high computation performances. Dynamic reconfiguration capabilities are also available on recent FPGAs which offer some reconfiguration delays of up to a few microseconds. Furthermore, FPGA programming model enables to leverage an important dataflow parallelism through its native parallel computational model in contrast to the sequential nature of DSPs. Thus, FPGA-based SDR is a quite old paradigm [5, 6], and most of the prototypes rely on intellectual properties (IP) described at the register-transfer level (RTL), therefore getting the SDR concept far away from its initial idea that is to say a software-only platform. Indeed, one of the issues related to FPGA-based SDR is the design flow, essentially based on hardware description languages (HDLs), which are used to program the applications. These languages, namely Verilog or VHSIC hardware description language (VHDL), represent an important burden and limit dramatically the programmability of the SDR platforms. In order tackle this issue, abstraction has been raised through software languages which were proposed to target FPGAs.

High-level languages (HLLs) are software languages that generate hardware description (RTL) from abstracted software specifications [7] for FPGA or ASIC targets. They raise the level of abstraction and bridge the gap between high-level algorithm designers and low-level circuit architecture designers. Their associated compiling frameworks generate RTL descriptions that fit the best to the specified application. We experienced with some of those high-level synthesis (HLS) tools and the flow depicted in this paper is essentially based on them.

In this paper, we are addressing the FPGA-based SDR and propose a methodology for rapid prototyping of the SDR applications. The main idea is to provide the SDR community with a design flow for specifying and implementing SDR waveforms fully running on FPGA-based platforms.

The major contribution of this paper is a design methodology consisting in a domain-specific language (DSL), which combines data frame information with dataflow computational model to synthesize an FPGA-SDR waveform. The aim is to hide the complexity of specifying an SDR waveform while automating all the control requirements from a high level data frame description. Furthermore, the HLS tools are employed to generate efficient signal processing blocks, at the RTL-level, while the compiling framework consistently builds the datapath and associates the control logic.

The rest of the paper is organized as follows. A discussion on the related work is given in Section 2. Subsequently, Section 2.3 states the problems which have motivated for this work. Section 3 details the methodology by first introducing the proposed DSL then describing each step of the language. Section 4 discusses the associated compiling framework, and Section 5 outlines some results. These results have been obtained on a Nutaq Perseus 6010 development board (Nutaq, Quebec, Canada) by prototyping both the PHY IEEE 802.15.4 and the PHY IEEE 802.11a. Finally, conclusions are drawn in Section 6.

2 RELATED WORK

2.1 Software-defined radio languages and middlewares

The main requirements in the SDR domain are essentially the configurability of the underlying platform, the programmability of the platform, and the portability of the application over different platforms [1]. Therefore, several proposals attempted to meet those requirements by using software-based approaches [8–14]. Indeed, software gives an abstraction level that enables more control over the hardware design flow. To this end, two complementary approaches have been proposed, namely the SDR-specific languages to design the waveform and the SDR middleware to provide the building environment. They both take advantage of the abstraction level given by the software.

The first approach consists in defining specific languages, (i.e., DSLs), which purpose is to simplify the prototyping process of an SDR waveform, that is to say the physical layer (PHY). Most of these languages proposed in the literature essentially target DSP-centric architectures through specific design flows [8–10]. The waveform description language (WDL) [8] enables implementing the overall PHY from a hierarchical decomposition. It is mixing graphical and state machine concepts to provide the user with facilities to specify a complete SDR-PHY. Processing elements are blocks within which a state machine locally handles both scheduling, thanks to handshake protocols, as well as the communication with the other blocks.

SPEX [9] is another language developed to specify SDR PHYs on single instruction multiple data (SIMD) processor using vector data type such as Matlab and also data type borrowed from SystemC. It is declined into three sub-languages, namely the Kernel SPEX defining the processing algorithm, the Stream SPEX handling the dataflow and modules interconnections, and finally the Synchronous SPEX for real-time constraints consideration. DiplodocusDF [10] is a modeling language that was proposed for implementing SDR PHYs on software-based platforms. It leverages a unified modeling language (UML)-like representation to model the SDR PHY and generates an executable to run on a software-based platform.

The second approach can be defined as a set of proposals for SDR standardization. They consist essentially in defining middlewares as the interfaces between the hardware and the application [11–14]. The core idea is to provide an environment, based on application programmable interfaces (APIs), to specify an SDR application while giving an emphasis to both the portability and the programmability of the application. The Software Communication Architecture (SCA) [11], initiated by the Joint Tactical Radio System (JTRS), is a major contribution in the software radio domain. It is defined as both a framework and a common standard for software radio specifications, and it is based on three major elements. The Core Framework handles via a hardware abstraction the installation, the configuration, the control, and the management of the waveforms. The ORB middleware serves to ensure the communication between the entities through client/server-like architecture. Both the Core Framework and the ORB leverage a real-time operating system to get access to the hardware resources. The Prismtech Spectra Core Framework (PrismTech Group Ltd., Stirlingshire, UK) [14] is a SCA-compliant framework that supports the deployment of waveform components on any mix of general purpose processor (GPP), DSP microprocessors, and FPGAs. FPGA functions are essentially programmed in VHDL-RTL. In the same way, the Platform and Hardware Abstraction Layer (P-HAL) [12] aims at designing specific radio applications independently of the hardware context. The underlying approach consists in abstracting the hardware platform by software functional units. Thus, it manages radio process real-time constraints, processing elements and communication issues, and enables the software functional units to be configured. The P-HAL defines four services, namely the *BRIDGE* that handles real-time constraints, the *SYNC* that synchronizes the concurrent processes, the *KERNEL* that schedules the software functional units, and the *STATS* that analyses the statistics of the functional units.

The GNU Radio [13] provides both the signal processing primitives and the environment to implement software radio applications running exclusively on a host PC. The interconnections within the waveform are written in Python, and the signal processing blocks together with some of the critical datapath are implemented in C++. It is usually combined with an external RF chip to generate radio waveforms or simply used for simulation purpose.

In summary, it is important to note that managing an SDR from a higher level of specification is a key element since it would provide a complete overview over the application at the early stages of the design process. Most of the proposals that we have discussed in this section target either software-based platforms or heterogeneous platforms composed of mix of GPPs, DSPs, and FPGAs. FPGA uniprocessor platforms are a promising alternative for SDR. Indeed, some research work [15] have already addressed this issue by developing FPGA-based uniprocessor SDR platform where the signal processing is entirely done on an FPGA. However, such platforms lack of programmability since FPGAs are programmed with low-level languages. In this context, HLS turns out to be a good candidate to achieve such a high level of abstraction when FPGA-based SDR is addressed.

2.2 High-level synthesis tools and flow

A traditional implementation of a waveform intended to run on hardware processors such as FPGA or ASIC fabrics often requires a manual HDL description. Those HDLs appeared to be relatively fastidious, error prone, and hard to maintain when it comes to specify huge and complex applications. In the early 1980s, some new approaches/languages, most of them inspired from the C language, suggested a more abstracted way to specify and implement the hardware circuit architecture. Known as HLL, this trend is still on the mainstream, and an interesting survey was proposed in [7]. One could make an analogy with software programming flows which employ the C language as entry point instead of pure assembly code. However, employing such high-level design flow still requires a good knowledge in hardware circuit architecture so as to achieve good design performance.

The majority of HLLs are academic research works, but commercial examples of such languages/tools have also been released, namely Catapult from Calypto (Calypto Design Systems, Inc., San Jose, CA, USA) and Vivado HLS from Xilinx (Xilinx Inc., San Jose, CA, USA). Figure 1 illustrates the Catapult design flow that we have experienced within the work presented in [16]. The first stage requires specifying the waveform from an algorithmic point of view. This specification allows a functional simulation of the application and it is more about deciding what the system does and how the computation is done. At this stage, some relevant aspects such as data sizing and communication protocols can also be explored. Then, those realistic specifications are fed to the synthesis tool together with a set of architectural and resource constraints. The compiler parses the specifications and the constraints to decide both a scheduling and resource allocation for the final design. In a successful case, it generates the RTL description of the specification which can be tested and synthesized for a specific FPGA target or ASIC fabric. Recently, OpenCL (Khronos Group, Beaverton, OR, USA) [17–19] has also been proposed as an abstraction to program FPGAs. It is argued that OpenCL has a native approach to express application parallelism; hence, it is a good candidate for designing parallel signal processing applications for FPGA fabrics.

These high-level languages and their compilers give an emphasis to the timing, area, or throughput constraints while making it easier to explore a set of solutions throughout design space exploration (DSE). Thus, HLS enables skipping several manual steps and gives an error-free path from abstract specification down to RTL description. In effect, by bypassing those steps, an important workload is being transferred to writing good specifications. A set of design optimization techniques such as loop pipelining or loop unrolling, which can be triggered from the specification, is also proposed by the HLS tools to achieve better design performance.

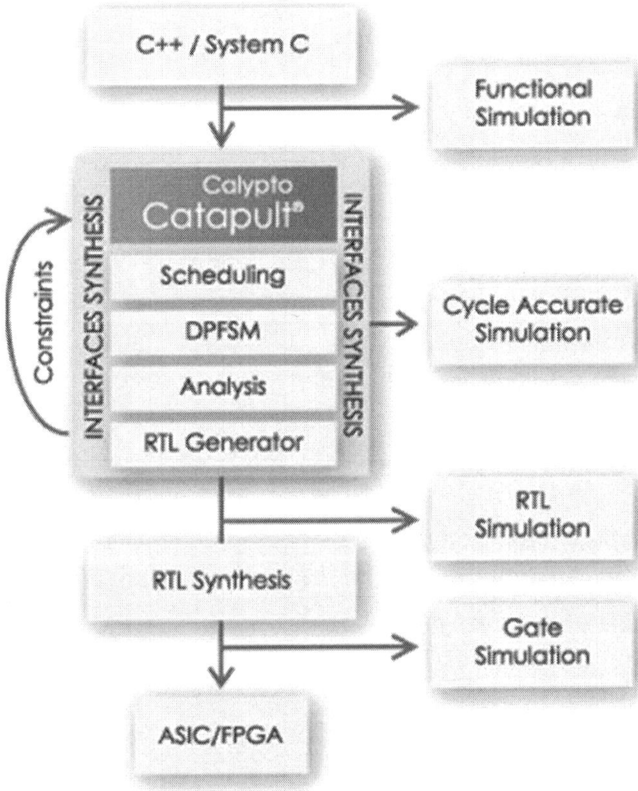

Figure 1. Catapult-C conception flow **[16]**.

2.3 Problem statement and motivations

The FPGA platforms have not extensively been considered for the implementation of SDR because of the programming model which is offered by this technology. Table 1 summarizes the SDR languages that have been proposed to achieve the high-level programmability of a target platform, its reconfiguration, and the portability of the application over it. Most the proposals that we have introduced in Section 2.1 use FPGA as hardware accelerators using in most of the case RTL description. They do not address the implementation of the SDR waveform in a uniprocessor FPGA platform.

As mentioned previously, HLS is a powerful means to prototype and synthesize waveform specifications down to circuit architecture. However, HLS has been thus far specialized in datapath designing rather than control. Indeed, complex control structures might require to be written entirely in HDL. Actually, HLS has been employed as a processor generator intended to be used as hardware accelerators. For instance, it does not properly address the specification and the implementation of state machines that are the mainstream approach for specifying complex control system. Thus, in the context of full FPGA-based SDR, HLS can be leveraged to increase the programmability of each signal processing block composing the SDR PHY dataflow graph whereas control requirements could be handled separately. In addition to this, employing different HLS tools so as to achieve various performance in a target design is a situation in which the control structure could be handled separately, as well. In the following sections, the authors propose an SDR PHY design methodology combining the model-driven engineering (MDE) for high-level description and the HLS for datapath designing.

3 DSL-BASED SDR WAVEFORM SPECIFICATION

3.1 Model-driven engineering for FPGA-SDR

The growth of the platform complexity exhibits the limitations of current programming languages. Furthermore, these platforms evolve rapidly while the application codes are still written and maintained manually. A mainstream approach to handle such platform evolution is the MDE [20]. It comprises both a DSL, which formalizes the application structure, behavior, and requirements in a declarative way, and a set of transformation engines and generators to generate multiple artifacts such as source code. The MDE approach ensures a 'correct-by-construction' development of an application.

Table 1. Summary of state-of-the-art SDR languages

Proposals	Programming language	Flexibility	Portability
WDL [8]	UML-based representation	Constrained specifications	n/a
SPEX [9]	Subset of the C++	n/a	DSP (VLIW and SIMD)
DiplodocusDF [10]	UML-based representation	Constraint profile	GPP and DSP
P-HAL [12]	Object-oriented C++	Real-time adaptation	GPP and DSP and FPGA
GNU Radio [13]	C++ and Python	Compile-time flexibility	GPP
Prismtech Spectra Core [14]	Model-based design and RTL IP cores	n/a	GPP and DSP and FPGA

n/a, not applicable.

The spearhead of the proposed methodology is the definition of a DSL to implement SDR waveforms running on FPGA uniprocessor platforms. A DSL, as opposed to the general-purpose languages (GPLs), is a computer programming language of limited expressiveness focused on a particular domain [21, 22]. In [21], they are declined into two variants, namely the internal DSL and the external DSL. Internal DSLs are languages that depend on a host language (generally a GPL). Their syntax is derived from the host language syntax and they benefit from the existing GPL compiling frameworks. An external DSL denotes a language with a custom syntax not depending on any GPLs. They are generally developed from scratch and require defining a specific compiling framework. Finally, the advantages of implementing a DSL are the improvement of the development productivity, the fact of facilitating the communication between domain expert through an explicit syntax, and above all, the usage of an alternative computational model.

The proposed methodology relies upon the MDE concept and deduces its computational model from a common feature of most of the telecommunication standards, that is, the data frame structure. The design flow synthesizes an efficient FPGA-based SDR waveform from both a specification of the data frame and the dataflow representation of the SDR waveform. These two features of the waveform are described in a novel external DSL. Figure 2 gives the generic DSL-based framework for an SDR-PHY description, which is divided into three related parts. The *Header* specifies different information that are later used both in the design flow and at compile time. Libraries of the required HLS-based functional blocks (FBs) are included together with the platform-specific information. Clocks and data rates are also highlighted in this part. The*Frame specification* part highlights the data frame structure for a given PHY. Thus, each field is described and the complete frame is specified afterwards. In the *Dataflow* part, both the interconnections and FB mapping are specified. It provides a natural dataflow representation (graph) of the PHY. Further details of the DSL are provided in the following parts by taking the PHY IEEE 802.11a as a use case.

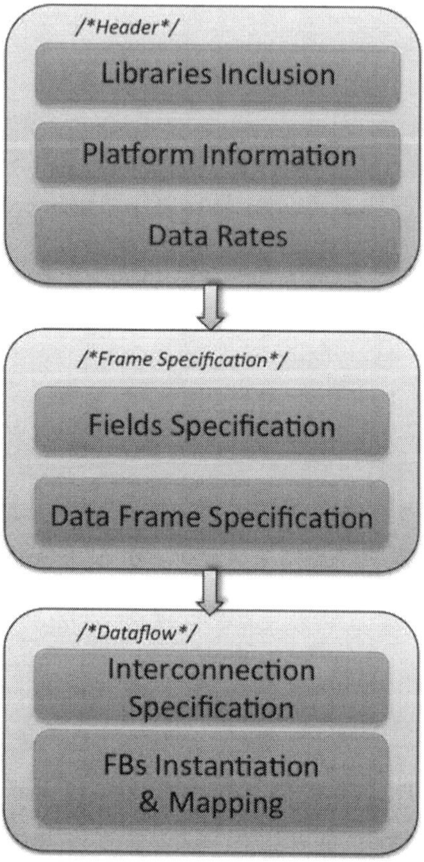

Figure 2. Framework of the PHY DSL-based description.

3.2 DSL-based frame specification

In most of the radio communication standards [23–25], the transmitted data are organized in data frames or packets. This structure ensures the interoperability of the solutions that are released by different vendors. A frame is composed out of a set of fields or subframes that carry either synchronization information or upper layer such as medium access control (MAC) data payload or frame-specific information.Moreover, the information nested in a given field can vary or remain unchanged in all the transmitted frames. For instance, synchronization data should always respect a regular pattern, whereas data payload can vary in terms of content or size. Thus, in the proposed DSL, each field is characterized depending on its fix or variable nature. As a result, two types of fields are identified, namely the constant fields and the variable fields. Figure 3 illustrates a field-based data frame structure of a PHY IEEE 802.11a standard where the SHORTPB and LONGPB are constant fields, whereas HEADER and DATA fields are variable.

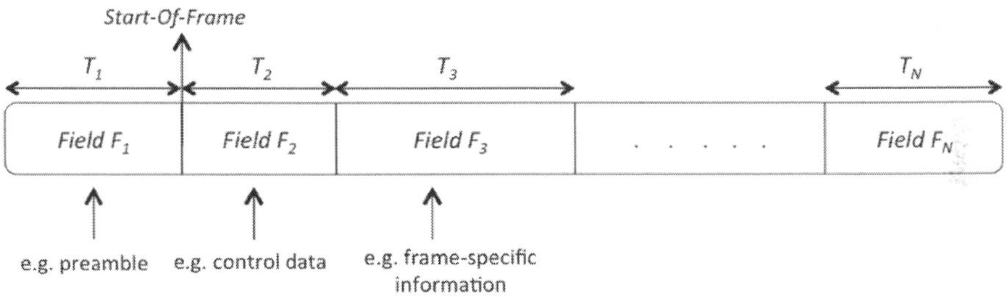

Figure 3. PHY IEEE 802.11a data frame and equivalent DSL declaration.

3.2.1 Field specification

In the DSL, the declarations of constant and variable fields are done with the key words *#fieldC* and*#fieldV*, respectively. They are followed by an arbitrary identifier that represents the field in the rest of the DSL source code. Following that, field-specific information such as data redundancy, size, and duration are defined within curly braces. These definitions enable to adapt the control when each field is transmitted or received.

Figure 4 shows a DSL-based source code description of the PHY IEEE 802.11a data frame previously shown in Figure 3. The PHY IEEE 802.11a frame is comprised of a short preamble (*SHORTPB*) appended for coarse synchronization. It is a known time domain data sequence used for signal detection, automatic gain control, and channel diversity selection. The short preamble is followed by a long preamble (*LONGPB*) field consisting of two orthogonal frequency-division multiplexing (OFDM) symbols used for channel and fine frequency estimation. The *HEADER* field carries frame-specific information such as the current modulation scheme and coding rate. The *DATA* field corresponds to the data from the upper layers to be transmitted.

```
/*Short training field specification*/
#fieldC SHORTPB{
    constant    ShTrainingSb: ./shpb.dat;
    redundancy  10;
    duration    8 us;
    }
/*Long training field specification*/
#fieldC LONGPB{
    constant    LgTrainingSb: ./lgpb.dat;
    redundancy  2;
    duration    8 us;
    }
/*Header(SIGNAL) field definition*/
#fieldV HEADER{
    data      hdpayloal;
    size      3 bytes;
    duration  4 us;
    }
/*DATA field specification*/
#fieldV DATA{
    data      dtpayload;
    maxsize   2312 bytes;
    minsize   0    bytes;
    }
/*OFDM PPDU specification*/
complex frame PPDU{
    SHORTPB, LONGPB, HEADER, DATA
    } sof after SHORTPB
```

Figure 4. DSL-based IEEE 802.11a PHY frame specification.

3.2.2 Data frame specification

A data frame is specified out of the instantiated fields with the key word *frame* followed by a frame identifier. Within curly braces, the set of fields composing the frame are listed. A frame can be either complex or real. Complex frames imply both an in-phase and a quadrature phase projection of the signal. Once a frame is specified, a *Start-Of-Frame* (*sof*) is designated among the constitutive fields. It denotes essentially a synchronization moment at the receiver. Thus, it enables to sketch the control of the waveform at the receiver.

The purpose of a frame declaration is twofold. On one hand, computation resources are optimized away in regard with the nature of the field. For instance, constant fields are one time computed and mapped to memory. The actual frame is built by consistently multiplexing those fields to the rest of the frame during transmission. On the other hand, the attributes of each field enable to dimension the appropriate control logic required in the waveform. This logic aims at sketching the datapath with energy efficiency considerations.

3.3 DSL-based dataflow

3.3.1 The underlying model of computation

Addressing the dataflow computation of an SDR waveform requires to define an appropriate model of computation (MoC). Thus, an SDR waveform can be modeled as a synchronous dataflow (SDF) graph [26] as implemented in the Ptolemy project [27]. SDF models dataflow applications in a graph-like representation, and the usage of SDF as the underlying MoC makes our approach more formal and high-level than some of the existing approaches such as GNU Radio [13] where no MoC has been defined. SDF defines actors, interconnected by channels that are transporting tokens (data). The channels are buffer memories that model infinite first-in-first-outs (FIFOs). An example of SDF signal flow graph is given in Figure 5, where *FB1*, *FB2*, *FB3*, and *FB4* denote FBs communicating through channels. An SDF implementation requires a control unit, and a typical SDF-based dataflow architecture is given in Figure 6, where the FBs depict the computing cores. Figure 6 can be interpreted as an implementation of the graph given in Figure 5. At the inputs and outputs of the FBs, FIFOs are interfaced to control the streaming flow through the graph. An important element that is making the waveform structure consistent is the control logic which purpose is to orchestrate the data routing and computing in the graph. Indeed, it provides the system with specific signals which are used to change the state of the system. This generic overview of the dataflow architecture clearly shows that for efficiency purposes, enhancements can be performed at three distinct levels, namely the FBs, the communication infrastructure, and finally the control unit. In this work, the control unit is automatically inferred and generated from the DSL-based specification of the waveform by means of a DSL compiler.

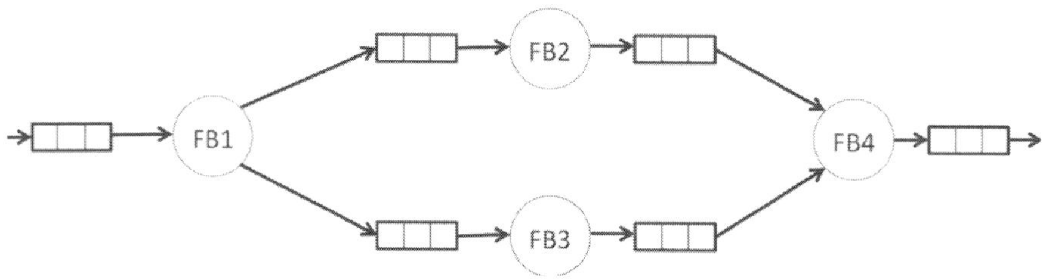

Figure 5. SDF signal flow graph example.

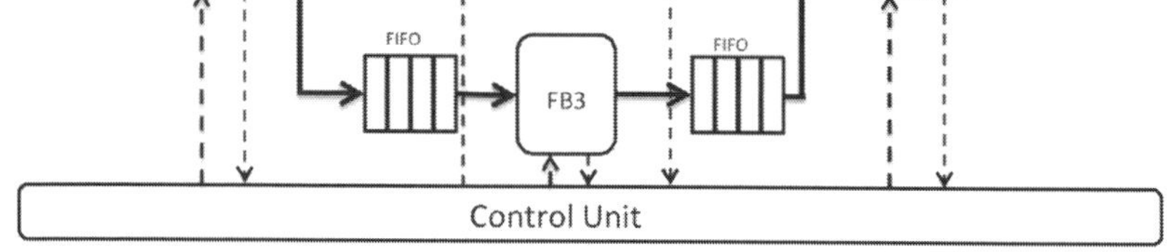

Figure 6. Typical SDF dataflow RTL architecture.

3.3.2 DSL-based dataflow description

A relevant step in the proposed design methodology is the assembly of the FBs into a waveform architecture. This step is automatically performed by the DSL compiler that is further detailed in the next section. The resulting waveform is intended to process the data frame specified in the DSL source code. Moreover, each block has to be synthesized according to some set of throughput and latency constraints. To this end, the dataflow structure of the final waveform is inferred from the DSL-based description of its datapath. In Figure 7, a DSL-based description of an IEEE 802.11a PHY is depicted, where the FBs are sourced from HLS-based libraries written in C++. As it can be noted, the description of each FB is made by specifying the set of fields, with the key word *processing*, that the block is intended to process. In addition to mentioning the fields of interest, their respective source (analog-to-digital converter (ADC) or another FB) is also highlighted in that description. Inside braces, input, and output are connected to the external world by making explicit or not the rate at which they work. Inputs and outputs are declared with the key words *read* and *write*, respectively. Further details are made explicit for synthesis purpose. Thus, the expected synthesis tool and various constraints are given in the description.

The proposed design flow is here to synthesize SDR waveforms. To this end, aiming at anticipating on the flexibility requirements, when adaptive coding modulation is implemented for instance, a flexible FB is declared *adaptive* within the DSL source code. In Figure 7, both the fast Fourier transform (FFT) and the Demapper blocks are declared adaptive. Indeed, these two blocks work in multi-mode, and it is often required to reconfigure them on the fly in order to work in a given mode. Thus, block-level reconfiguration is addressed early in the design process. For a complete waveform to be synthesized, both the transmitter (TX) and the receiver (RX) have to be described.

A DSL compiler has been implemented to parse the entire waveform description and synthesize all the artifacts required to implement the waveform. This compiler is introduced and detailed in the next section.

```
/* Cyclic Prefix Removal*/
cpremoval_i: ip CpRemoval processing LONGPB
    HEADER DATA from ADC
    {
      read adc_data on port frame_in at fe;
      read sync0    on port sync_data0;
      read sync1    on port sync_data1;
      write cpRemov on port frame_out at fe;
      synthesis     #catapultc;
      constraint    latency 1;
    }
/* Coarse Time-Frequency Synchronization*/
ctfs_i: ip CoarseTimeFreqSync processing
    SHORTPB from ADC
    {
      read adc_data on port frame_in at fe;
      write sync0   on port sync_data0;
      synthesis     #catapultc;
    }
/*FFT instantiation*/
fft_i: adaptive ip FFT processing LONGPB
    HEADER DATA from cpremoval_i
    {
      read cpRemov   on port fft_in  at fe;
      write cplx_sbl on port fft_out at fs;
      synthesis      #catapultc;
      constraint     latency N;
    }
/* Fine Time synchronization*/
 fts_i: ip FineTimeSync processing LONGPB
     from fft_i
     {
      read cplx_sb  on port cplx_fts at fe;
      write sync1   on port sync_data1;
      synthesis      #catapultc;
     }
/* LongPreamble-based Channel Estimation*/
equa_i: ip ChannelPhaseTrack processing
      LONGPB from fft_i
      {
      read   cplx_sb    on port fft_in_eq at fs;
      write cplx_sb_eq on port eq_out    at fs;
      synthesis             #catapultc;
      }
/* De-mapping*/
demapper_i: adaptive ip DeMapper processing
     HEADER DATA from fft_i
     {
      read cplx_sb_eq  on port cplx_in at fs;
      write coded_bit  on port bit_out at fc;
      synthesis             #catapultc;
     }
```

Figure 7. DSL source code for a PHY IEEE 802.11a receiver.

4 DSL COMPILER

4.1 Compiling framework

The proposed DSL enables to capture, for a given waveform, several extra information like the PHY data frame structure or the adaptive nature of some of the FBs. This description is parsed and synthesized into the actual waveform intended to run on FPGA fabrics. The main interface language that is employed in this flow is the *.tcl* scripting language. Indeed, the *.tcl* language is proposed by most of the electronic design automation (EDA) tools as entry point. This scripting language is leveraged in the proposed design methodology to automate several steps throughout the synthesis process. HLS tools, for instance, are interfaced with *.tcl* scripts that are generated by the DSL compiler. Indeed, for each FB instantiated in the DSL, a *.tcl* script will be generated by the compiler. Afterwards, those scripts are used to synthesize the desired RTL description of the block. In addition, after generating the appropriate *.tcl* scripts, the DSL compiler collects the FB RTL descriptions and implements the datapath of the desired SDR waveform as a top level design. A controller is also inferred from the DSL-based description. It is implemented as a hierarchical finite state machine (HFSM) that is automatically generated after parsing the source code. The structure and the working modes of the finite state machine (FSM) are deduced from both an algorithm and the description provided by the DSL. Tcl scripting is also used to interface the Xilinx synthesis tools when it comes to synthesize the bitstream of the waveform. Figure 8 illustrates the compiling framework that is made up of four parts. The first part consists in modeling the waveform in the proposed DSL. Then, this description is parsed to generate *.tcl* scripts for each HLS-based FB. A heterogeneous approach is also envisioned in this methodology so as to interconnect FBs issued from different HLS tools. Thus, some key words such as *#catapult*, *#vivadohls*, and *#rtl* enable to target Catapult-C, Vivado HLS, and native RTL blocks, respectively. The second part is the core compiler where each script is used to synthesize (at the RTL level) the desired blocks while a control unit is automatically inferred and generated. The connection of all the FBs into a datapath is also performed automatically in this step together with the assembly of waveform which consists of the dataflow unit (datapath) and the control unit. The third part consists in the integration of the waveform into the platform with the help of the generated scripts. However, this step is not fully automated and requires the user to deal with the synthesis tools. The fourth stage operates in parallel with the others and deals essentially with verification and validation. In the following section, we discuss the validation aspects of the proposed design flow.

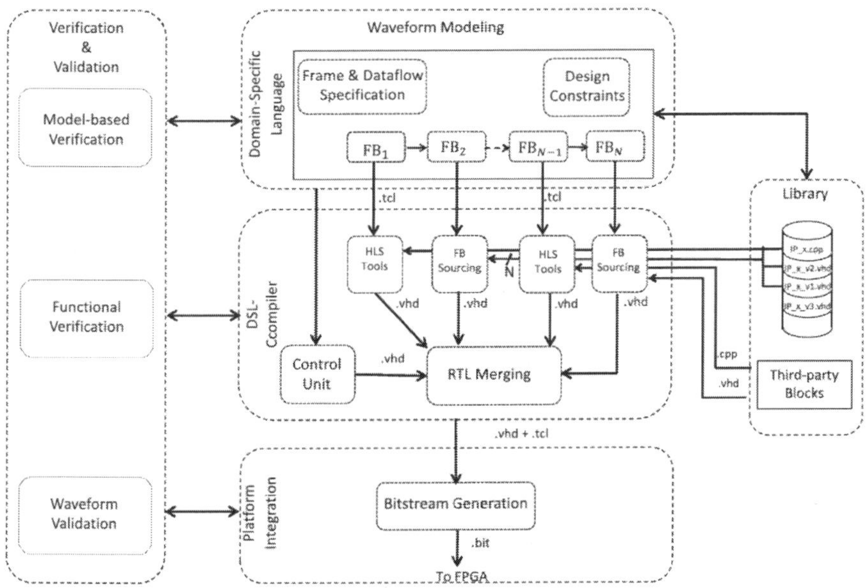

Figure 8. Top-down FPGA-SDR design flow.

4.2 Verification and validation framework

Verification and validation (V&V) processes are very important in a design flow because they ensure that the final design meets with the requirements. They can be time consuming to be performed, but they enable to prove correctness and reliability in the various steps of design and implementation. In the proposed design as illustrated in Figure 8, the V&V is declined into three steps, namely the *Model-Based Verification*, the *Functional Verification*, and the *Waveform Validation*. The *Model-Based Verification* relies on the MDE concept and includes formal verification, dataflow analysis, and model checking. The*Functional Verification* relies first on the verification provided by the HLS tools which enables to verify each generated FB from a C/C++ test bench. The data frame specification is used to generate the stimuli for the test bench. The final waveform is verified from a generated VHDL test bench whose outputs are compared with predetermined *golden* outputs. Finally, the *Waveform Validation* takes place after bitstream synthesis. It consists essentially in testing the waveform on the platform so as to analyze its performance. Contrary to the first two steps that are performed automatically, this step is by now performed manually, and the authors are investigating on how to automate such validation process from the high-level specifications.

4.3 Frame-based SDR waveform controller

A frame is generally considered at distinct levels, namely the bit level, the symbol level, and optionally at the sample level. It is mainly characterized by its duration, its source (e.g., a FB), and its composition (a set of fields). This structure gathers exploitable information that are leveraged to achieve better waveform control performance. The duration of each field for instance can help generate the read and write clock signals during the appropriate slot of time. In addition, each block within the flow graph is meant to perform a given action on a specific set of fields. Once this action terminates, the block may no longer be required, then disabled. For instance, some FBs may address only synchronization and some others address only data decoding. It is then convenient to control the activation and deactivation of each FB.

The automatically generated controller is a hierarchical FSM working in both TX and RX modes. Its overall structure is given in Figure 9, where the dash lines denote parallel states. In the TX mode, the controller consists of two major states called *super-states*. First is the *IDLE* super-state corresponding to the inactive state of the transmitter. After detecting a start signal from the MAC layer for example, it switches from the *IDLE* to the *FRAMING* super-state where data coding is sketched. Generally speaking, dataflow transmitters are feed-forward architectures then less complex to implement as compared to their associated receiver. The *FRAMING* super-state is declined into three parallel sub-states, namely the*CODING* state, the *INSERT* state, and finally the *BL-RECONF* state. In the *CODING*, the dataflow computation described in the DSL is performed. The output samples are fed to the digital-to-analog converters (DACs) prior to RF stage. In parallel to the *CODING* state, an *INSERT* state is active. This state manages the insertion of specific data in the frame, both at the time and frequency domains. Considering the standards using an OFDM modulation, they require to inject pilot symbols for coherent detection. Moreover, a data frame often includes constant fields (e.g., preamble) that remain the same in all the transmitted frames. For the purpose of reducing the overall computation, such fields are one-time computed and inserted (at run-time) at the sample level in the frame before DACs. The *BL-RECONF* state handles the block-level (fine-grained) reconfiguration of the transmitter. Modern standards require certain blocks to be adaptive (ACM), i.e., changing their properties on-the-fly. One approach consists in hard coding all the configuration of the block once, then using software controlled switch to select the desired configuration at run-time. A second approach is to reconfigure the block when a given configuration is desired. It is a suitable approach which fits the best to the paradigm of SDR and would require partial reconfiguration capabilities in the context of FPGA.

In the RX mode, the FSM is composed out of the three super-states. An *IDLE* state, as in TX mode, denotes the inactive state of the receiver. In this state, the receiver monitors the environment seeking for an incoming signal. Once a signal is detected, through an received signal strength indicator (RSSI) for instance, the receiver switches from the *IDLE* state to the *PRE-SOF* state. The *PRE-SOF* state consists essentially of synchronization tasks as imposed by most of the standards. Once the system enters the*PRE-SOF* state, a set of synchronization elements has to be detected and computed within a certain delay. If not, the system returns in the *IDLE* state. These synchronization element detection and computation are associated to the *sof* event which is defined in the DSL-based frame specification that was lately introduced. An *sof* detection makes the system switch from *PRE-SOF* to *POST-SOF* where a coherent data decoding is sketched. The *POST-SOF* state is declined into three parallel sub-states, namely the *DECODING* state where most of the signal processing is required, the *SYNC-TRACK* state in which the system keeps on tracking synchronization elements, and finally the *BL-RECONF* state to handle the run-time block-level reconfiguration like in TX mode.

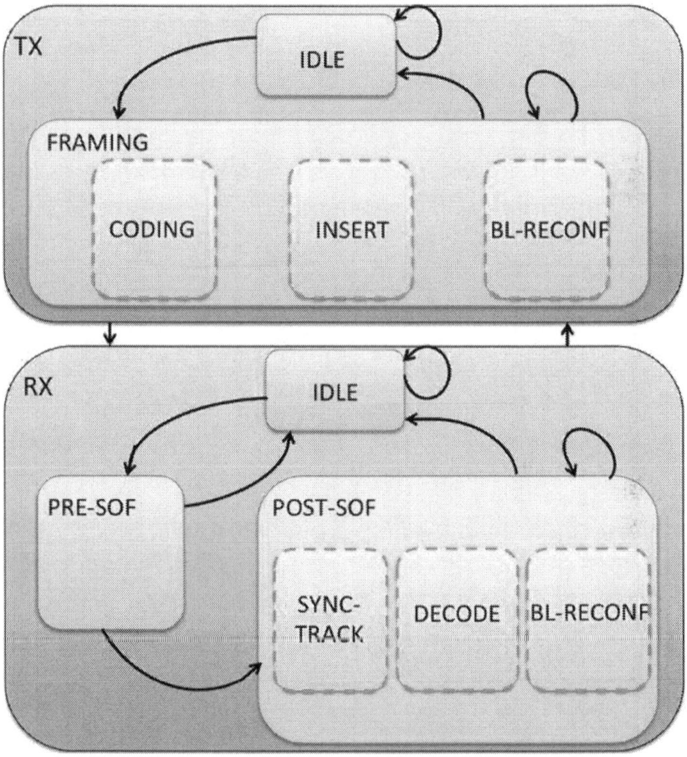

Figure 9. Transceiver hierarchical FSM.

In each of the states (TX and RX), a set of dataflow computation is intended. In the context of FPGA, the datapath is one time mapped to dedicated resources and ready to operate as soon as the FPGA is powered on. One of the roles of the controller is to distribute the clock signal to activate or deactivate the FBs when required. We leverage the properties of the data frame together with the intrinsic structure of the datapath (dataflow) to build the control unit. First, a data frame F is as a collection of fields, i.e,

$$F = \cup_{i=1}^{N} F_i, \tag{1}$$

where F_i denotes the i th field. Each field F_i is characterized by its duration T_i, its *constant,* or *variable*nature *State* of its transported data *Payload*:

$$F_i = \{T_i, \text{State}, \text{Payload}\}. \tag{2}$$

The duration T_F of the overall frame F is computed as,

$$T_F = \sum_{i=1}^{N} T_i. \tag{3}$$

The datapath, on both the transmitter and receiver side, is a set of interconnected FBs as illustrated in Figure 6. They are characterized by their latency (L), throughput (TP), and input and output data rates ($f_{in}$and f_{out}). For each block, when the inputs and outputs rate are known, they can be directly managed using enable signals. Moreover, each block is activated or deactivated on a per-field basis since computation happens to be specific to a given field. Thus, let FB_j be the j th FB within the dataflow graph:

$$\text{FB}_j = \left\{f_{\text{in}_j}, f_{\text{out}_j}, L_j, \text{TP}_j\right\}. \tag{4}$$

Assuming that FB_j processes the field F_i of duration T_i at an input rate of f_{in} and output rate of f_{out}, the block requires being enabled a number of clock cycles equal to

$$k_{i,j} = T_i f_{\text{in}}. \tag{5}$$

Thus, each block is affected a time slot to process a field when this field is traversing the graph. They are then activated depending on the ongoing field. To achieve this, the controller decides a starting moment for each block in the graph. This starting time is computed by considering both the graph structure and the properties (latency and throughput) of each block composing it. Indeed, each state is associated to a datapath, and once the system enters a state, the processing starts with a specific block that is tagged as a reference block. The activation moment of the remaining blocks in the datapath is then estimated by computing their distance to the reference block based on the latency and the throughput of the blocks preceding them. This algorithm has been integrated into the presented SDR PHYs design flow.

5 EXPERIMENTATION AND VALIDATION

5.1 Testbed description and waveform implementation results

The experimentation of the proposed DSL-based design methodology was carried out on an FPGA-based platform. It consisted in describing and automatically implementing both IEEE 802.15.4 and IEEE 802.11a transceivers.

The testbed is composed of a Nutaq (ex-Lyrtech) Perseus 6010 development board. Perseus 6010 is an advanced mezzanine card designed around a Virtex-6 FPGA with fabrics flexibility and an external memory. It also benefits from multiple high-pin-count add-on FPGA mezzanine card (FMC)-based cards. An FMC-based Radio 420x daughter board is used as full duplex SDR agile RF front-end with 12 bits ADC and DAC at up to 40 mega-samples per second.

The integration of the applications is partly made by using generated *.tcl* scripts as entry point to the synthesis tools. Moreover, in order to demonstrate the feasibility of the concept, a first test has been made without the DSL on the same platform and the results were published in [28].In Figure 10, the testbed is presented. Figure 11 on the other hand, illustrates the set of equipment utilized in this experimentation. It includes two Nutaq platforms (TX and RX) and some measurement tools such as ADS vector signal analyzer (VSA), spectrum analyzer, and timing scopes. The PHY IEEE 802.15.4 transceiver was first prototyped, and the corresponding baseband signals are also shown in Figure 10 through a Chipscope capture. The spectrum corresponding to transmitted signal is observed using a spectrum analyzer, and VSA Agilent (Agilent Technologies, Santa Clara, CA, USA) was also used to demodulate the transmitted signal, thus validating the IEEE 802.15.4 waveform. Moreover, we have developed an OFDM transceiver whose corresponding transmitted signal spectrum is given in Figure 12.

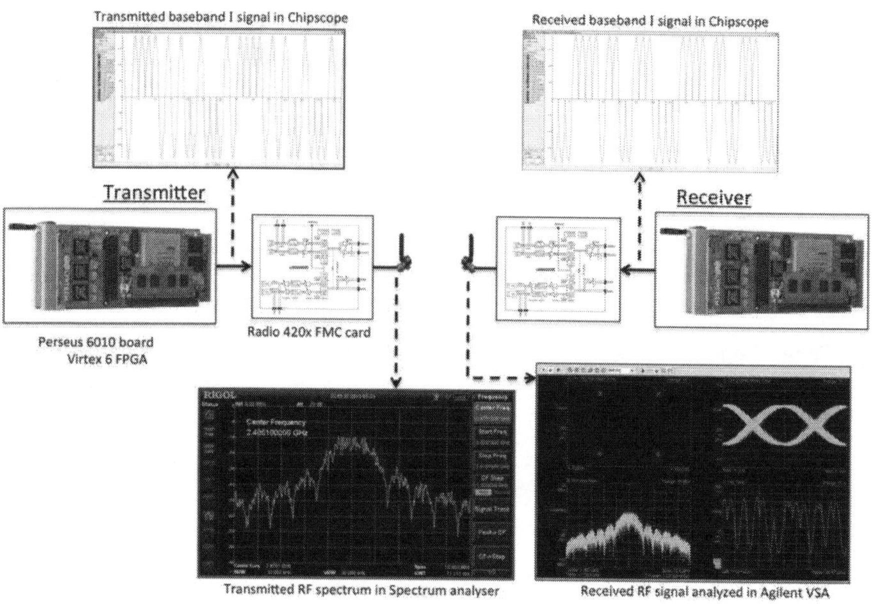

Figure 10. Nutaq boards and signal analysis snapshots.

5.3 Synthesis results and design space exploration

Table 2 gives the synthesis results for the two waveform receivers. The results are collected after place and route and are intended to show that the proposed flow allows to complete the whole design process. Resource optimization can be performed from a higher level through the HLS tools. Indeed, this flow also enables automatic DSE for a given FB. The exploration aims essentially at meeting performance requirements and represents an important add value to the HLS tools. They make it possible within a few clicks to explore various solutions of the same design. In Figure 13, a DSE is performed on a *Decoder*block, part of the PHY IEEE 802.15.4, in order to trade off between the area and the throughput of the block. Each curve on this figure corresponds to a level of internal loop pipelining which represents how often, in clock cycles, a loop iteration is started. Thus, the less the initiation interval (II), is the deeper the pipeline is. One can see from these curves that low throughput in cycles (high in frequency) is achieved when the design is pipelined to a maximum (II = 1). Loop unrolling (*U*) impacts considerably the design throughput. However, both loop unrolling and pipelining require more resources; hence, an increasing area as can be seen in Figure 14 shows a DSE for a 256-point FFT, performed with Catapult-C in order to obtain different solutions for same FB. The DSE is performed automatically from the scripts generated by the DSL compiler. The exploration of the FFT block exhibits an increasing number of slices versus the achievable data rate. Hence, suitable solution can be chosen to compose the desired waveform.

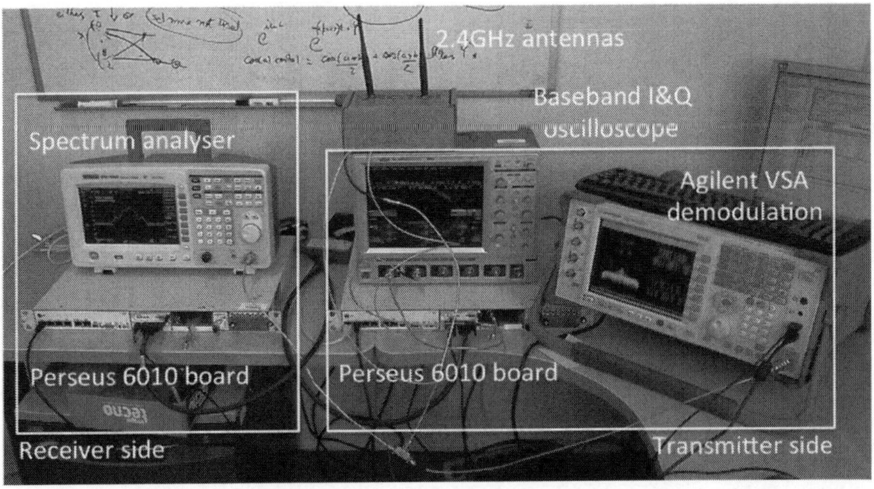

Figure 11. Experimental testbed.

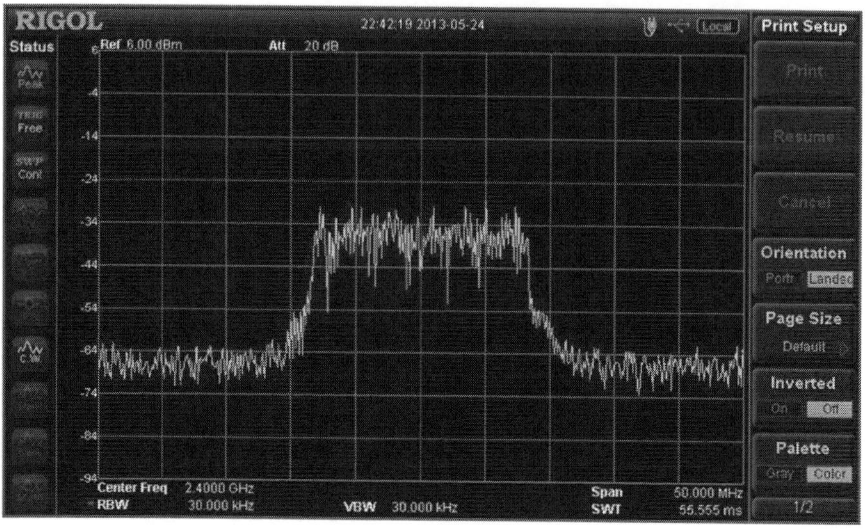

Figure 12. IEEE 802.11a transmitted spectrum.

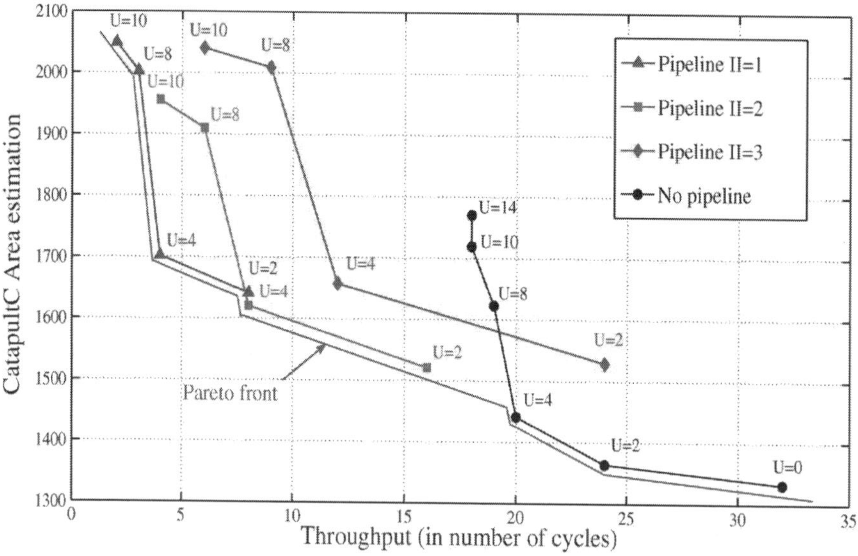

Figure 13. Design space exploration on PHY IEEE 802.15.4 ***Decoder*** block.

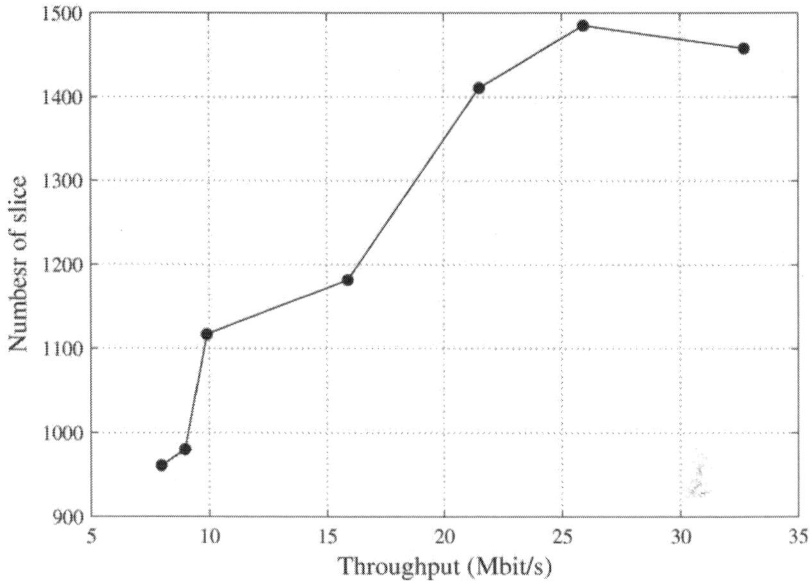

Figure 14. Resource estimation versus data rate of the IEEE 802.11a receiver.

Table 2. Resource estimation for the IEEE 802.15.4 and IEEE 802.11a receivers

	Slices	FF	LUT	DSP	BRAM
IEEE 802.15.4	543	1630	1058	1	0
IEEE 802.11a	961	803	2832	8	5

To conclude, the current version of the flow handles block-level configuration; it enables to select the architecture of a *adaptive* block depending on the constraints. This compile-time reconfiguration takes advantage of the HLS capabilities. An extension would be to make the generated controller able to manage at run-time the handover between two configurations of an *adaptive* block. In practice, it could leverage the dynamic and partial reconfiguration features available on recent FPGA devices. To this end, each *adaptive* block could be interfaced with large memory resources to store the streaming data when a reconfiguration is required.

6 CONCLUSIONS

In this paper, we have discussed a design flow which purpose is to enable rapid implementation of SDR applications on FPGA-based platforms. The proposed flow relies upon a DSL which provides a software abstraction to model the waveform. The specified waveform generation results from the analysis of their associated data frame and dataflow structure. Moreover, HLS capabilities are also featured with this flow, aiming at shortening design implementation time.

A case study has been performed through two examples, namely a PHY IEEE 802.11a transceiver and a PHY IEEE 802.15.4 transceiver. It results in a fast method for prototyping SDRs on FPGA devices with considerable flexibility to achieve different design goals. The current perspectives aim at enriching the processing block libraries and integrate different HLS tools within the flow. Another aspect that we will investigate is the use of dynamic and partial reconfiguration features on FPGA which are now missing in the depicted flow.

ACKNOWLEDGEMENTS

The authors would like to thank the anonymous reviewers for their comments and suggestions which helped improve this paper.

REFERENCES

1. Mitola J: Software radios: survey, critical evaluation and future directions. *IEEE Aerospace Electron. Syst. Mag*1993, 8(4):25-36.

2. Dardaillon M, Marquet K, Risset T, Scherrer A: Software defined radio architecture survey for cognitive testbeds. In *IEEE International Wireless Communications and Mobile Computing Conference (IWCMC)*. Limassol, Cyprus; 2012:189-194.

3. Anjum O, Ahonen T, Garzia F, Nurmi J, Brunelli C, Berg H: State of the art baseband DSP platforms for software defined radio: a survey. *EURASIP J. Wireless Commun. Netw* 2011, 2011: 5. 10. 1186/1687-1499-2011-5

4. Jondral JF: Software-defined radio: basics and evolution to cognitive radio. *EURASIP J. Wireless Commun. Netw* 2005, 2005: 275-283.

5. Cummings M, Haruyama S: FPGA in the software radio. *IEEE Commun. Mag* 2010, 37(2):108-112.

6. Stefano AD, Fiscelli G, Giaconia CG: An FPGA-based software defined radio platform for the 2.4 GHz ISM band.*Res. Microelectronics Electron.* 2006, 73-76. doi:10.1109/RME.2006.1689899

7. Edwards SA: The challenges of synthesizing hardware from C-like languages. *IEEE Des. Test Comput* 2006, 23(5):375-386.

8. Willink ED: The waveform description language: moving from implementation to specification. *IEEE Mil. Commun. Conf. (MILCOM 2001)* 2004, 1: 208-212.

9. Lin Y, Mullenix R, Woh M, Mahlke S, Mudge T, Reid A, Flautner K: SPEX: a programming language for software defined radio. In *Software Defined Radio Technical Conference and Product Exposition (SDR-Forum 06)*. Orlando, FL, USA; 2006.

10. Gonzales-Pina J, Ameur-Boulifa R, Pacalet R: DiplodocusDF, a domain-specific modeling language for software defined radio applications. In *38th EUROMICRO Conference on Software Engineering and Advanced Applications (SEAA)*. Cesme, Izmir, Turkey; 2012:1-8.

11. Jianxin G, Xiaohui Y, Jun G, Quan L: The software communication architecture specification: evolution and trends. In *IEEE Conference on Computational Intelligence and Industrial Applications (PACIIA)*. Wuhan, China; 2009.

12. Gelonch A, Revès X, Marojevik V, Ferrús R: P-HAL: a middleware for SDR applications. In *SDR Forum Technical Conference*. Orange Country, CA, USA; 2005.

13. GNU Radio: The free and open software radio ecosystem.

14. PrismTech Corporation: *Prismtech spectra SDR: spectra CF high performance low footprint SCA core framework*. PrismTech Corp., France; 2014.

15. The WARP Project http://warp.rice.edu

16. McCloud S: *Catapult-C, synthesis-based design flow: speeding implementation and increasing flexibility*. White Paper, Mentor Graphics; 2004.

17. Altera: *Implementing FPGA design with the OpenCL Standard*. White Paper, Altera Corporation; 2013.

18. Shagrithaya K, Kepa K, Athanas P: Enabling development of OpenCL applications on FPGA platforms. In *IEEE 24th International Conference on Application-Specific Systems, Architectures and Processors (ASAP)*. Washington, D.C., USA; 2013:26-30.

19. Economakos G: ESL as a gateway from OpenCL to FPGAs: basic ideas and methodology evaluation. In *16th Panhellenic Conference on Informatics*. Piraeus, Attica, Greece; 2012:80-85.

20. Schmidt DC: Model-driven engineering. *IEEE Comput* 2006, 39(2):25-31.

21. Fowler M, Parsons R: *The Addison-Wesley Signature Series: Domain-Specific Languages*. Pearson, Indianapolis; 2011.

22. Pasha A, Derrien S, Sentieys O: System level synthesis for wireless sensor node controllers: a complete design flow. *ACM Trans. Des. Automation Electron. Syst. (TODAES)* 2011, 17(1):2-1224.

23. IEEE: *IEEE Std 802.15.4: IEEE Standard for Information Technology: Wireless Medium Access Control (MAC) and Physical Layer (PHY)*

Specifications for Low-Rate Wireless Personal Area Networks (WPANS). IEEE, Piscataway; 2006.

24. IEEE: *IEEE Standard for Local and Metropolitan Area Networks: Part 16: Air Interface for Fixed Broadband Wireless Access Systems*. IEEE, Piscataway; 1999.

25. IEEE: *Supplement to IEEE Standard for Information Technology: Wireless LAN Medium Access Control (MAC) and Physical Layer (PHY) Specifications*. IEEE, Piscataway; 2001.

26. Lee EA, Messerschmitt DG: Synchronous data flow. *Proc. IEEE* 1987, 31(1):24-35.

27. Eker J, Janneck J, Lee EA, Liu J, Liu X, Ludvig J, Sachs S, Xiong Y: Taming heterogeneity - the Ptolemy approach. *Proc. IEEE* 2003, 91(1):127-144.

28. Bahtnagar V, Ouedraogo GS, Gautier M, Carer A, Sentieys O: An FPGA software defined radio with a high-level synthesis flow. In *IEEE Vehicular Technology Conference (VTC-Spring13)*. Dresden, Germany; 2013:1-5.

Chapter 4

Evaluation of Titanium Alloys Fabricated Using Rapid Prototyping Technologies—Electron Beam Melting and Laser Beam Melting

Mari Koike [1], Preston Greer [1], Kelly Owen [1], Guo Lilly [1], Lawrence E. Murr [2,*], Sara M. Gaytan[2], Edwin Martinez [2] and Toru Okabe [1]

[1]Department of Biomaterials Science, Baylor College of Dentistry, Texas A&M Health Science Center, 3302 Gaston Ave., Dallas, TX 75246, USA

[2]Metallurgical and Materials Engineering Department, University of Texas at El Paso, El Paso, TX 79968, USA

ABSTRACT

This study characterized properties of Ti-6Al-4V ELI (extra low interstitial, ASTM grade 23) specimens fabricated by a laser beam melting (LBM) and an electron beam melting (EBM) system for dental applications. Titanium alloy specimens were made into required size and shape for each standard test using fabrication methods. The LBM specimens were made by an LBM machine utilizing 20 μm of Ti-6Al-4V ELI powder. Ti-6Al-4V ELI specimens were also fabricated by an EBM using 40 μm of Ti-6Al-4V ELI powder (average diameter, 40 μm: Arcam AB®) in a vacuum. As a control, cast Ti-6Al-4V ELI specimens (Cast) were made using a centrifugal casting machine in an MgO-based mold. Also, a wrought form of Ti-6Al-4V ELI (Wrought) was used as a control. The mechanical properties, corrosion properties and grindability (wear properties) were evaluated and data was analyzed using ANOVA and a non-parametric method ($\alpha = 0.05$). The strength of the LBM and wrought specimens were similar, whereas the EBM specimens were slightly lower than those two specimens. The hardness of both the LBM and EBM specimens was similar and slightly higher than that of the cast and wrought alloys. For the higher grindability speed at 1,250 m/min, the volume loss of Ti64 LBM and EBM showed no significant differences among all the fabrication methods. LBM and EBM exhibited favorable results in fabricating dental appliances with excellent properties as found for specimens made by other fabricating methods.

KEYWORDS

rapid prototyping; titanium alloy; mechanical properties; grindability; corrosion behavior; dental applications

1. INTRODUCTION

Rapid prototyping and manufacturing (RP or RPM) is an emerging technology that has revolutionalized product development and fabrication [1]. The method, which is often called layered manufacturing, solid free-form fabrication, and 3D printing, is a significant technological breakthrough in the product manufacturing industry [2]. Compared to the conventional material forming processes, the part is fabricated by additive processes through a gradual-building of solid material from powder layers to the required shape from profiles created using CAD, X-ray computer tomography (CT), magnetic resource imaging (MRI) scanning, *etc*. Since this method requires no fixtures and tooling, a considerable reduction in the cost and lead time can be achieved. The first RP technology emerged as early as 1987 and used a laser for materials processing. More recently developed systems employ an electron beam in sintering and melting materials. In this article, these processing methods are referred to as laser beam melting (LBM) or selective laser melting (SLM) processes; or electron beam melting (EBM) processes. The LBM process is also commonly called selective laser melting (SLM). At first, this method was developed to produce industrial parts has now been considered as an economical processes for the fabrication medical and dental prostheses. A number of articles have been published with respect to the capabilities of these methods, the mechanism of the additive fabrication processes, properties of products made with these technologies, and applications. Typical articles include those by Murr *et al.* [3,4] where titanium and titanium alloys have been considered to make medical and dental prostheses using these additive technologies. Since the use of an inert gas or a vacuum is a necessity for a quality laser and electron beam fabrication, respectively, this is ideal for fabricating titanium components which are easily oxidized in air. The purpose of the present article was to compare the mechanical properties and some other relevant properties for biomedical applications of a titanium alloy (Ti-6Al-4V ELI) fabricated using the LBM and EBM methods.

2. MATERIALS AND METHODS

2.1. EBM and LBM Systems

Figure 1 shows comparative schematic views for the EBM (Figure 1(a)) and the LBM (or SLM) (Figure 1(b)) systems. The EBM system in Figure 1(a) utilizes a vacuum environment similar to other electron optical systems such as an SEM. Electrons generated in the gun (1) are focused (2) and electromagnetically scanned. (3) Powder is fed by gravity from cassettes (4) and raked into layers (5) across the build table. The building specimen (6) is lowered on the build table (7) with each layer-melt cycle. The SLM system in Figure 1(b) utilizes a purified gas environment (either argon or nitrogen). The laser beam enters the system at (1), is deflected by a mirror system at (2), and focused in a lens at (3). Powder in a cassette system at (4) is spread by a raking system at (6) over the build platform at (5). Excess powder is reused as shown at (7).

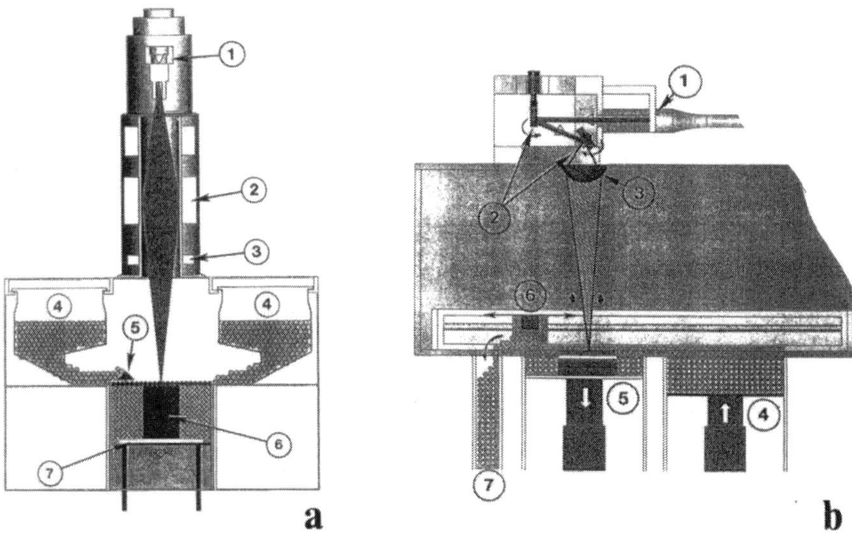

Figure 1. Schematic drawings of an electron beam melting (EBM) system (**a**) and a selective laser melting system (**b**). See text for descriptions. (After Murr *et al.* [4]).

The specimen compartment houses the powder hoppers to supply the metal powder and the rake or powder distributor to spread the powder during the layering process on a build table, on which a designed object or component are built up layer by layer.

The fabrication of a 3D object goes through several stages as shown in Figure 2 for the EBM process. At first, a CAD model of an object is produced into data formatted in stl. using a digital file obtained by computer tomography (CT scan) of the object with a designed dimension. The equipment builds a metal powder layer which is spread each time at a thickness of approximately 100 μm thick, from the bottom up, by selectively scanning the focused electron beam first, to preheat or sinter specific areas of the metal powder layer as directed by the 3D CAD model. The pre-heating process at lower beam power is needed to lightly sinter the powder to prevent the metal powder from spreading. Then, the same selected areas are melted using full beam power, resulting in the formation of a molten pool and solidifying it into a fully dense layer with a fine-scale microstructure. The table is then lowered, and a new powder layer is spread to continue building the 3D object. In the EBM processing, these three basic processes, powder spreading, pre-heating and melting, are repeated until the 3D object is completely fabricated according to the design. The operation of fabricating a 3D objective in the LBM equipment is basically similar to that for the EBM equipment. However, major differences between two systems, EBM and LBM, are the thickness of the powder layer (100 μm *vs.* 40 μm). The building speed of the LBM system is more rapid than the EBM system (~10^4 mm/s, respectively). This gives rise to more rapid cooling especially for small size specimens fabricated by LBM. Typical operational conditions for each process are summarized in Table 1.

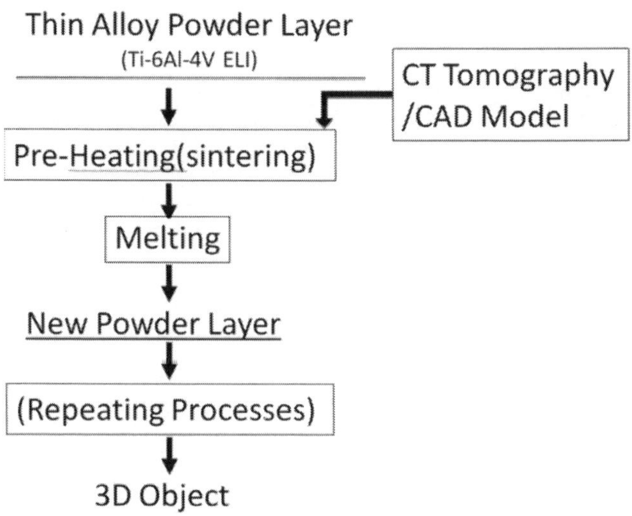

Figure 2. Flow sheet of fabricating 3D object using EBM.

2.2. Fabrication of Specimens

Each equipment manufacturer specifies an alloy powder that is allowed to build components when the equipment is used. For Arcam A2, the EBM system, the spherical alloy powder of Ti-6Al-4V ELI (ASTM Grade 23, Arcam℘ AB) with the average particle size of 40 μm was used, whereas for EOSINT M270, the LBM system, the average 20 μm of Ti-6Al-4V ELI spherical particle alloy powder (ASTM Grade 23, EOS) was used. The nominal chemical compositions of each powder are listed in Table 2. Using each alloy powder, for each corresponding equipment, three types of specimens, dumbbell-shaped specimens (20 mm gauge length, 3 mm diameter) for the tensile test; and two kinds of plate specimens (10 mm × 10 mm × 2 mm or 30 mm × 30 mm × 4 mm) for the metallography, the evaluation of corrosion behavior and grindability were fabricated.

Table 1. Operative conditions for EBM *vs.* LBM systems.

Process	Laser Beam Melting (EOSINT M270)	Electron Beam Melting (Arcam A2)
Environment	argon/nitrogen	
Vacuum/Helium		
Temperature	700 °C	700 °C
Power	5,500 W	7,000 W
Efficiency	High	High
Powder (average size)	20 μm	40 μm
Scan Speed	10^4 mm/s	10^2 m/s
Charging	No	Yes
Beam/melt/pool	0.1–0.5 mm	0.2 mm–1.2 mm
Layer thickness	50–100 μm	100 μm
Building speed	7–8 mm/h	6–7 mm/h

Table 2. Nominal chemical composition (w/o) of the Ti-6Al-4V ELI powder used for EBM and LBM system.

Process	Al	V	C	Fe	O	N	H	Ti
EBMPowder (ArcamAB)	6.0	4.0	0.03	0.10	0.10	0.01	<0.003	Balance
LBM powder(EOS)	6.0	4.1	0.02	0.10	0.08	0.01	0.0024	Balance

2.3. Optical Metallography

Alloy plates (10 mm × 10 mm × 2 mm, n = 2) were metallographically polished and etched using a hydrofluoric acid-based solution [5]. The prepared surfaces were examined using an optical microscope (Epiphot 200, Nikon, Japan). For the LBM and EBM specimens, planes both parallel and perpendicular to the beam direction were examined.

2.4. Electron Microscopy

Plate specimens were sliced into 1 mm of the thickness and mechanically ground and polished up to 1,200 grit. As for the final polish, 0.3 mm diamond paste was used. After polishing and rinsing in the acetone and ethanol, specimens were etched using a solution consisting of 100 mL H_2O, 2.5 mL HF and 5 mL HNO_3. The etched samples were observed directly in Hitachi 4800 field-emission scanning electron microscope (FESEM) utilizing secondary electron (SE) image at an accelerating voltage of 20 kV.

In addition, sections were cut from the LBM and EBM plate specimens and ground and polished to a thickness of approximately 0.2 mm. Standard 3 mm transmission electron microscope (TEM) disc were punched from these thinned sections, dimpled on both sides and electropolished using a Struers Tenupol-5 dual-jet unit using a solution consisting of 0.9 L methanol to which 50 mL H_2SO_4 was added. The electropolishing solution was cooled to −10 °C and the electropolishing voltage varied between 15 and 25 V at 5 A to observe the characteristic polishing plateau. These voltage conditions varied for the different microstructures and crystallographic (α + β) mixtures in particular. The resulting electron transparent thin sections were then examined in a Hitachi H-8000 analytical TEM at 200 kV accelerating potential; utilizing a goniometer-tilt stage.

2.5. Mechanical Properties

Tensile properties were tested (n = 4) for the dumbbell specimens prepared using the LBM and EBM system and cast specimens at a crosshead speed of

0.25 mm/min at room temperature. Yield strength at 0.2% offset (YS), ultimate tensile strength (TS), modulus of elasticity (E) and percent elongation (El) were determined. Typical testing procedures employed are given in an earlier report [6].

2.6. Microhardness

The Vickers microhardness was determined with a 200 g load and 15 s dwell time at more than 300 μm below the surface using a microhardness tester (FM-7, Future Tech, Tokyo, Japan). The microhardness of four randomly chosen areas was determined on two specimens for each metal (n = 8). The procedures for the determination of the hardness are given elsewhere [6].

2.7. Grindability

Both LBM and EBM plate specimens (30 mm × 30 mm × 4 mm,) were cut into rectangular shapes of 8 mm x 30 mm by slicing them parallel to the direction of the beam, which is perpendicular to the plane of the stacking layers. Both surfaces of the 8 mm × 30 mm plate were ground 0.5 mm so that the resultant thickness of the specimens was reduced to 3 mm. On the other hand, the cast specimens were ground from castings of 3.5 mm × 8.5 mm × 30.5 mm, so that the thickness after the removal of the α-case from the both surfaces was 3 mm. In addition, plates of a similar dimension (3.0 mm × 8.0 mm × 30. mm) were cut from the wrought Ti-6Al-4V ELI pieces and used for test. Grindability (n = 8) was evaluated as volume loss (mm^3) after grinding for one minute, using a SiC wheel of specimens (13 mm diameter, 1.5 mm thick: 703–120, Brasseler USA, USA) by applying 100 gf at 1,250 m/min. The testing method used for this part of the evaluation was similar to that in a previous study [6]. One of the side walls of 30 mm × 3 mm of the specimens was placed perpendicular to the circumferential surface of the SiC wheel so that the direction of the grinding was parallel to the layer of the LBM and EBM specimen. The volume of metal ground, evaluated by a reduced weight of specimens, was used to compare the grindability among the various metals [7].

2.8. Corrosion Behavior

The corrosion characteristics of the specimens were evaluated using a potentiodynamic polarization technique. Evaluation of the corrosion behavior was performed (n = 4) in a modified Tani-Zucchi synthetic saliva maintained at 37 °C as previously reported [8]. Specimen used was plates of 10 mm × 10 mm × 2 mm. A rough surface from the LBM, EBM and wrought plates and the α-case layer of cast specimens were removed. The open circuit potential (OCP: V), polarization resistance (Rp: MΩ•cm^2), corrosion current density (I_{corr}: A/cm^2) and passivation current density at 500 mV (I_{pass}: A/cm^2) were evaluated using a potentiostat (Model 273; EG&G Princeton Applied Research, Princeton, NJ, USA). For the potentiodynamic corrosion tests, the open circuit potential was evaluated up to 16 hours in the aerated electrolyte. Following the OCP measurement, determination of linear polarization and cathodic polarization were conducted in aerated conditions and anodic polarization in deareated conditions over the ranges and scanning rate as previously reported [8]. A summary of the experimental conditions is given in Table 3.

2.9. Statistical Analysis

The results for all tests, except for corrosion testing, were analyzed using one-way ANOVA and the Tukey's test at $\alpha = 0.05$. The data from the corrosion tests were statistically analyzed by Kruskai-Walls H test at a significance level of $\alpha = 0.05$.

Table 3. Experimental conditions for determination of corrosion behavior.

Methods	**Atmosphere**	**Potential ranges (mV)**	**Scan rate (mV/sec)**	**Corrosion parameters**
Open-circuit potential (OCP)	-	-	-	OCP: **OCP** (mV) 16 h
Linear polarization	Aerated (Air + 10% CO_2)	−8 < OCP to OCP < +8	0.1	Polarization resistance: $\mathbf{R_P}$ ($M\Omega \cdot cm^2$)
Potentiodynamic cathodic polarization	-	OCP to 300 < OCP	0.167	Cathodic Tafel slope: β_c (V/decade)
Potentiodynamic anodic polarization	Deaerated (N_2 + 10% CO_2)	20 0< OCP to 2000 > OCP	0.167	Anodic Tafel slope: β_a (V/decade) Corrosion current density: I_{corr} (A/cm^2) $I_{corr} = \beta_a\beta_c/2.3\ R_P\ (\beta_a+\beta_c)$ Pasive current density at 500 mV: I_{pass} (A/cm^2)

3. RESULTS

3.1. Exterior Appearance

Figure 3 compares the external appearances of a LBM-fabricated Ti-6Al-4V ELI specimen, an EBM-fabricated Ti-6Al-4V ELI specimen, a cast specimen and a plastic dumbbell pattern used as the template for preparing a mold for casting the tensile specimens. In Figure 4, an enlarged view of the gauge section of the LBM, EBM and cast dumbbell specimen are also included. The EBM fabricated specimen has a much rough surface with a rippled, exterior appearance.

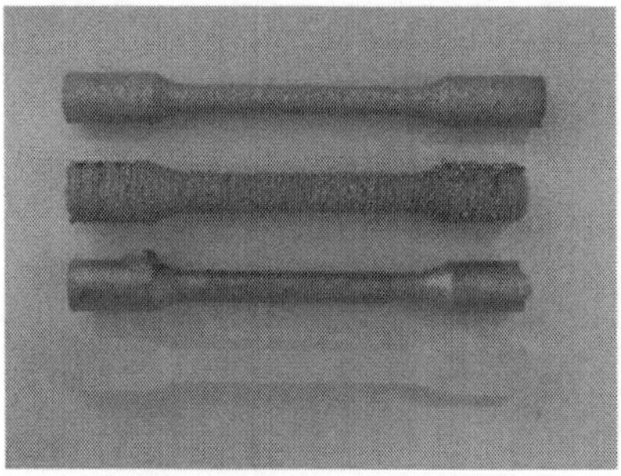

Figure 3. Exterior appearance of (**a**) an LBM specimen; (**b**) an EBM specimen; (**c**) a cast Ti-6Al-4VELI specimen; and (**d**) a plastic dumbbell pattern.

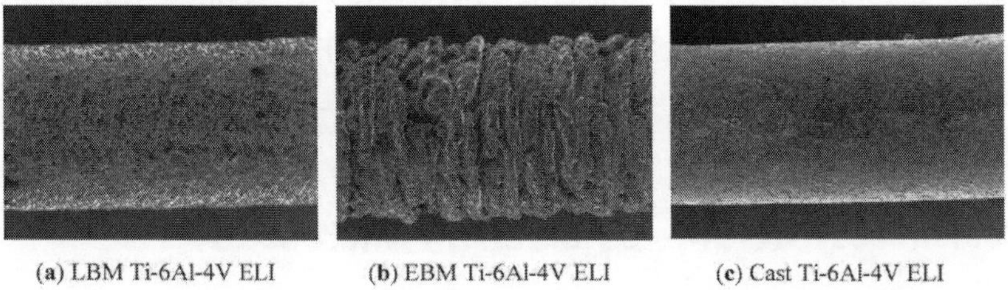

Figure 4. Enlarged views of (**a**) an LBM specimen; (**b**) an EBM specimen; (**c**) a cast Ti-6Al-4V.

3.2. Microstructures by Optical Microscopy

The microstructures of all those four type of tested alloys shows in Figure 5. Compared to the microstructure of an interior area of the cast specimens, which is away from the α-case layer, all other three types of the specimens, LBM, EBM and wrought specimens all had much finer α-β lamellar structures. The lamellar structure in the cast specimen was much courser than others.

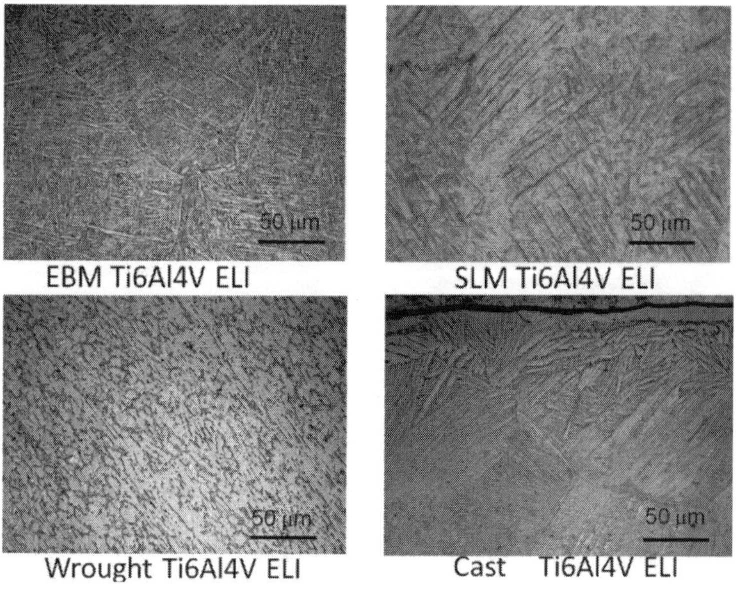

Figure 5. Typical microstructure of (**a**) an LBM specimen; (**b**) an EBM specimen; (**c**) a cast Ti-6Al-4V ELI specimen and (**d**) a wrought specimen.

3.3. Microstructures by Electron Microscopy

Figure 6(a) shows optical (light) micrograph for α-Ti-6Al-4V microstructure of EBM specimen. The dark (or black) in this picture is β. Bottom picture of Figure 6(b) shows SEM view of EBM structure as in top, indicating prominent acicular α-plates. The SEM and Spectrum resulting from EDS analysis for EBM Ti-6Al-4V specimen are shown in Figure 7. On the other hand, top view inFigure 3 shows optical micrograph with mixture of α-phase and α′martensite in the LBM specimen. Bottom view in Figure 8 is corresponding SEM view. Figure 9 indicates TEM views of EBM α-phase, while that of LBM consists of mixed α-α′ (with some twinning in α). Figure 10 is the TEM pictures showing that EBM specimen has α-phase in Ti-6Al-4V, and dark areas separating α-phase grains is β. Figure 10 is a magnified TEM view of α-grains in EBM Ti-6Al-4V specimen, showing dislocations. The α-phase grains in Figure 11 are inclined to the specimen surface. Average grain size is ~800 nm (0.8 μm). Figure 12 is a TEM view of α-α′martensite and twinned α on the LBM specimen.

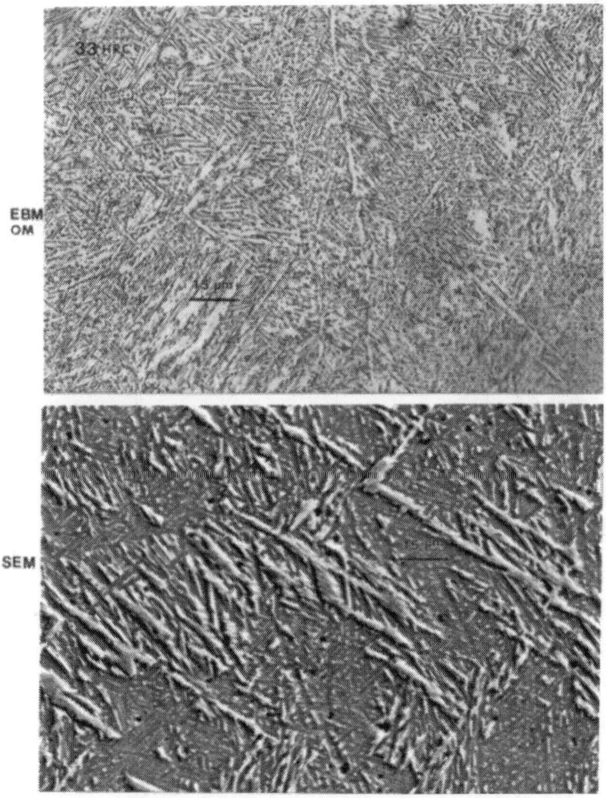

Figure 6. (EBM) Top shows optical (light) micrograph for α-Ti-6Al-4V microstructure. Dark (or black) is β. Bottom shows SEM view of EBM structure as in top. Prominent acicular α-plates.

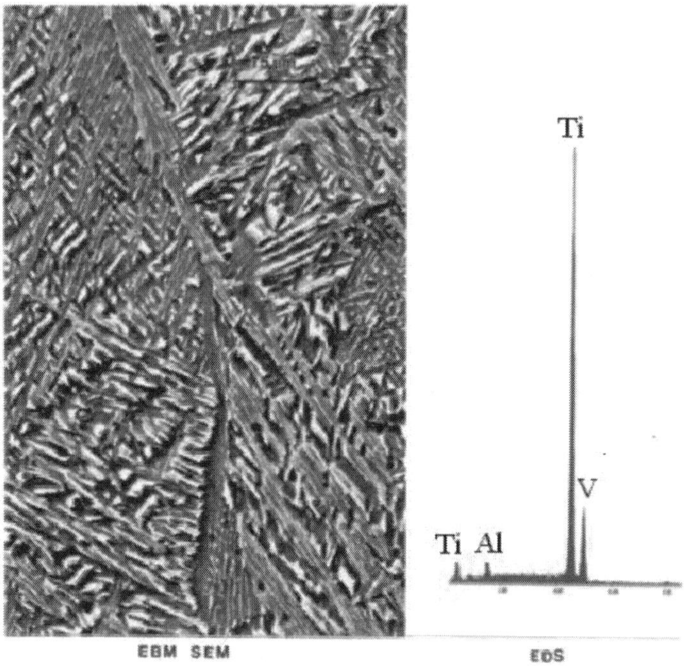

Figure 7. SEM and EDS for EBM Ti-6Al-4V.

3.4. Mechanical Properties

Figure 13 summarizes the yield strength, tensile strength and elongation of each type of Ti-6Al-4V ELI specimens. The mechanical properties for the wrought specimens were obtained from manufacturer's data sheet. The strength of the LBM and wrought specimens were similar whereas those of the EBM specimens were somewhat lower than those two specimens. In the properties of the cast specimens, note that the yield strength is the lowest among all types of specimens ($p < 0.05$). Figure 14 shows the measured interior, bulk microhardness numbers for each type of alloy specimens. The hardness of both the LBM and EBM specimens was similar and roughly 25% higher than that of the cast and wrought alloys ($p > 0.05$). However, as shown in the optical micrographs in Figure 6(a) and Figure 8(a), the EBM-product hardness measured using a Rockwell C-scale indenter is slightly lower than the SLM-product hardness: 33 HRC *versus* 34

HRC. This is also reflected in the mechanical property data in Figure 13 where both the yield stress and the UTS are roughly 11% higher for the SLM product than the EBM product. This is somewhat reversed from the micorindentation hardness comparisons shown in Figure 14. The elongations for both the EBM and LBM (SLM) products are low in contrast to wrought Ti-6Al-4V in particular, and the EBM product elongation is only about 2%. This is in contrast to elongations of more than 12% reported earlier by Murr *et al.* [9]. Correspondingly, the yield and UTS were more than 30% higher for EBM-fabricated products (Murr *et al.*, 2010 [9]).

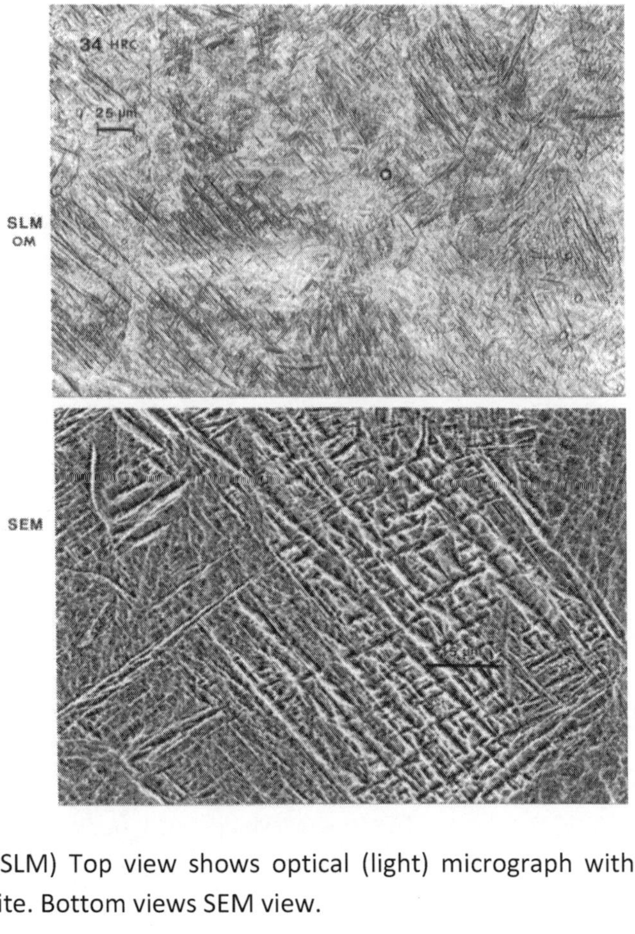

Figure 8. (SLM) Top view shows optical (light) micrograph with primarily α'martensite. Bottom views SEM view.

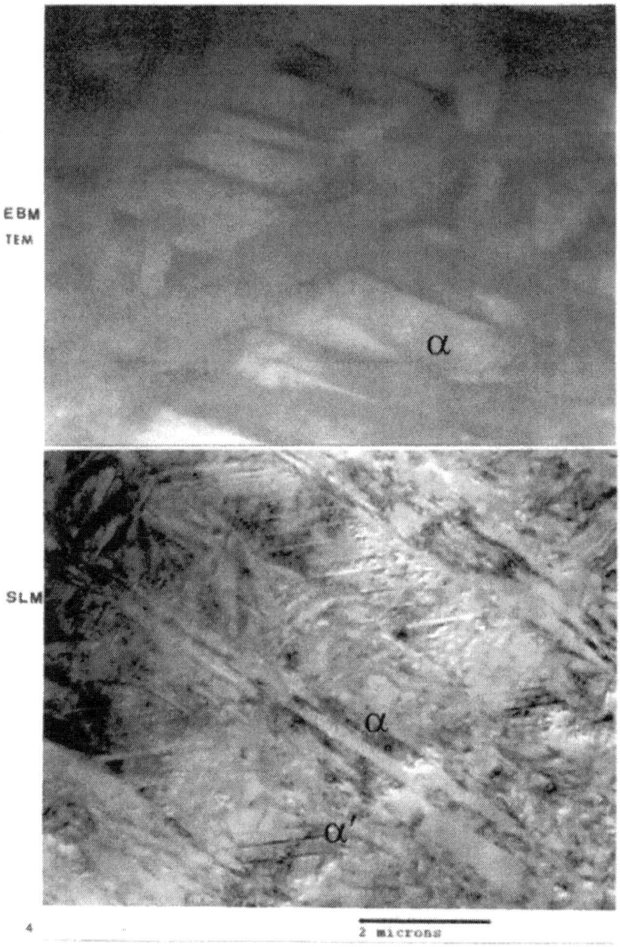

Figure 9. TEM views of EBM-α-phase and SLM mixed α-α′ (with some twinning in α).

These "variances" are due in part to the fact that the oxygen content for ELI-Ti-6Al-4V powders utilized in this comparative study for EBM *versus* SLM (LBM) varied significantly. The nominal oxygen content for powder is ~0.12% oxygen, but the recycled EBM powder exhibited an oxygen level of 0.34%, roughly 3 times the nominal content. Correspondingly, the LBM powder contained only 0.14% oxygen, and this is in contrast to 0.11% oxygen for the wrought product. Consequently, the interstitial oxygen present in the EBM product is probably responsible for the higher microindentation hardness shown in Figure 14 and the significantly degraded mechanical properties shown in Figure 13.

Figure 10. TEM of EBM showing α-phase in Ti-6Al-4V. Dark areas separating α-phase grains is β.

3.5. Grindability

The grindability for each type of the Ti-6Al-4V ELI specimens for the wheel speeds of 500 and 1.250 m/min are shown in Figure 15. For the higher grindability speed at 1.250 m/min, the grindability of the cast specimen was significantly lower when compared to that of the other specimens ($p < 0.05$). On the other hand, at 500 m/min, no significant difference was found among all types of the specimens tested ($p > 0.05$).

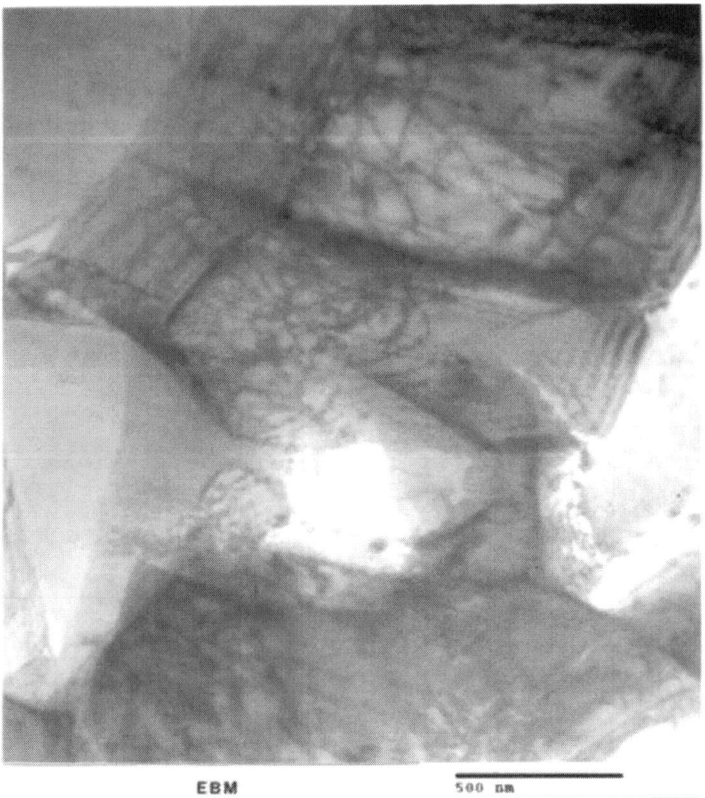

Figure 11. Magnified (TEM) view of α-grains in EBM Ti-6Al-4V sample showing dislocations. α-phase grains are inclined to the specimen surface. Average grain size is ~800 nm (0.8 μm).

3.6. Corrosion Behavior

Table 4 summarizes the corrosion parameter determined specimen using the different fabrication methods. No significant differences were seen in the OCP and the passivation current density among all the fabrication methods. On the other hand, the Kruskai-Walls H test shows significant differences in the polarization resistance (R_p; $p = 0.4$) and the corrosion current density (I_{corr}: $p = 0.2$) among all the fabrication methods. The LBM and wrought specimens showed better corrosion resistance compared to that of the EBM specimens and cast specimens. This is certainly related to the fact that in the EBM and cast specimens the α-phase dominates, the acicular α plates are larger than the α'-martensite in the SLM components. In the wrought specimens, there is considerably more β than in the EBM or cast specimens, and the α and β regions are smaller as shown in Figure 5(d).

Figure 12. TEM view of SLM α-α'martensite and twinned α.

4. DISCUSSION

In the present study, the microstructures and mechanical properties, grindability and corrosion behavior of the Ti-6Al-4V ELI specimens fabricated by different layer manufacturing techniques were investigated along with conventional cast and wrought fabrication technologies. The Ti-6Al-4V ELI specimens were prepared using newly introduced rapid prototyping machines, a laser beam melting (LBM) or SLM system and an electron beam melting (EBM) system. The tensile data of the LBM and EBM fabricated specimens were compared with those of cast and wrought Ti-6Al-4V ELI. It was interesting to examine the microstructures of all those four types of tested specimens. Compared to the microstructure of an interior area of the cast specimens, which is away from the α-β lamellar structures. The lamellar structure in the cast specimen was much courser than others.

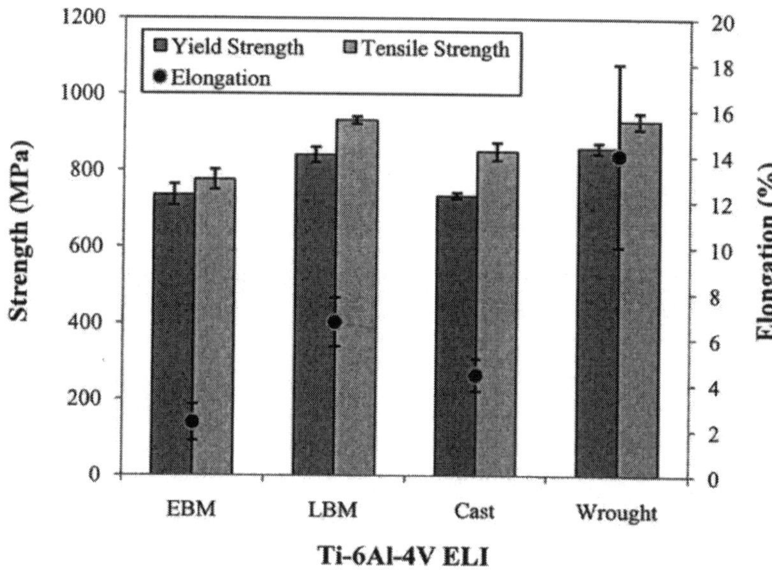

Figure 13. Mechanical properties of metals using different fabrication methods.

While differences in microstructures for the EBM and SLM-fabricated products as shown inFigure 5, Figure 6, Figure 7, Figure 8, Figure 9, Figure 10, Figure 11, Figure 12 and Figure 13 can account for some variances in properties and performance, differences in oxygen content complicate this issue as noted earlier. It is, however apparent, as noted by Murr *et al.* [9], that LBM fabrication of Ti-6Al-4V products, especially having smaller dimensions, produce more rapid cooling than EBM fabrication, resulting in transformation to α′martensite in various proportions. This microstructure refinement appears to have a significant effect on the corrosion potential which may be especially significant for dental applications. However, if sufficient care is taken to utilize only low oxygen content powder for EBM fabrication, the microstructures may be manipulated to exhibit better mechanical properties and other performance features implicit inFigure 13, Figure 14, Figure 15 and Figure 16.

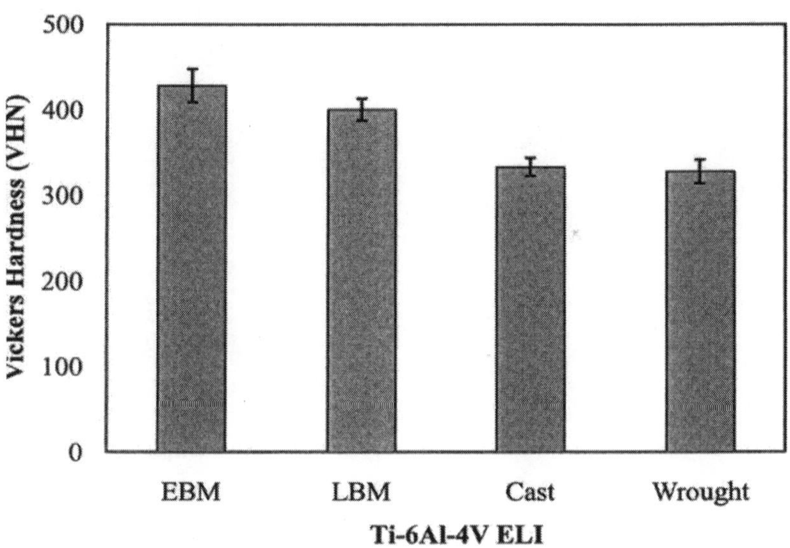

Figure 14. Bulk hardness of Ti-6Al-4V ELI specimens using different fabrication methods.

It is interesting to note that for the manufacture of small dental implant products, there seems to be little advantage of one melt process over the other. Figure 13 illustrated a small increment of strength for SLM processing over EBM processing while Figure 14 indicated a small hardness increase of EBM fabrication over SLM fabrication. Moreover, both EBM and SLM processing exhibited harder products than wrought or cast products (Figure 14). In contrast, there was no difference in grindability for EBM or SLM products and no corrosion difference. Fundamentally, fine α′-martensite produced by SLM processing, and this similarity in microstructure behavior is consistent with the mechanical property responses noted above. Laser melting has been shown to allow finer surface structure control than electron beam melting, and this may be a concern for the production of dental implants in particular.

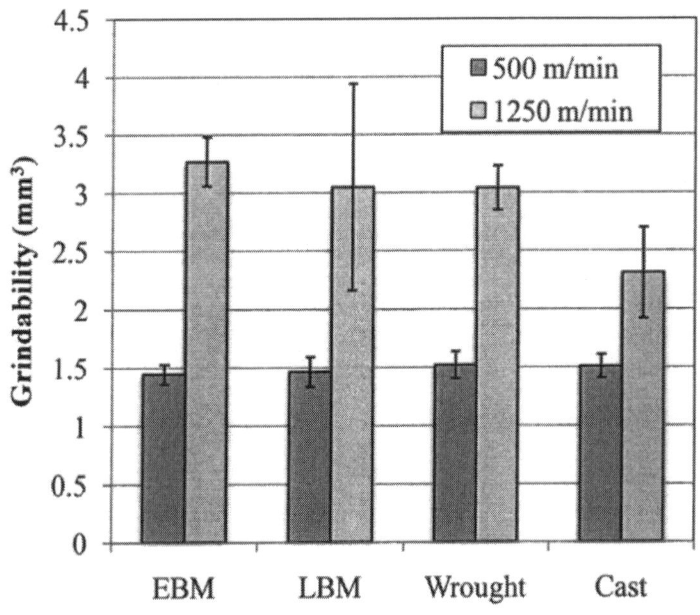

Figure 15. Grindability of Ti-6Al-4V ELI specimens using different fabrication methods.

Recently, Murr *et al.* [9] have shown that open-cellular structures and complex cellular (or porous)-solid monoliths can be fabricated by EBM for potential biomedical implant applications. This could include dental implants which could be fabricated with low density, porous stems with low stiffness (or Young's modulus) for bone stress shielding reduction.

Table 4. Corrosion characteristics of specimens tested.

	OCP (mV)		Rp (MW)		icorr (nA/cm^2)		ipassive (nA/cm^2)	
LBM	−239	(18) [a]	1.81	(0.5) [a]	23	(8) [a]	870	(179) [a]
EBM	−246	(81) [a]	0.44	(0.3) [b]	199	(90) [b]	1645	(583) [a]
Cast	−243	(18) [a]	0.75	(0.7) [b,c]	199	(158) [b]	1137	(752) [a]
Wrought	−159	(18) [a]	1.36	(0.5) [a,c]	49	(25) [a]	837	(249) [a]

Values are means (one standard deviation) for properties of tested alloys. Identical letters indicate no statistical differences ($p > 0.05$).

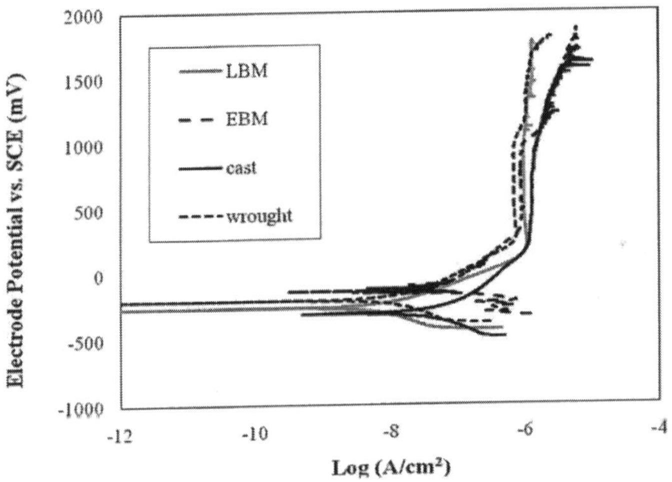

Figure 16. Typical anodic polarization behavior of Ti-6Al-4V ELI specimens using different fabrication methods.

5. CONCLUSIONS

The Ti-6Al-4V ELI specimens fabricated using the electron beam melting (EBM) or the laser beam melting (LBM) systems had a sound microstructure and mechanical properties. Grindability was found to be comparable to those of wrought and cast Ti-6Al-4V ELI specimens. These newly introduced metal-fabrication techniques can be used in preparing numerous types of medical and dental prostheses. Further studies are needed to thoroughly examine specimens prepared at various fabrication conditions to develop optional parameters for properties testing, including dimensional accuracy, corrosion characteristics, fatigue properties, *etc.*

ACKNOWLEDGMENTS

The Authors gratefully acknowledge Hideki Fujii, Nippon Steel Corp., Chiba Japan, for analyzing the oxygen content of the specimens. In addition, the Authors gratefully appreciated Gilbert Chahine and Radovan Kovacevic at Research Center for Advanced Manufacturing, Department of Mechanical Engineering, Southern Methodist University for making electron beam melting (EBM) specimens, and EOS GmbH in Germany for making laser beam melting (LBM) specimens.

REFERENCES

1. Das, S.; Wohlert, M.; Beaman, J.J.; Bourell, D.L. Producing metal parts with selective laser sintering/hot isostatic pressing. *J. Manag.* **1998**, *50*, 17–20.

2. Lü, L.; Fuh, J.Y.H.; Wong, Y.S. *Laser-Induced Materials Sand Processes for Rapid Prototyping*; Kluwer Academic Publishers: Boston, MA, USA, 2001.

3. Murr, L.E.; Esquivel, E.V.; Quinones, S.A.; Gaytan, S.M.; Lopez, M.I.; Martinez, E.Y.; Medina, F.; Hernandez, D.H.; Martinez, E.; Martinez, J.L.; *et al.* Microstructures and mechanical properties of electron beam-rapid manufactured Ti-6Al-4V biomedical prototypes compared to wrought Ti-6Al-4V. *Mater. Char.* **2009**, *60*, 96–105.

4. Murr, L.E.; Quinones, S.A.; Gaytan, S.M.; Lopez, M.I.; Rodela, A.; Martinez, E.Y.; Hernandez, D.H.; Martinez, E.; Medina, F.; Wicker, R.B. Microstructure and mechanical behaviorof Ti-6Al-4V produced by

rapid-layer manufacturing, for biomedical applications. *J. Mech. Behav. Biomed. Mater.* **2009**, *2*, 20–32.

5. ASM Handbook Committee. *Metals Handbook*, 9th ed.; Metallography and Microstructures, American Society for Metals: Metals Park, OH, USA, 1985; Volume 9.

6. Koike, M.; Ohkubo, C.; Sato, H.; Fujii, H.; Okabe, T. Evaluation of cast Ti-Fe-O-N alloys for dental applications. *Mater. Sci. Eng. C* **2005**, *25*, 349–356.

7. Koike, M.; Chan, K.S.; Okabe, T. Dental titanium casting at baylor college of dentistry—Update. In *Innovations in Titanium Technology*; Gungor, M.H., Imam, M.A., Froes, F.H., Eds.; TMS: Warrendale, PA, USA, 2007; pp. 199–208.

8. Koike, M.; Cai, Z.; Fujii, H.; Brezner, M.; Okabe, T. Corrosion behavior of cast titanium with reduced surface reaction layer made by a face-coating method. *Biomaterials* **2003**, *24*, 4541–4549.

9. Murr, L.E.; Gaytan, S.M.; Medina, F.; Martinez, E.; Martinez, J.L.; Hernandez, D.H.; Machado, B.I.; Ramirez, D.A.; Wicker, R.B. Characterization of Ti-6Al-4V open cellular foams fabricated by additive manufacturing usingelectron beam melting. *Mater. Sci. Eng. A*2010, *527*, 1861–1868.

Chapter 5

Fast Prototyping of Sensorized Cell Culture Chips and Microfluidic Systems with Ultrashort Laser Pulses

Sebastian M. Bonk [1], Paul Oldorf [2], Rigo Peters [2], Werner Baumann [1] and Jan Gimsa [1,*]

[1]Chair of Biophysics, University of Rostock, Rostock 18057, Germany

[2]SLV Mecklenburg-Vorpommern GmbH, Rostock 18069, Germany

ABSTRACT

We developed a confined microfluidic cell culture system with a bottom plate made of a microscopic slide with planar platinum sensors for the measurement of acidification, oxygen consumption, and cell adhesion. The slides were commercial slides with indium tin oxide (ITO) plating or were prepared from platinum sputtering (100 nm) onto a 10-nm titanium adhesion layer. Direct processing of the sensor structures (approximately three minutes per chip) by an ultrashort pulse laser facilitated the production of the prototypes. pH-sensitive areas were produced by the sputtering of 60-nm Si_3N_4 through a simple mask made from a circuit board material. The system body and polydimethylsiloxane (PDMS) molding forms for the microfluidic structures were manufactured by micromilling using a printed circuit board (PCB) milling machine for circuit boards. The microfluidic structure was finally imprinted in PDMS. Our approach avoided the use of photolithographic techniques and enabled fast and cost-efficient prototyping of the systems. Alternatively, the direct production of metallic, ceramic or polymeric molding tools was tested. The use of ultrashort pulse lasers improved the precision of the structures and avoided any contact of the final structures with toxic chemicals and possible adverse effects for the cell culture in lab-on-a-chip systems.

KEYWORDS

rapid prototyping; micro sensor chip; ITO; oxygen; pH; picosecond laser; cell monitoring system; top-down approach

1. INTRODUCTION

The development of multifunctional microfluidic systems calls for the integration of sensors and actuators such as electrical sensors and heating or pump elements, all of which are routinely manufactured using well-established microelectronic fabrication techniques. Microfluidic components are also produced using photolithographic technology, especially in basic research [1]. Nevertheless, injection molding is unrivalled amongst the various polymer technologies used in the mass production of microfluidic components. Microinjection molding, hot embossing, or hot shaping are alternatives for low volume production or prototyping [2].

The materials used in biotechnological and medical applications must comply with certain requirements, e.g., biocompatibility or stability against heat sterilization. These requirements are challenging with respect to the physical and chemical properties, especially in lab-on-a-chip devices for long-term cell monitoring or for micro-reaction techniques in Micro Total Analysis Systems (μTAS) [3]. Unfortunately, glass, as the material of choice, requires special adaptations in the production methods [4]. For low volume production or prototyping, photolithography techniques are time-consuming and costly due to their high number of processing steps. Often, the outdated (4-inch) disk-wafer technology is used, which restricts the size and the degrees of freedom in the individual chip design [5].

To increase the frequency of prototype realization and for small batch series (a requirement in basic research), it is necessary to implement fast design cycles using flexible and fast production technologies. This strategy shortens development times and test cycles in the research-intensive field of microfluidic systems development. As a consequence, rapid prototyping techniques are gaining increasing importance because they help reduce costs through more efficient employment of human resources.

To our knowledge, lasers are routinely used in the production of precise circuit board structures as small as 50-µm wide [6,7], whereas the photolithographic technology dominates thin layer structuring, especially of platinum or ITO layers on silicon or glass [8,9]. With respect to the conventional long-pulse lasers, ultrashort pulse lasers improve the quality of ablation because a higher percentage of their pulse energy is employed in evaporation instead of melting processes [10,11]. This is another reason why the technology is gaining importance in the surface modification of thin layers [12] or in the industrial production of solar cells [13].

In some cases, laser techniques were used by other authors for the production of channels or recesses in microfluidic systems [4,14,15,16].

Here, we present a new prototyping technology for sensorized microfluidic cell-culture systems, which is based on a combination of different applications of an ultrashort pulse laser system. The system consists of a polycarbonate body with inlets and outlets for fluids, as well as a polycarbonate lid (*cf.* Section 2.4). The lid bears the microfluidic structure, which was imprinted in polydimethylsiloxane (PDMS). In the assembled system, the microfluidic structure is sealed by a microscopic glass slide, which bears the thin layer-sensor structures.

The polycarbonate body was produced using a standard printed circuit board (PCB) micromilling machine. Here, this machine was also used to produce the PDMS molding tools for imprinting the microfluidic structures into the PDMS lid. More precise, high temperature-stable molding tools, which are needed for hot embossing, injection molding or hot shaping, could be produced from ceramic wrought materials (Keralpor99, Kerafol GmbH, Eschenbach, Germany). Direct laser structuring is an alternative to the common photolithographic production of PDMS molding tools, e.g., from SU-8 or silicon [1,17]. In our system, the microfluidic structure was confined by a microscopic glass slide on the bottom. The slide carried amperometric Clark oxygen sensors, potentiometric pH and impedimetric cell adhesion sensors interdigitated electrode structures (IDES) that were originally developed with photolithographic techniques and redesigned for laser structuring after testing [18].

Our new technology circumvents the use of clean rooms and toxic or harmful chemicals, thereby shortening manufacturing times. This technology allows for the use of a wide variety of wafer formats. Here, we present sensorized chips that were produced from cheap microscopic glass slides. Together with a microfluidic PDMS structure, they allow for long-term (days to weeks) cell culture and on-line registration of sensor readouts.

2. EXPERIMENTAL SECTION

2.1. Laser Structuring of Platinum and ITO Layers

Microscope slides (NK72.1, Carl Roth, Karlsruhe, Germany) were cleaned with aqueous 10% Tickopur W77 cleaning solution (BANDELIN electronic GmbH & Co. KG, Berlin, Germany) in an ultrasonic bath and dried in a pressurised air stream. The slides were sputtered with 130 nm of platinum on a 15-nm titanium undercoating using a magnetron sputter system (Ardenne LA-320S, VON ARDENNE GmbH, Dresden, Germany). The chips were structured by ablation with a picosecond laser (TruMicro 5X50, TRUMPF Laser- und Systemtechnik GmbH, Ditzingen, Germany) using a high-precision micromachining system (GL.5, GFH GmbH, Deggendorf, Germany). The laser could be switched between three wavelengths, 1030 nm (fundamental frequency), 515 nm (second harmonic frequency), and

343 nm (third harmonic frequency). The positioning precision of the system was better than 1 µm. The structure designs were drawn in AutoCAD 2010 (Autdesk, Inc., San Rafael, CA, USA) and directly exported into the laser control system as DXF-files [19]. For chip structuring, platinum or ITO (CEC020, Präzisions Glas & Optik GmbH, Iserlohn, Germany) were ablated from the microscope slide at a wavelength of 343 nm with a pulse frequency of 400 kHz with a pulse energy of 1.25 µJ, and an effective spot diameter of 10 µm. At 1000 mm/s driving, the pulse spot overlapped approximately 80%. To ensure the microscopic transparency of the chip areas without sensor structures, platinum areas were ablated in bidirectional stripes of 8-µm distance. This ablation step could be omitted in ITO structuring (Figure 1). For both materials, the sensor structures were outlined in a final step at 100 mm/s driving, a pulse frequency of 40 kHz and a pulse energy of 1.25 µJ. To compensate for the size of the laser spot, the outlines of the structures were enlarged by 6 µm in the AutoCAD files.

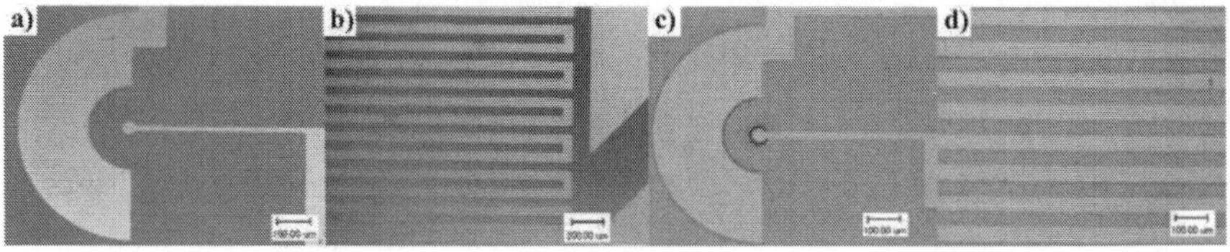

Figure 1. Platinum (**a**,**b**) and indium tin oxide (ITO) (**c**,**d**) structures of the oxygen sensors with a circular working electrode spot and semi-circular counter electrodes (**a**,**c**), as well as interdigitated electrode structures (IDES) with a50-µm pitch (**b**,**d**). The on-chip-sensor connectors were insulated in a following processing step.

2.2. Laser Structuring of Silicon Nitride (Si_3N_4)

After structuring, the chips were cleaned again, as described above, and sputtered with a 200-nm Si_3N_4 passivation layer (300 s at 400 W in high frequency mode). For a thicker passivation layer, another chip batch was passivated with 1000 nm of Si_3N_4 (GeSiM mbH, Grosserkmannsdorf, Germany) using a PE-CVD process. Si_3N_4 was chosen because of its chemical, electrical and optical characteristics, as well as its biocompatibility. A second laser-processing step was executed to create windows in the passivation layer for the external chip connectors and the sensors. Si_3N_4layers of both thicknesses were ablated at 1000 mm/s driving, a pulse frequency of 200 kHz and a pulse spot overlap of approximately 70%. To remove the Si_3N_4 passivation layer only and not the platinum layers, a maximum pulse energy of 1.0 µJ was used. To produce pH sensors in a final step, a 60-nm Si_3N_4 layer was sputtered through four openings in a PCB, which was used as a cheap and simple mask.

2.3. Laser Structuring of Molding Tools by Laser Ablation

In an attempt to overcome the limitations of the stereo-lithographic (material, aspect ratio) and micro-milling techniques (precision, surface roughness), the laser system was used to create new molding tools for microfluidics. A wrought aluminum oxide ceramic chip was laser processed in the same system with at a wavelength of 1030 nm, a pulse energy of 125 µJ, 2000 mm/s driving and a pulse rate of 200 kHz. A structure depth of 240 µm was reached after 20 repetitions.

2.4. Cell Culture System and Microfluidics Fabrication

Figure 2 presents the cell culture system consisting of a body with fluidic connectors and a lid with a central PDMS membrane. An outside ring and inner spacer structures confined the microfluidic cell culture volume. All of the polycarbonate parts, *i.e.*, the system's body, lid and the PDMS molding tools for the microfluidic structures, were produced by a PCB micromilling machine (CCD 2, BUNGARD Elektronik, Windeck, Germany). The body and lid were designed in AutoCad and milled in an 8-mm polycarbonate plate, whereas the molding tools were milled in polymethyl methacrylate

(PMMA) because of its better grindability with smaller milling tools (<500 µm in diameter). For the larger fluidic body structures of the cell culture system, Teflon® could also be used for the molding tools. Because of its low surface adhesion, Teflon® has advantages in the separation of the PDMS parts from the casting molds, though it is delicate to mill with small tools.

To produce the PDMS parts, PDMS monomer (Sylgard 184, Dow Corning Inc. Midland, MI, USA) was degassed, injected into the molding tools and cured for 4 h at 70 °C. After removing the molded parts, the bottom side of the PDMS body was manually coated with a very thin layer of uncured PDMS before the body was fixed to the chip under pressure and cured for a second time. For improved PDMS adhesion, the polycarbonate parts and the chip surfaces were coated with a bonding agent (GRUN G790, Wacker Chemie AG, München, Germany) before PDMS injection. After curing the PDMS, the microfluidic connectors were glued to the body. The connectors were shortened syringe needles fixed with their plastic connectors in cross-shaped notches of the body (Figure 2). The notches hindered rotation of the syringe heads and facilitated the attachment of Luer lock connectors. The removable lid enabled access to the culturing volume and the integration of 3D scaffolds.

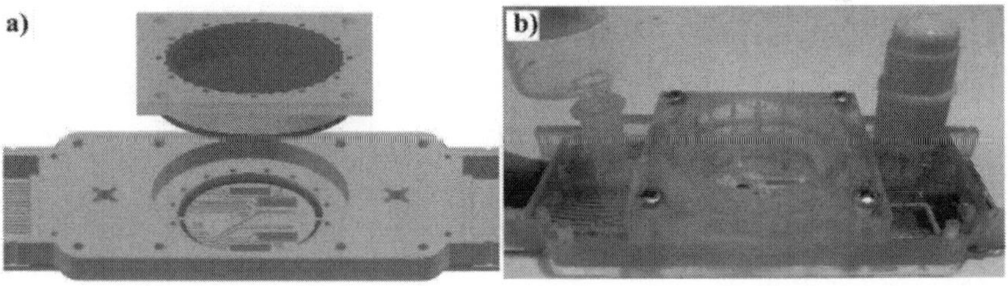

Figure 2. Computer-aided design of the microfluidic system (**a**) with the body (bottom) and lid (top) milled in polycarbonate (light turquoise). The blue polydimethylsiloxane (PDMS)-imprinted parts (gasket with fluidic channels in the body and PDMS membrane in the lid) confine the fluidic volume. The laser-structured chip (green) is glued to the lower PDMS surface. (**b**) The assembled cell culture system with a flexible printed circuit board connector (lower left), as well as a syringe and syringe-injection cap on the left and right inlets, respectively.

2.5. Cell Culture

To verify the biocompatibility, a mouse osteoblast precursor cell line (MC3T3-E1) was used. These cells, which are a common model system for bone regeneration, were obtained from the German collection of microorganisms and cell culture (DMSZ GmbH, Braunschweig, Germany). The cells were cultured in an incubator at 37 °C with 95% humidity and 5% CO_2. The cells were grown to confluence in 50-mL cell culture flasks (25 cm^2; Greiner bio-one, Frickenhausen, Germany) in alpha medium (order No. F 0925) supplemented with 1% penicillin/streptomycin (stem solution: 100 U/mL penicillin and 100 µg/mL streptomycin) and 10% foetal bovine serum (all purchased from Biochrom AG, Berlin, Germany). After the cells grew to confluence, they were trypsinated in phosphate-buffered saline supplemented with 0.05% trypsin and 0.02% EDTA (PAN Biotech GmbH, Aidenbach, Germany) and were diluted before subculture or transfer to the microfluidic systems.

For cell culture in the microfluidic systems, carbonate-free alpha medium (P03-2510, Pan Biotech, Aidenbach, Germany) was supplemented as described above and buffered with 20 mM HEPES (Carl Roth, Karlsruhe, Germany). For cell seeding, 500 µL of the cell suspension with up to 500,000 cells/mL (corresponding to 50,000 cells per culture system) were injected by slow flushing of the system. Then, the system was closed with a medium-filled 6-mL syringe at the inlet and a syringe injection cap as a cannula injection port at the outlet (Figure 2). For medium exchange, an empty, open syringe with a 0.6-mm cannula was plugged into the injection port, and 500 µL of medium from the filled syringe was slowly flushed through the system.

3. RESULTS AND DISCUSSION

3.1. Structuring of Platinum and ITO

For processing, the sputtered chips were aligned with the limit stop of the laser workbench. The determination of the optimal laser parameters (power, driving, pulse rate, and pulse spot overlap) for structuring platinum or ITO layers required several pre-runs. Less than 3 min per chip were needed with the optimized laser process (chip area of 11.5 cm^2). The structures could be manufactured with widths less than 20 µm and minimal distances of 10 µm. The smallest on-chip structures were the working electrodes of the oxygen sensors with 40-µm diameter and a conducting path with 20-µm width.

The edge roughness of the structures was usually in the range of ±1.5 µm. We found that this result was less due to a problem of the beam guidance but primarily a consequence of the inhomogeneous ablation in the outer zones of the laser spot where the ablation depended on the trace curvature and the materials (Figure 3).

As observed in Figure 4, the distances between the IDES fingers were approximately 2 µm wider than expected, whereas their width was approximately 2 µm too small. This small mismatch between the design and manufactured structure resulted from an insufficient offset correction.

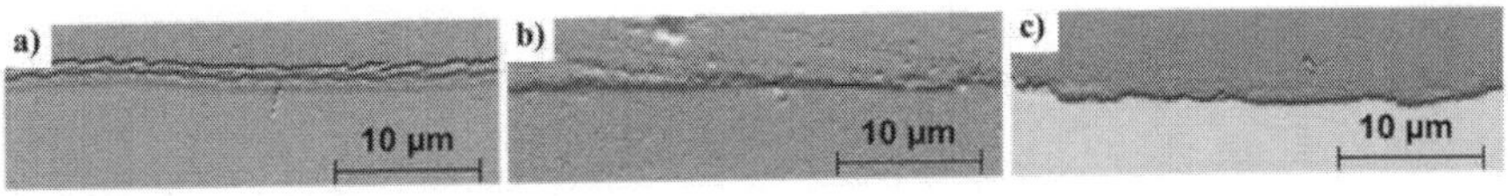

Figure 3. Edge quality of an IDES finger controlled by colour contrasted atomic force microscopic images. (**a**) ITO on glass; (**b**) platinum on glass; (**c**) photolithographically (photo mask) produced chip (GeSiM®).

Despite the ease of small offset corrections, small circular structures are more difficult to produce. The effective laser driving, *i.e.*, the linear distance between three pulse spots, is decreased in curved areas, which led to an increased pulse spot overlap, a stronger removal of material, and even some ablation of the glass carrier (see Figure 1c, oxygen working electrode). This problem will either be solved in a preliminary approach by a modification of the laser parameters in the individual software files for curved structures or with the next update of the driver software of the manufacturer of the laser positioning system (GFH GmbH).

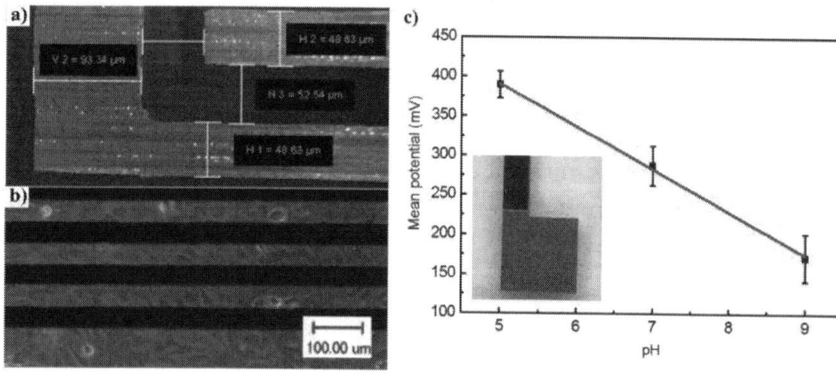

Figure 4. Images of a platinum IDES. (**a**) Scanning electron microscopy image with dimensions. (**b**) Confluent cells above the IDES. (**c**) Sensitivity test of a Si_3N_4 sensor layer on platinum (insert: pH sensor with 1.4 × 1.4 mm^2 electrode area). The data represent measurements with six chips in pH-buffered solutions with pH values of 5, 7, and 9. The straight line corresponds to a sensitivity of −53.8 ± 1.8 mV/pH.

3.2. Structuring of Si_3N_4

The laser parameters for processing the Si_3N_4 passivation layer were confined to a very small window by the underlying platinum and ITO structures of the IDES and oxygen sensors or the peripheral chip contacts. Within this window, 200-nm layers of Si_3N_4 could be removed without removing the platinum layer [19]. The ablation efficiency depended on the underlying substrate. The ablation of Si_3N_4 from glass required higher pulse energy than that over platinum because the ablation thresholds for Si_3N_4 were reduced over glass. Nevertheless, for platinum, the process led to roughening of the surfaces due to the punctual ablation (see the IDES in Figure 4). Interestingly, the 200- and 1000-nm Si_3N_4 layers could be removed using the same laser parameters, sustaining the theory of the effects at the Si_3N_4-platinum or Si_3N_4-glass interfaces that influenced the ablation process [13].

To produce pH sensors, 60 nm of Si_3N_4 were deposited on the laser-manufactured platinum structures. The chips were tested for their stabilities and pH sensitivities by measurements in standard buffer solutions with pH values of 5, 7 and 9 against an Ag/AgCl microelectrode (Microelectrode Inc., Bedford, NH, USA). The chips provided reproducible potentials 10 s after medium exchange. They were kept in the solution at room temperature for up to 600 s to confirm the stability of their readouts. The potentials were linearly dependent on the pH in the range from 5 to 9 at a sensitivity of −53.8 ± 1.8 mV/pH. This sensitivity was comparable to the sensitivity of ISFETS with a Si_3N_4-gate passivation layer [20].

3.3. Structuring Molding Tools by Laser Ablation

Laser manufacturing of molding tools from wrought aluminum oxide ceramic chips was fast and provided a very good surface quality (Figure 5). Per ablation scan, a depth of approximately 12 µm was obtained with 2000 mm/s driving and a repetition rate of 200 kHz. For our structures, the area-specific processing time of approximately 3600 mm^2/min per scan largely referred to the actual ablated area. A structure depth of 240 µm was reached after 20 repetitive scans, resulting in a 5 min processing time for the surface of the 30 × 30 mm^2 moulding tool (Figure 5a).

The moulding tool for the large sensor chip with a final depth of 465 µm was processed with modified parameters (Figure 5b). The driving and repetition rate were increased to 4000 mm/s and 400 kHz, respectively. This modification reduced the manufacturing time to approximately 35 min for 42 scans despite the larger surface of the tool.

The small tilts of the vertical structures were caused by optical effects in the ablating process (see the laser scanning microscope images in Figure 5). We believed that the resulting tilts in the fluidic channel walls would be advantageous in finally stripping the mold from the cast. If necessary, the tilts could be reduced by using special trepanning optics. Nevertheless, the smooth removal of the cured PDMS molds from the ceramic tools required the use of a mold release agent.

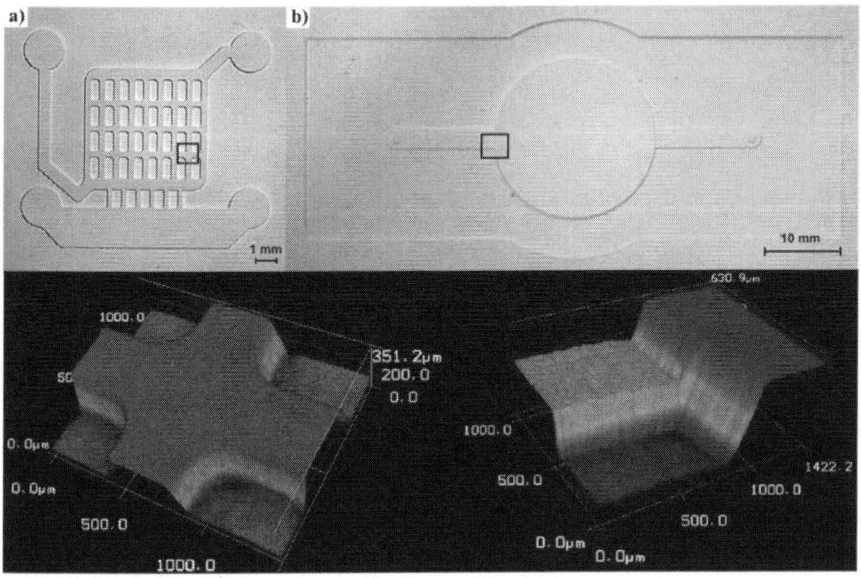

Figure 5. Two ceramic mold chips processed by laser ablation. Black squares mark the positions of the laser scanning microscope images below the mold images. (**a**) A 30 × 30 mm^{2}chip for a microfluidic pattern with 240-µm channel height. (**b**) Larger structure (33 × 76 mm^2) for the cell culture system with heights of approximately 230 µm (horizontal inlet and outlet channels) and 465 µm (circular area). Please note that the measures given in the images for the vertical scaling refer to a larger measuring frame.

3.4. Cell culture

MC3T3-E1 cells showed good proliferation in the microfluidic cell culture systems, reaching confluence approximately three days after seeding. The cells adhered to the Si_3N_4, as well as the platinum surfaces without surface coatings, e.g., with poly-D-lysin or laminin [5,18], suggesting that the laser ablation-induced surface roughness may improve cell adhesion [21,22]. Interestingly, the aqueous cell culture medium evaporated through the

PDMS lid, resulting in the formation of perturbing gas bubbles. Bubble formation was likely enhanced by the roughness of the cutting edges of the mold structures, which may have been transferred to the PDMS surfaces. In our system, the bubble formation could be suppressed by overlaying the lid of the cell culture system with deionized water, allowing for cell culture times longer than 10 days.

4. CONCLUSIONS AND OUTLOOK

The use of micromachined bodies and molding tools produced by the well-established PDMS technology in combination with ultrashort pulse laser micromachining of the sensor chips enabled fast prototyping of sensorized microfluidic cell culture systems without any photolithographic processing steps. We could produce thin-layer structures on glass chips with resolutions of approximately 10 µm. The use of this system reduced the fabrication times because the ablation of larger chip areas for microscopy could be spared. The optical transparency of the ITO substrates improved the microscopic analysis of the cell culture.

Fresh pH-sensitive Si_3N_4 layers were finally sputtered on the laser-machined structures. The layers showed a very good sensitivity of −53.8 ± 1.8 mV/pH when compared with ISFETs with Si_3N_4 gate passivation layers [23].

Our cell culture systems could be vapor sterilized and easily modified by remolding the PDMS structures of their lids. MC3T3-E1 cells could be cultured longer than 10 days with good cell adhesion to the laser-manufactured chip surfaces even without further surface modifications. The gas permeability of the PDMS lid ensured 100% air saturation in the culture medium, which may be desirable for the cells but could cause bubble formation. Smoother molds produced, for example, by laser processing, would likely reduce this problem in future microfluidic designs.

Ultrashort pulse laser techniques could also be used to produce casting molds for PDMS molding or even hot embossing of PMMA. This would require robust, temperature-stable casting molds manufactured, for example, from aluminium oxide ceramics. Our prototypes were produced in 3 to 35 min with a resolution of approximately 10 µm in the horizontal direction and approximately 13 µm in the vertical direction. This resolution outperformed that of the currently available stereo-lithographic 3D printers.

For the current system, a machine hour costs approximately €220, resulting in processing costs of €5 per ITO chip in a 60-chip batch. This system also allowed for the production of holes or recesses for advanced microfluidic designs (not shown). The maximum driving of our system of up to 4000 mm/s will be improved in the next generation of ablation systems.

ACKNOWLEDGMENTS

The authors are grateful to the German Research Council (DFG) for their funding of the graduate school GRK1505 "WELISA". We would like to thank Dr. Steffen Howitz (GeSiM GmbH, Grosserkmannsdorf) for help in the chip production, as well as Reik Modrozynski (Institute of Biophysics, University of Rostock) for his help with the cell culture. The authors would also like to thank Dipl.-Ing. Jürgen Josupeit and the group of Prof. Dr. Mathias Nowottnick (Institute of Electronic Appliances and Circuits, University of Rostock) for granting access and operating the magnetron sputter system.

AUTHOR CONTRIBUTIONS

Sebastian M. Bonk designed all experiments with the microfluidic cell culture system. The laser experiments were performed by Paul Oldorf. Jan Gimsa, Werner Baumann, and Rigo Peters contributed knowledge, devices, materials, and reagents. Sebastian M. Bonk provided a manuscript draft. He was financed by grants to Jan Gimsa who finalized the manuscript.

REFERENCES

1. Chiriacò, M.S.; Primiceri, E.; D'Amone, E.; Ionescu, R.E.; Rinaldi, R.; Maruccio, G. EIS microfluidic chips for flow immunoassay and ultrasensitive cholera toxin detection. *Lab Chip***2011**, *11*, 658–663.

2. Shah, J.J.; Geist, J.; Locascio, L.E.; Gaitan, M.; Rao, M.V.; Vreeland, W.N. Capillarity induced solvent-actuated bonding of polymeric microfluidic devices. *Anal. Chem.* **2006**, *78*, 3348–3353.

3. Kovarik, M.L.; Gach, P.C.; Ornoff, D.M.; Wang, Y.; Balowski, J.; Farrag, L.; Allbritton, N.L. Micro Total Analysis Systems for Cell Biology and Biochemical Assays. *Anal. Chem.* **2012**, *84*, 516–540.

4. Khan Malek, C.; Robert, L.; Boy, J.-J.; Blind, P. Deep microstructuring in glass for microfluidic applications. *Microsyst. Technol.* **2006**, *13*, 447–453.

5. Koester, P.J.; Buehler, S.M.; Stubbe, M.; Tautorat, C.; Niendorf, M.; Baumann, W.; Gimsa, J. Modular glass chip system measuring the electric activity and adhesion of neuronal cells—Application and drug testing with sodium valproic acid. *Lab Chip* **2010**, *10*, 1579–1586.

6. Zheng, H.; Gan, E.; Lim, G.C. Investigation of laser via formation technology for the manufacturing of high density substrates. *Opt. Lasers Eng.* **2001**, *36*, 355–371.

7. Moorhouse, C.J.; Villarreal, F.; Wendland, J.J.; Baker, H.J.; Hall, D.R.; Hand, D.P. Enhanced peak power CO_2 laser processing of PCB materials. *Proc. SPIE* **2005**, *5827*, 438–444.

8. Ahadian, S.; Ramón-Azcón, J.; Ostrovidov, S.; Camci-Unal, G.; Hosseini, V.; Kaji, H.; Ino, K.; Shiku, H.; Khademhosseini, A.; Matsue, T. Interdigitated array of Pt electrodes for electrical stimulation and engineering of aligned muscle tissue. *Lab Chip* **2012**, *12*, 3491–3503.

9. Yang, L.; Li, Y.; Griffis, C.L.; Johnson, M.G. Interdigitated microelectrode (IME) impedance sensor for the detection of viable Salmonella typhimurium. *Biosens. Bioelectron.* **2004**, *19*, 1139–1147.

10. Sugioka, K.; Cheng, Y. Ultrafast lasers—Reliable tools for advanced materials processing.*Light Sci. Appl.* **2014**, *3*, e149.

11. Gattass, R.R.; Mazur, E. Femtosecond laser micromachining in transparent materials. *Nat. Photonics* **2008**, *2*, 219–225.

12. Ahmmed, K.; Grambow, C.; Kietzig, A.-M. Fabrication of Micro/Nano Structures on Metals by Femtosecond Laser Micromachining. *Micromachines* **2014**, *5*, 1219–1253.

13. Bovatsek, J.; Tamhankar, A.; Patel, R.S.; Bulgakova, N.M.; Bonse, J. Thin film removal mechanisms in ns-laser processing of photovoltaic materials. *Thin Solid Films* **2010**, *518*, 2897–2904.

14. Liao, Y.; Song, J.; Li, E.; Luo, Y.; Shen, Y.; Chen, D.; Cheng, Y.; Xu, Z.; Sugioka, K.; Midorikawa, K. Rapid prototyping of three-dimensional microfluidic mixers in glass by femtosecond laser direct writing. *Lab Chip* **2012**, *12*, 746–749.

15. Talary, M.S.; Burt, J.P.; Rizvi, N.H.; Rumsby, P.T.; Pethig, R. Microfabrication of biofactory-on-a-chip devices using laser ablation technology. *Proc. SPIE* **1999**, *3680*, 572–580.

16. Müller, T.; Gradl, G.; Howitz, S.; Shirley, S.; Schnelle, T.; Fuhr, G. A 3-D microelectrode system for handling and caging single cells and particles. *Biosens. Bioelectron.* **1999**, *14*, 247–256.

17. Cho, C.-H.; Cho, W.; Ahn, Y.; Hwang, S.-Y. PDMS–glass serpentine microchannel chip for time domain PCR with bubble suppression in sample injection. *J. Micromech. Microeng.* **2007**,*17*, 1810–1817.

18. Buehler, S.M.; Stubbe, M.; Gimsa, U.; Baumann, W.; Gimsa, J. A decrease of intracellular ATP is compensated by increased respiration and acidification at sub-lethal parathion concentrations in murine embryonic neuronal cells: Measurements in metabolic cell-culture chips. *Toxicol. Lett.* **2011**, *207*, 182–190.

19. Peters, R.; Oldorf, P. Novel Applications of Ultra-short Pulsed Lasers. *Opt. Photonik* **2012**, *7*, 30–33.

20. Baumann, W.H.; Lehmann, M.; Schwinde, A.; Ehret, R.; Brischwein, M.; Wolf, B. Microelectronic sensor system for microphysiological application on living cells. *Sens. Actuators B Chem.* **1999**, *55*, 77–89.

21. Gimsa, U.; Iglič, A.; Fiedler, S.; Zwanzig, M.; Kralj-Iglič, V.; Jonas, L.; Gimsa, J. Actin is not required for nanotubular protrusions of primary

astrocytes grown on metal nano-lawn. *Mol. Membr. Biol.* **2007**, *24*, 243–255.

22. Matschegewski, C.; Staehlke, S.; Birkholz, H.; Lange, R.; Beck, U.; Engel, K.; Nebe, J.B. Automatic Actin Filament Quantification of Osteoblasts and Their Morphometric Analysis on Microtextured Silicon-Titanium Arrays. *Materials* **2012**, *5*, 1176–1195.

23. Schöning, M.J.; Ronkel, F.; Crott, M.; Thust, M.; Schultze, J.W.; Kordos, P.; Lüth, H. Miniaturization of potentiometric sensors using porous silicon microtechnology. *Electrochim. Acta* **1997**, *42*, 3185–3193.

Chapter 6

Rapid algorithm prototyping and implementation for power quality measurement

Krzysztof Kołek and Krzysztof Piątek

AGH University of Science and Technology, al. A.Mickiewicza 30, Kraków 30-059, Poland

ABSTRACT

This article presents a Model-Based Design (MBD) approach to rapidly implement power quality (PQ) metering algorithms. Power supply quality is a very important aspect of modern power systems and will become even more important in future smart grids. In this case, maintaining the PQ parameters at the desired level will require efficient implementation methods of the metering algorithms. Currently, the development of new, advanced PQ metering algorithms requires new hardware with adequate computational capability and time intensive, cost-ineffective manual implementations. An alternative, considered here, is an MBD approach. The MBD approach focuses on the modelling and validation of the model by simulation, which is well-supported by a Computer-Aided Engineering (CAE) packages. This paper presents two algorithms utilized in modern PQ meters: a phase-locked loop based on an Enhanced Phase Locked Loop (EPLL), and the flicker measurement according to the IEC 61000-4-15 standard. The algorithms were chosen because of their complexity and non-trivial development. They were first modelled in the MATLAB/Simulink package, then tested and validated in a simulation environment. The models, in the form of Simulink diagrams, were next used to automatically generate C code. The code was compiled and executed in real-time on the Zynq Xilinx platform that combines a reconfigurable Field Programmable Gate Array (FPGA) with a dual-core processor. The MBD development of PQ algorithms, automatic code generation, and compilation form a rapid algorithm prototyping and implementation path for PQ measurements. The main advantage of this approach is the ability to focus on the design, validation, and testing stages while skipping over implementation issues. The code generation process renders production-ready code that can be easily used on the target hardware. This is especially important when standards for PQ measurement are in constant development, and the PQ issues in emerging smart grids will require tools for rapid development and implementation of such algorithms.

KEYWORDS

Automatic code generation, Flicker, PLL, Power quality, Rapid prototyping, Simulink, Synchronisation

1. INTRODUCTION

Smart Grids offer an opportunity for effective power system management and utilisation of distributed and renewable energy resources. Efficient utilisation of the grid includes maintaining power supply (voltage) quality and emission (current) quality according to the specified limits. These limits can be set by the regulator, provided by standards or grid codes, or even agreed as part of an energy supply contract. The requirement of measuring the power quality (PQ) parameters has increased the interest in applications using signal processing techniques for PQ measurement. Comprehensive overviews of this problem are presented in [1,2]. These books describe classical methods of PQ analysis as well as the application of advanced techniques like neural networks, wavelet transform, and machine learning methods. It is clear that there is a need for increasingly complex PQ metering algorithms.

On the other hand, PQ metering is defined by standards, e.g. EN 61000-4-30. These standards define voltage quality measurement and provide implementation details needed to build a PQ meter. Consequently, algorithms for a PQ meter include not only signal processing techniques, but also data aggregation, gapless measurement, and synchronization with line voltage waveforms or time references, etc.

Because further requirements for PQ are constantly developing, there is a need for a rapid development platform for new algorithms. A rapid development framework should enable fast modelling, testing, and hardware implementation. The framework would be useful for preparing a reference PQ meter to test algorithms for PQ measurement or event classification in the field, prepare test procedures for upcoming certification processes, or test new ideas for PQ metering. This framework should enable rapid modelling, facilitate model validation and testing, as well as enable automatic code generation for different hardware platforms, including code generation for microprocessors and reconfigurable FPGA devices.

The conventional V-model of software development includes specification, design, implementation, integration, testing, and verification and validation stages. This implementation process is performed manually and is time intensive. The complexity of PQ measurement algorithms and the requirement for short development cycles motivate the investigation of a more efficient, reliable, and cost-effective alternative. Model-Based Design (MBD), adapted to the development of measurement algorithms, is here considered as an option. The MBD approach to the development of measurement algorithms consists of five steps:

1 Modelling input test signals and defining reference responses to the test inputs

2 Synthesis of measurement algorithms (Computer-Aided Engineering (CAE) tools are heavily used at this stage.)

3 Simulation of measurement algorithms excited by the test sequences

4 Tuning the algorithms to achieve compliance of the simulated responses with reference responses

5 Synthesis of the algorithms on a target hardware platform

The MBD approach focuses on modelling and simulation, hence most of the development time is independent of target hardware. Moreover, some CAE packages automatically convert the models into a source code library, which simplifies and accelerates the synthesis stage. The automatic code generation method reduces the number of errors that appear during manual coding.

Several attempts have been made to design rapid development methods for power systems algorithms. In [3], an analysis of CAE tools such as MATLAB/Simulink and dSpace/TargetLink describes how they perform fundamental steps such as physical modelling, simulations, control algorithms design and testing, hardware evaluation, parameter optimization, and finally code generation for real-time software implementations. As an example, the development of a controller for a low power single-phase transformerless inverter was presented. The development, verification, and implementation stages of automatic code generation to implement over/under-power protection functions and MATLAB/Simulink active power filter control blocks are given in [4] and [5], respectively. The active power filter allows the rapid on-line tuning of the filter's parameters, selection of control algorithms, and can be applied to generate code for microcontrollers. Kirubakaran et al. in [6] presented a Digital Signal Processing (DSP) controller for a fuel-cell based system. MATLAB/Simulink was used to generate Pulse Width Modulation (PWM) signals for the TMS320F2812 DSP. The same DSP was applied to implement a unity power factor PWM rectifier and shunt active power filter, as described in [7]. The automatic code generation in the MATLAB/Simulink environment for the fixed-point DSP was presented. A slightly different development path is given in [8]. Simulink diagrams are automatically converted to C code, afterward converted to assembly language, and finally transferred to a DSP for execution.

SCADA systems are considered to be the target platform for algorithms generated in Simulink. In [9], a Simulink implementation of a grid load forecast algorithm was given. The Simulink diagram was applied to automatically generate OPen Connectivity (OPC) Data Access and Modbus/TCP servers. The servers were "embedded" into a SCADA for real-time load prediction.

More specifically, PQ algorithms have been investigated. McGranaghan and Santoso in [10] presented a summary of the problems encountered during both offline and online analyses of PQ algorithms. In [11], a discrete model of the IEC 61000-4-15 flickermeter was presented. The full discrete flickermeter channel, developed as Simulink diagram, is shown, however the aim of this model is only simulation, and hence the implementation path is not considered. An implementation method for a Simulink algorithm that conforms the IEEE 1459-2000 standard for measurement of electric power quantities is presented in [12]. The MATLAB xPC Target toolbox was used to run the code generated automatically from the Simulink diagram on a PC computer. The methods defined by the IEC 61000-4-30 standard were investigated in [13]. The modelling and analysis of the algorithms were carried out in a MATLAB/Simulink environment. The algorithms were then automatically executed on a dSPACE DS 1104 board.

In addition, studies on the compliance of automatically generated code with safety standards were performed. Krizan et al. in [14] dealt with the usability of automatically generated C code in critical applications. Compliance with the DO-178C and DO-331 standards were presented. DO-178C and DO-331 address the entire software development cycle, from functional specification to software verification. The DO-178C and DO-331 are documents used by certification authorities such as the Federal Aviation Administration, European Aviation Safety Agency and Transport Canada to approve software for aerospace systems. In [15], the authors used the IEC

61508 standard and investigated options for running automatically generated code on safety PLCs. Stages for code generation, evaluation, and conversion before the code was applied in safety systems were presented.

Finally, some effort has been made to generate automatic code for reconfigurable FPGA circuits and their applications in power systems. Mekonnen et al. in [16] presented the simulation of a complete full-bridge PWM converter for a solar grid-tie inverter that also provided the benefits of auto VHDL-code generation for an RMS-based digital controller. In [17], a rapid prototyping platform for photovoltaic power inverters was presented. The hardware-in-the-loop approach was used to develop and validate PWM signals for different converter topologies. The control strategies are developed as Simulink diagrams, and the goal of the platform is the automatic VHDL code generation for Xilinx FPGAs.

The scope of this paper covers the development of algorithms for PQ metering while following the MBD approach. The algorithms developed and validated first as models are then transferred to C code automatically. The MATLAB/Simulink CAE plays a central role during the development. The generated code is executed on a hardware platform and real-time processing results are compared to the measurement generated by a commercial reference device. The implementation path for two example algorithms is presented. The algorithms are chosen because of their importance in PQ metering. The authors' intention is to show not the novelty of the algorithms but rather the rapid implementation issues.

1.1 Rapid prototyping

1.1.1 Rapid prototyping approach

The main advantage of the rapid prototyping approach is the ability to focus on the problem while omitting the details of its implementation. Development is carried out in an environment that offers a high level of abstraction, and the implementation on a hardware platform is performed by automatically generated code in the target programming language. The differences with respect to the classical software development process can be shown using the example of a filter design. The classical approach requires the selection of the filter structure, the calculation of parameters, and, finally, the implementation of the filter in a programming language. The rapid prototyping path is reduced to giving the type and parameters of the filter bandwidth. The source code of the filter procedures is then generated automatically. This approach results in ability to rapidly test and verify the proposed strategy while at the same time reducing the number of programming errors.

The MATLAB/Simulink stages of design and implementation of a measurement algorithm are shown in Figure 1. A data processing algorithm is developed as a Simulink diagram and then excited by test data vectors until the results are compliant with the reference results. At this point in the process, the design consists entirely of simulations without any references to the hardware on which the designed algorithm is intended to run.

The implementation on target hardware requires the replacement of simulation inputs and outputs by real signals. The interface can be established by controlling A/D and D/A converters, using files or databases, or over standard communication protocols such as Modbus, OPC Data Access, or OPC Unified Architecture. Modern processors map the A/Ds and D/As as memory, and communication protocol buffers also are allocated in memory, hence, without loss of generality, it can be assumed that in each case, communication is performed by reading and writing to memory locations. To switch from simulation to execution by a microprocessor, only the simulated inputs and outputs need to be swapped for memory access blocks.

At this stage, the C code can be automatically generated. The *MATLAB Coder* [18] and *Simulink Coder*[19] packages are required to translate a Simulink diagram into equivalent C procedures. The generated code contains three sets of procedures: initialisation procedures executed once when the calculations begin, solver procedures that calculate the model at each sampling period, and termination procedures. Usually, the metering algorithms do not have a specific operating time, so the termination procedures are never called.

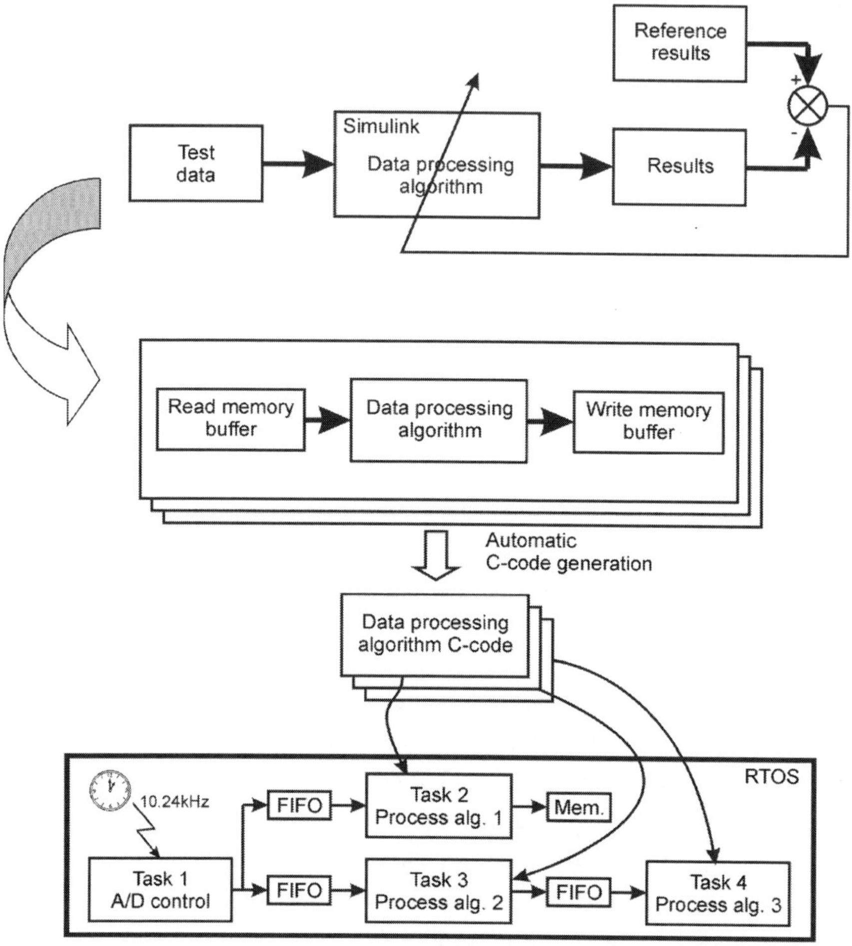

Figure 1. Stages of rapid prototyping approach.

The generated code is functionally equivalent to the Simulink diagram. The solver procedures read data from the defined memory location, carry out the calculations, and store the results to the given memory addresses. In the case of a PQ metering application, the Simulink diagrams implement calculations for root mean square values (RMS), spectrum, asymmetry, and flicker, resulting in the automatic generation of a PQ measurement library.

The C procedures, generated from Simulink diagrams, are used to create tasks in a real-time operating system (RTOS). The data comes directly from

A/D converters with a sampling frequency of 10.24 kHz. The A/Ds measure phase voltages and line currents, and the A/D results are stored in First In-First Out (FIFO) queues that trigger the execution of the tasks. The FIFO is a buffer where samples are stored until the following tasks become ready for execution, synchronizing the data source to the data consumer, and preventing any measurement points from being lost. The tasks read voltages and currents by accessing the FIFO memory and perform calculations for every incoming data sample. Inter-task communication is performed over memory locations, as was defined in the Simulink diagrams.

An alternative to the C-code generation path, the HDL Coder [20] package converts Simulink diagrams into Verilog or VHDL descriptions (see [16] and [17] as examples). HDL code is synthesizable and can be implemented as an FPGA module. However, unlike C-code procedures, HDL modules may not perform floating point calculations, and the algorithms must be converted into a fixed-point representation. The*Fixed-Point Designer* [21] toolbox supports this conversion, however, the conversion is usually time-consuming and sometimes may not even be possible.

1.1.2 Hardware platform

The Mars Starter Kit evaluation board from Enclustra was selected as the test hardware platform [22]. The board contains Zynq integrated circuits from Xilinx. The Zynq units contain within the single integrated circuit a dual-core ARM Cortex A9 processor equipped with the double precision floating point extension, reconfigurable FPGA fabric equipped with gates, registers, and RAM resources as well as communication cores (see Figure 2). An external A/D converter board is connected to measure grid voltages and currents. The board is equipped with Analog Devices AD7980 1MSPS, 16-bit, successive approximation analogue-to-digital converters. The A/Ds are controlled by an IP (intellectual property) core implemented in the FPGA. The core is developed in the VHDL language and operates as a component of the FPGA, as a kind of simple coprocessor. The A/D converters require the sequence of control signals to be generated with accuracy on the order of a few dozen of nanoseconds. Such accuracy cannot be achieved in programming, and has to be implemented as a silicon circuit.

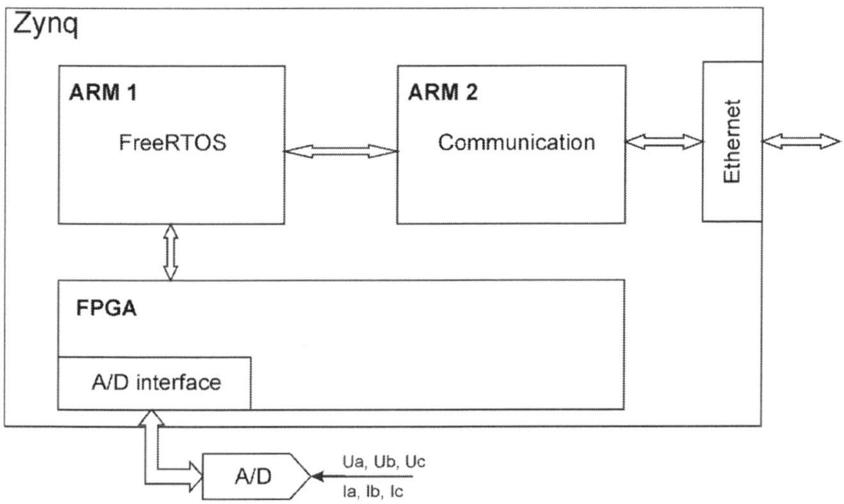

Figure 2. Zynq hardware platform.

One ARM processor runs the FreeRTOS real-time operating kernel. FreeRTOS tasks are created directly from the code generated automatically from Simulink diagrams. The second ARM processor runs a Linux distribution and is responsible mainly for implementing communication with the device via Ethernet.

The laboratory prototype of the flickermeter is shown in Figure 3. It consists of two boards—one equipped with the Zynq, memory, interfaces, and connectors to the communication channels. The second one operates as an interface to the analogue inputs.

The prototype has compact dimensions, but also has enough computational power to implement the chosen measurement algorithms. The worst case CPU utilisation of the ARM 1 processor is 7% when running the synchronisation and flicker calculation algorithms. The average ARM 2 utilisation is 5% when running the Modbus/TCP server in the Linux environment.

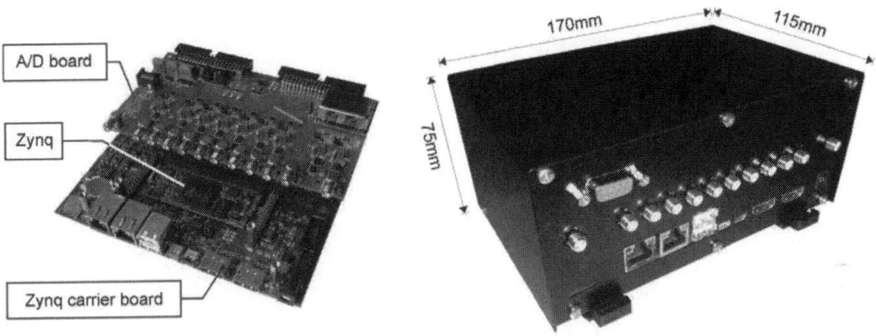

Figure 3. Laboratory flickermeter prototype.

1.2 Case studies

1.2.1 Synchronization with line voltage

A significant part of the PQ metering process is synchronisation with the linc voltage. The PQ metering standards, namely EN 61000-4-30 and EN 61000-4-7, define strict requirements in this area. In particular, all quantities should be measured within 10 cycle intervals for 50 Hz systems (for 60 Hz systems 12 cycles are required). In addition, RMS measurements for event detection and flicker reference values must be measured by means of a sliding one cycle interval that moves in half-cycle steps. Consequently, correct detection of a cycle is crucial. A typical phase locked loop (PLL) could be used for this task; however, it can be prone to voltage disturbances (e.g. harmonic distortion) or events (e.g. voltage dips). For three phase systems, the asymmetry could also affect a typical PLL system. Therefore, a robust implementation of the PLL is an important task in order to make a PQ meter operate correctly.

The PLL technique is a subject of great interest, and many PLL architectures and applications have been presented (e.g. [23-26]). The Enhanced PLL (EPLL) contains an adaptive notch filter and provides a higher degree of insensitivity to variable-frequency input signals. A detailed description of the EPLL structure is given in [23,27-29]. This structure has been selected to demonstrate the proposed rapid implementation method.

Figure 4 presents the Simulink diagram of the EPLL. The *Reference sin generator* block is the source of test data (see Figure 1). The *RefSin* output generates the sine wave for which amplitude, phase, and frequency are disturbed. The output of the EPLL is a sine signal denoted as *u(t)*. The EPLL also outputs the detected amplitude, frequency, and phase, marked respectively as *A(t), w0(t),* and *phase(t)*. The*Compare* scope acquires the simulation results and is used to compare the response of the EPLL to the reference signals.

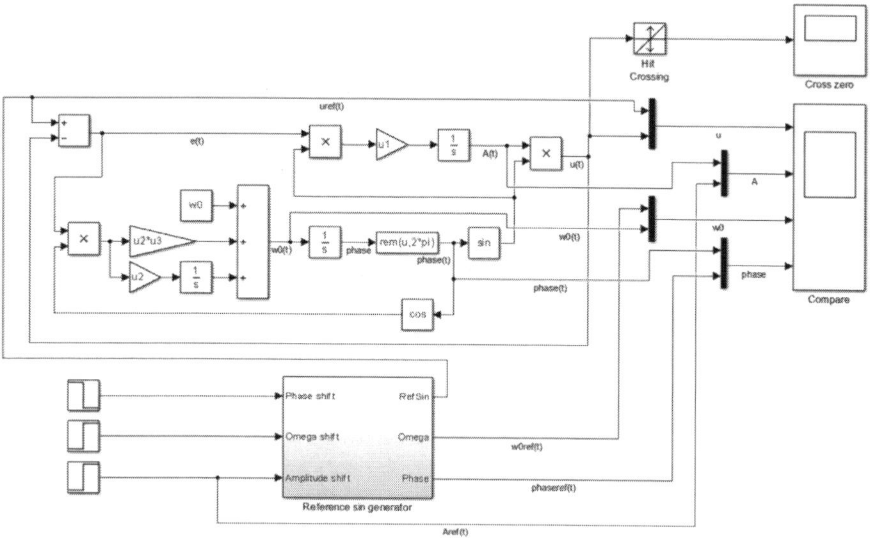

Figure 4. EPLL - simulation diagram.

The *Hit Crossing* block detects the zero crossing points of the sine signal generated by the EPLL. It is used for synchronising the PQ measurement algorithms to the power signal. Correct detection of the amplitude, frequency, and phase by the EPLL indicate the synchronous operation of the loop. The difference between the reference sine signal *uref(t)* and the EPLL output *u(t)* is used to tune the loop. However, only the zero crossing signal is used for the measurement algorithms.

The EPLL tuning requires calculation of the *u1, u2,* and *u3* gains (see Figure 4). The parameter values were determined by numerical optimization of the loop response to the test excitation. The response to a step change in amplitude, frequency, and phase was tested. The following cost sub-functions were applied:

$$J = \begin{bmatrix} \sqrt{\sum_{i=0}^{N-1} \left(u(iT_0)-u_{\text{ref}}(iT_0)\right)^2} \\ \sqrt{\sum_{i=0}^{N-1} \left(A(iT_0)-A_{\text{ref}}(iT_0)\right)^2} \\ \sqrt{\sum_{i=0}^{N-1} \left(w(iT_0)-w_{\text{ref}}(iT_0)\right)^2} \\ \sqrt{\sum_{i=0}^{N-1} \left(\text{phase}(iT_0)-\text{phase}_{\text{ref}}(iT_0)\right)^2} \end{bmatrix}$$

where T_0 is the sampling period, u_{ref} and u are respectively input and output sine signals of the loop, A_{ref} and A are respectively reference and measured amplitudes, w_{ref} and w are respectively reference and measured pulsation values, $phase_{ref}$ and *phase* are respectively reference and measured phase values, and N is the number of samples during the numerical optimisation experiment. The sampling frequency was set to 10.24 kHz. The optimisation procedure can be defined as:

$$\left[u_{1\text{opt}}, u_{2\text{opt}}, u_{3\text{opt}}\right] = \min_{u_1, u_2, u_3} W * J$$

where W is a four element row vector of non-negative constants. The optimisation is performed in the MATLAB environment by calling the *fminsearch* function [30].

The selection of the W vector elements determines the optimal u_{1opt}, u_{2opt} and u_{3opt} values and finally the behaviour of the EPLL. For the flicker measurement, the EPLL is used to synchronise the algorithm to the grid signal when the loop output signal $u(iT_0)$ follows the input signal $u_{ref}(iT_0)$. The optimal loop parameters are calculated for W such that only the first element is a non-negative value and the remaining elements are set to zero. During the optimisation, the reference sine signal is disturbed by step phase, frequency, and amplitude changes. The calculated optimal values are:

$$\left[u_{1opt}, u_{2opt}, u_{3opt}\right] = \left[3\,919.07,\quad 147.7206,\quad 208.1230\right]$$

For test purposes, the optimised loop is applied not to the simulated signal but to synchronise to the real grid signal measured in the university power laboratory. The total harmonic distortion (THD) of the signal is 2.95% and, additionally, the signal is disturbed by a $-\pi/6$ rad step phase change, 5% frequency step, and 30% amplitude sag. The disturbances of the phase, frequency, and amplitude appear respectively at 60, 120, and 180 ms. The results are shown in Figure 5. The upper diagram presents input test signal u_{ref} and the sinusoidal response of loop u. The bottom left picture shows the difference between u_{ref} and u. The time period between the moments when the u_{ref} and u signals cross the zero voltage level is given in the bottom right diagram.

The miscellaneous sets of vector W values enable us to switch the EPLL into amplitude, frequency, or phase measurement modes and exemplify the flexibility of the proposed approach.

After simulation and optimisation phases, the test signal sources are replaced by memory access drivers. The updated diagram is given in Figure 6. The input driver *Ua* and the output drivers *Cross zero, EPLL sin, Amplitude, Omega,* and *Phase* are created as Simulink level-2 C-code S-functions [31]. The S-functions access memory buffers and operate as interfaces between the Simulink blocks and to the remaining flickermeter blocks.

The diagram is used to automatically generate code. The generation procedures call the input S-function to read the input signal from the memory hexadecimal address FCA0000, run the EPLL algorithm, and call the output S-functions to store the results to memory locations from EA000000 to EA000010. When running the generated software in real time, it is essential that the execution takes place with the same sampling period as during code generation.

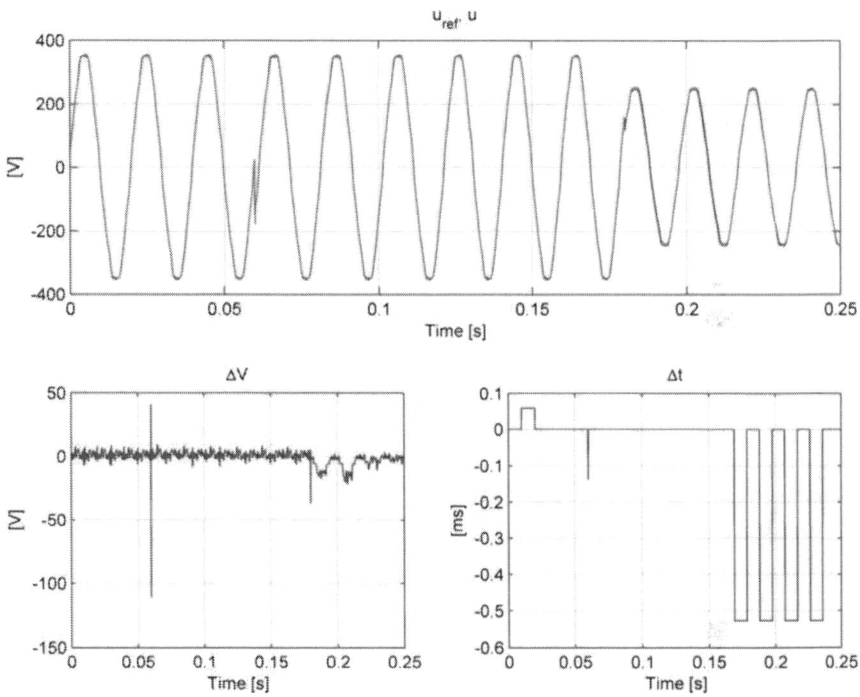

Figure 5. EPLL synchronisation to a real signal.

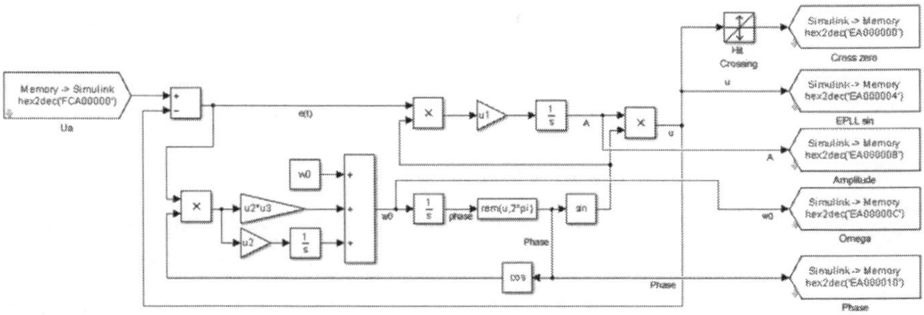

Figure 6. EPLL - diagram prepared for code generation.

The steps presented during the EPLL implementation can be applied to other algorithms. The next section presents the rapid development path of the flicker measurement algorithm. However this approach can also be applied to the development of the remaining PQ algorithms, and even to the development of control strategies.

1.2.2 Flicker implementation

A nontrivial example of rapid prototyping and implementation of a metering problem is the flickermeter. Light flicker measurement and the flickermeter are described in detail in standard EN 61000-4-15. Basically, the meter consists of several blocks (see Figure 7(a)).

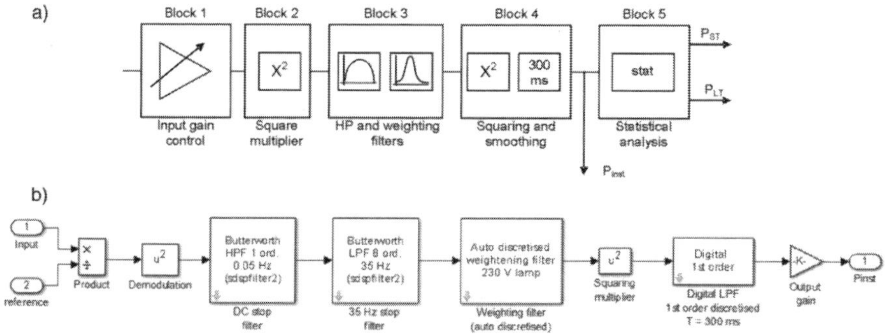

Figure 7. Block diagram and its Simulink model for instantaneous flicker computation. **Block diagram of the IEC flickermeter according to the standard EN 61000-4-15** (a) **and its sample model for instantaneous flicker computation in MATLAB/Simulink** (b).

The flickermeter is described in the standard as an analogue device, i.e. all signal processing blocks are defined in the analogue domain. The reason for this is that at the time of the standard creation, the flickermeter was intended to be single device built using standard electronic parts. Nowadays, the flicker severity measurement is a function of a digital meter

(PQ analyser) but the algorithms for computing short-term flicker P_{ST} and long-term flicker P_{LT} must follow the description in the standard. In state-of-the-art devices, all the operations on the input signal are done in the digital domain. Consequently, the problem of implementing a flickermeter in a digital processor requires discretisation of the analogue blocks and implementation of the discrete transfer functions. The considered blocks are (see Figure 7(a)):

1 Input gain control block: in the standard, the block operates as a voltage adaptor and signal conditioning unit and provides initial scaling. In the digital model, the block provides only the scaling, which is done by dividing the input signal by the reference signal. The reference signal is the half-period RMS value processed by the first order digital filter with a 27.3 s time constant (as defined in the standard). The filter has to be designed and implemented in the digital domain.

2 Square multiplier block: the squaring operation resembles the behaviour of an incandescent lamp. The block, together with the high pass filter from the next block, operates as a demodulator. A digital implementation of this algorithm is straightforward.

3 High pass filter and the weighting filter: the blocks consist of three filters. The first high pass filter eliminates the DC component of the voltage, and the standard suggests a first order filter with a −3 dB at 0.05 Hz cut-off frequency. The second filter is a low pass one, and the standard requires a sixth order Butterworth filter with a −3 dB at 35 Hz cut-off frequency (for 230 V systems). A digital implementation of the filter requires utilisation of filter design tools in order to evaluate the parameters of the filter. The last filter is the co-called weighting filter. It simulates the spectral properties of the human visual system. The filter is described as a Laplace transfer function model:

$$G(s) = \frac{k\omega_1 s}{s^2 + 2\lambda s + \omega_1^2} \cdot \frac{1 + s/\omega_2}{(1 + s/\omega_3)(1 + s/\omega_4)}$$

where the parameters k, λ, and $\omega_i (i = 1...4)$ are described in the standard and are different for 230 V and 110 V systems. Therefore the first operation is to obtain the discrete transfer function so the frequency response of the analogue filter and the discrete implementation are similar in the frequency domain.

4 Squaring and smoothing: this block performs two functions, it simulates the eye-brain perception by means of a squaring operation and emulates the memory effect of the brain. The effects can be implemented as the sliding mean operator, however the standard suggests the utilisation of a first order filter with a 300 ms time constant. The output of this block is instantaneous flicker P_{inst}.

5 Statistical analysis: this is the only block that utilises digital data processing to obtain its output: P_{ST} and P_{LT} flicker levels. The computation is based on the percentiles computation and calculates the flicker according to the formula:

$$P_{ST} = \sqrt{0.0314P_{0.1} + 0.0525P_{1s} + 0.0657P_{3s} + 0.28P_{10s} + 0.08P_{50s}}$$

where:

$$P_{50s} = (P_{30} + P_{50} + P_{80})/3$$
$$P_{10s} = (P_6 + P_8 + P_{10} + P_{13} + P_{17})/5$$
$$P_{3s} = (P_{2.2} + P_3 + P_4)/3$$
$$P_{1s} = (P_{0.7} + P_1 + P_{1.5})/3$$

and P_x is the x-th percentile of the values of P_{inst} logged during a specified time interval, where $x$is 0.1, 0.7, 1, 1.5, 2.2, 3, 4, 6, 8, 10, 13, 17, 30, 50, 80. The interval can vary from 1 to 15 m, however, the EN 61000-4-30 standard assumes 10 m for a typical flicker severity evaluation. This conforms with the interval set by EN 61000-4-30 for PQ evaluation. The evaluation of P_{LT} is performed using 12 samples of P_{ST}, hence the long-term flicker describes the flicker severity for the last 2 h. Because the block is actually a discrete implementation in a digital processor, it requires numerical procedures for sorting and mathematical calculation.

The MATLAB/Simulink package provides toolboxes and blocksets for both digital and analogue system design and analysis. Therefore, implementation of the flickermeter in MATLAB/Simulink follows the development stages of the rapid development method. The basic structure of the Simulink diagram that implements the signal processing stages is shown in Figure 7(b). Note that the model closely resembles the description in the standard. Each filter defined by spectral properties is defined in the *z* domain by means of standard tools available in the MATLAB/Simulink package. The weighting filter requires special procedures. In [11], the transfer functions of the filters were obtained analytically by defining the filter in the *s* domain and next using a Bilinear Transform to obtain the transfer function in the *z* domain. This procedure does not match the rapid implementation approach. Filter parameters in the flickermeter blocks are strictly defined in the standard, but their selection depends on the voltage level. On the other hand, there are several discretisation methods and the choice can affect the properties of the flickermeter. The discretisation also depends on sample time, which is related to the hardware platform, and therefore can be unspecified at modelling time. Consequently, the best option is to discretise the filter numerically and let the software perform all necessary computations. The MATLAB/Simulink package supports this operation by providing commands for the immediate discretisation of transfer functions. This functionality is used to obtain a fully automatic discretisation of the weighting filter. Therefore, the filter is defined in the*s* domain and then numerically discretised using MATLAB commands.

The validation of the model and recalibration can also be done in the simulation environment. It requires additional blocks for test signal generation. The test signals are strictly defined in the EN 61000-4-15 standard. Figure 8 shows a sample flickermeter validation framework.

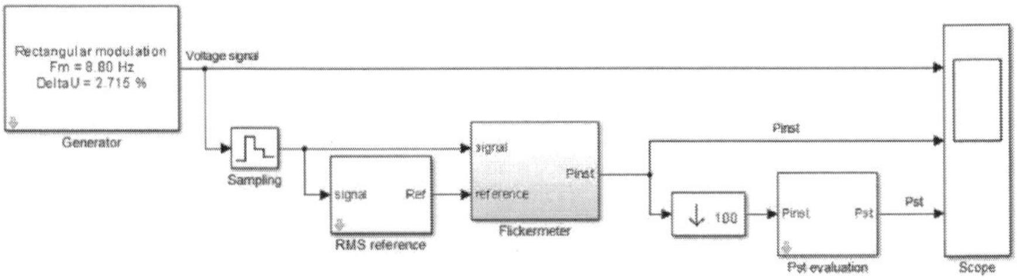

Figure 8. The flickermeter model testing framework.

As in the case of the EPLL implementation in the flickermeter diagram, the signals are reconnected to the driver blocks to access the measurements and store the P_{ST} and P_{LT} values. The C code is automatically generated from the Simulink diagram, compiled, and executed in real-time by the Zynq hardware platform.

1.2.3 Results of the flicker algorithm

The results of the generated flickermeter are shown in Figure 9. The diagram presents 24 hours of measurements. The upper diagram presents two P_{ST} values: one generated by the reference class A PQ analyser (A-eberle PQI-D) and the second generated by the test hardware platform described in Section II B. The Zynq test device ran the code generated automatically from the Simulink diagram. The reference PQ meter is a class A meter (according to IEC 61000-4-30) with the metering uncertainty defined by the standard, e.g. for voltage, the uncertainty is ± 0.1% of declared voltage (i.e. the grid's nominal). Flicker uncertainty is 5% and is defined by IEC 61000-4-15. For the test device, the metering was done by means of voltage transducers of type LV 25-P [32]. According to the data sheet, the overall accuracy of the transducers is 0.9% of the voltage range, which is 400 V in this case.

The meters were arranged in the PQ metering laboratory in which the building mains was available for metering. The meters were connected to the same voltage signals so the comparison refers to the real metering situation.

The lower diagram presents the difference between the data series. The difference can be explained by the accuracy of the sensors. For the hardware platform, typical off-shelf transducers were used with a conditional board not designed for precise measurements. On the other hand, the typical error allowed in the standard for P_{ST} is 5% when $P_{ST} = 1$.

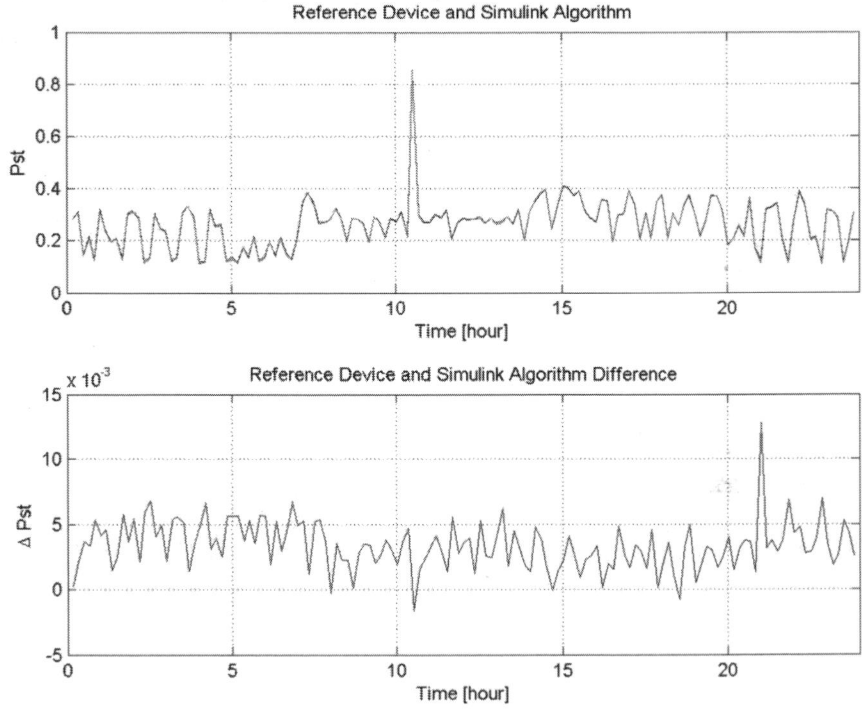

Figure 9. The flickermeter results.

2. CONCLUSIONS

This article presented a method of rapid code generation for implementing and testing of PQ algorithms. The method covers not only the PQ meter development, but also the preparation of the certification tests and procedures. The MBD approach shortens the time from an idea to an operating device. A user is supported by the functions of a CAE package, can focus on the problem itself, and skip the laborious implementation details of the algorithms under development. In the presented case, Simulink was used as the CAE platform. The efficiency of the presented development path becomes apparent in the implementation of the flicker calculation algorithm. The flickermeter channel consists of a series of filters and data processing blocks. It was first developed and validated in simulation, the C code was then generated and implemented on a real hardware platform. The correctness of the implemented algorithm was confirmed by the match of the generated flicker values with the results of the commercial reference metering device.

PQ measurements have recently become an important topic that has resulted in different regulatory documents. An example is the differences between the EN 50160 standard for supply quality and national regulations. The standard requires e.g. RMS voltage within ± 10% limits in relation to the nominal (or declared) value for low voltage networks. However, in some countries, the limits are different, e.g. in France, the admissible change is from −10% to +6%, and in Spain, it is ± 7%. In addition, the statistical measure differs: the standard requires computation of the 95 and 100 percentiles. The grid codes in Poland for a transmission system require a 99 percentile for flicker and voltage distortion when a wind farm connection is considered. There are also parameters not required in the standard but required in the grid codes, e.g. the THFF (telephone harmonic form factor). The metering interval is also subject to change, e.g. in Norway, a 1 minute interval is used. On the other hand, there is the possibility of change of the limit values, percentile, or even metering interval in the future. This requires additional work in the software of a PQ meter to make the change possible. The real problem arises when non-standard algorithms are required, e.g. the localization of a PQ disturbance source. This functionality is very useful when the introduction of PQ contracts is considered. However, the existing algorithms are not ready for implementation because of lack of efficiency.

The ability to easily add a new algorithm with new functionality to a PQ meter is clearly necessary. Rapid prototyping and implementation makes it possible to test the algorithm and produce the code without manual implementation.

This study highlights the need for a flexible and rapid development method for devices to meet the as yet non-existing standards. The presented approach is a step towards satisfying these demands.

ACKNOWLEDGEMENTS

This work was supported by the AGH University of Science and Technology under European Regional Development Found, Subsidy no POiG.01.03.01-30-056/12 and by the AGH University of Science and Technology KIC-ASS Grant no 7.7.120.7037.

REFERENCES

1. MHJ Bollen, IYH Gu, *Signal processing of power quality disturbances* (IEEE Press, New York, NY, USA, 2006)
2. A Zobaa, MM Canteli, R Bansal (eds.), *Application of Signal Processing in Power Quality Monitoring*, in *Power Quality Monitoring, Analysis and Enhancement*) (InTechOpen, 2012).
3. RV Dell'Aquila, L Balboni, R Morici, *A new approach: modeling, simulation, development and implementation of a commercial grid-connected transformerless PV inverter, SPEEDAM International Symposium on Power Electronics, Electrical Drives, Automation and Motion, 1422–1429*, 2010.
4. X Yang, B Kirby, Q Zhao, Y Ma, F Xu, *Model-based design process for product development of substation IEDs, 2nd IEEE International Conference & Exhibition (ENERGYCON)*, 2012, pp. 968–974.
5. G Adam, A Zbanţ, G Livint, *New Simulink control block for single phase shunt active power filters, 8th International Symposium on Advanced Topics in Electrical Engineering (ATEE)*, 2013, pp. 1–4.
6. A Kirubakaran, S Jain, RK Nema, DSP-controlled power electronic interface for fuel-cell-based distributed generation. IEEE Trans. Power Electron. **26**(12), 3853–3864 (2011).
7. K Vardar, T Sürgevil, E Akpinar, *Rapid prototyping applications on three-phase PWM rectifier and shunt active power filter*. (International Conference on Electrical and Electronics Engineering, 2009), p. 258–262

8. P Meena, KU Rao, D Ravishankar, *Real-time detection and analysis of PQ disturbances with DSP using MATLAB embedded link to code composer studio*. (Third International Conference on Power Systems, 2009), p. 1–5.

9. K Kołek, K Piątek, P Włodarczyk, Rapid algorithm prototyping for SCADA applications, (Advances in Electrical and Computer Engineering, in press)

10. MF McGranaghan, S Santoso, Challenges and trends in analyses of electric power quality measurement data. EURASIP J. Adv. Signal Process **57985**, 1–6 (2007).

11. LW White, S Bhattacharya, A Discrete, MATLAB-Simulink flickermeter model for power quality studies. IEEE Trans. Instrum. Meas. **59**(3), 527–533 (2010).

12. MI Milanes, V Minambres, E Romero, F Barrero, *Quality meter of electric power systems based on IEEE standard 1459-2000*. (Compatibility and Power Electronics, 2009), p. 86–92.

13. M Rogóż, Z Hanzelka, *The design and construction of a power quality parameters recorder*. 9th International Conference. (Electrical Power Quality and Utilisation, 2007), p. 1–6.

14. J Krizan, L Ertl, M Bradac, M Jasansky, A Andreev, *Automatic code generation from MATLAB/Simulink for critical applications*. (IEEE 27th Canadian Conference on Electrical and Computer Engineering (CCECE), 2014), p. 1–6.

15. MH Schwarz, H Sheng, A Sheleh, J Boercsoek, *IEEE/ACS International Conference on Computer Systems and Applications, 1058 – 1063 (2008)*, 2008, pp. 1058–1063.

16. ET Mekonnen, J Katcha, K Parker, *An FPGA-based digital control development method for power electronics*. (IECON 38th Annual Conference on IEEE Industrial Electronics Society, 2012), p. 222–226.

17. R Selvamuthukumaran, R Gupta, Rapid prototyping of power electronics converters for photovoltaic system application using Xilinx System Generator. IET Power Electron. **7**(9), 2269–2278 (2014).

18. MATLAB Coder. User's guide, http://www.mathworks.com/help/pdf_doc/coder/coder_ug.pdf. Accessed 5 December 2014

19. Simulink Coder. User's guide, http://www.mathworks.com/help/pdf_doc/rtw/rtw_ug.pdf. Accessed 5 December 2014

20. HDL coder, http://www.mathworks.com/products/hdl-coder/. Accessed 5 December 2014.

21. Fixed-point designer. User's guide, http://www.mathworks.com/help/releases/R2014b/pdf_doc/fixedpoint/FPTUG.pdf. Accessed 5 December 2014.

22. Mars Starter Kits, http://www.enclustra.com/en/products/hardware-kits/mars-starter-kits/. Accessed 18 October 2014.

23. A Gupta, A Porippireddi, VU Srinivasa, A Sharma, M Kadam, Comparative study of single phase PLL algorithms for grid synchronization applications. IJECT **3**(4), 237–245 (2012)

24. S Shinnaka, A Robust, Single-phase PLL system with stable and fast tracking. IEEE Trans. Ind. Appl. **44**(2), 624–633 (2008).

25. M Karimi-Ghartemani, M Mojiri, A Safaee, JA Walseth, SA Khajehoddin, P Jain, A Bakhshai, A new phase-locked loop system for three-phase applications. IEEE Trans. Power Electron. **28**(3), 1208–1218 (2013).

26. XQ Guo, W Wy, HR Gu, Phase locked loop and synchronization methods for grid-interfaced converters: a review. PRZEGLĄD ELEKTROTECHNICZNY (Electric Rev) **87**(4), 182–187 (2011)

27. B Singh, SR Arya, Implementation of single-phase enhanced phase-locked loop-based control algorithm for three-phase DSTATCOM. IEEE Trans. Power. Deliv. **28**(3), 1516–1524 (2013).

28. M Karimi-Ghartemani, JA Walseth, *Using the EPLL algorithm as a preprocessor for fault analysis*. (11th International Conference on Information Science, Signal Processing and their Applications (ISSPA), 2012), p. 1377–1382.

29. M Karimi-Ghartemani, M Karimi-Ghartemani, Linear and pseudolinear enhanced phased-locked loop (EPLL) structures. IEEE Trans. Ind. Electron. **61**(3), 1464–1474 (2014.

30. Optimization toolbox user's guide, MathWorks, http://www.mathworks.com/help/pdf_doc/optim/optim_tb.pdf. Accessed 18 October 2014

31. Simulink. Developing S-functions, MathWorks, http://www.mathworks.com/help/pdf_doc/simulink/sfunctions.pdf. Accessed 04 December 2014

32. Voltage Transducer LV 25-P, http://www.lem.com/docs/products/lv%2025-p.pdf. Accessed 04 December 2014.

Chapter 7

Prototyping Advanced Control Systems on FPGA

Stéphane Simard, Jean-Gabriel Mailloux and Rachid Beguenane

Department of Applied Sciences, University of Quebec at Chicoutimi, 555 boul. de l'Universit´e, Chicoutimi, QC, Canada

ABSTRACT

In advanced digital control and mechatronics, FPGA-based systems on a chip (SoCs) promise to supplant older technologies, such as microcontrollers and DSPs. However, the tackling of FPGA technology by control specialists is complicated by the need for skilled hardware/software partitioning and design in order to match the performance requirements of more and more complex algorithms while minimizing cost. Currently, without adequate software support to provide a straightforward design flow, the amount of time and efforts required is prohibitive. In this paper, we discuss our choice, adaptation, and use of a rapid prototyping platform and design flow suitable for the design of on-chip motion controllers and other SoCs with a need for analog interfacing. The platform consists of a customized FPGA design for the Amirix AP1000 PCI FPGA board coupled with a multichannel analog I/O daughter card. The design flow uses Xilinx

System Generator in Matlab/Simulink for system design and test, and Xilinx Platform Studio for SoC integration. This approach has been applied to the analysis, design, and hardware implementation of a vector controller for 3-phase AC induction motors. It also has contributed to the development of CMC's MEMS prototyping platform, now used by several Canadian laboratories.

1. INTRODUCTION

The use of advanced control algorithms depends upon being able to perform complex calculations within demanding timing constraints, where system dynamics can require feedback response in as short as a couple tens of microseconds. Developing and implementing such capable feedback controllers is currently a hard goal to achieve, and there is much technological challenge in making it more affordable. Thanks to major technological breakthroughs in recent years, and to sustained rapid progress in the fields of very large scale integration (VLSI) and electronic design automation (EDA), electronic systems are increasingly powerful [1, 2]. In the latter paper, it is rightly stated that FPGA devices have reached a level of development that puts them on the edge of microelectronics fabrication technology advancements. They provide many advantages with respect to their nonreconfigurable counterparts such as the general purpose micropocessors and DSP processors. In fact, FPGA-based digital processing systems achieve better performance-cost compromise, and with a moderate design effort they can afford the implementation of a powerful and flexible embedded SoCs. Exploiting the FPGA technology benefits for industrial electrical control systems has been the source of intensive research investigations during last decade in order to boost their performances at lower cost [3, 4]. There is still, however, much work to be done to bring such power in the hands of control specialists. In [5], it is stated that the potential of implementing one FPGA chip-based controller has not been fully exploited in the complicated motor control or complex converter control applications. Until now, most related research works using FPGA devices are focusing on designing specific parts mainly to control power electronic devices such as space vector pulse width modulation (SVPWM) and power factor correction [6, 7]. Usually these are implemented on small FPGAs while the main control tasks are realised sequentially by the supervising processor system, basically the DSP. Important and constant improvement in FPGA devices, synthesis, place-and-route tools, and debug capabilities has made FPGA prototyping more available and practical to ASIC/SoC designers than ever before. The validation of their hardware and software on a common platform can be accomplished using FPGA-based prototypes. Thanks to the existing and mature tools that provide automation while maintaining flexibility, the FPGA prototypes make it now possible for ASIC/SoC designs to be delivered on time at minimal budget. Consequently, FPGA-based prototypes could be efficiently exploited for motion control applications to permit an easy modification of the advanced control algorithms through short-design cycles, simple simulation, and rapid verification. Still the implementation of FPGA-based SoCs for motion control results in very complex tasks involving SW and HW skilled developers. The efficient IP integration constitutes the main difficulty from hardware perspective while in software side the issue is the complexity of debugging the software that runs under real-time operating system (RTOS), in real hardware. This paper discusses the choice, adaptation, and use of a rapid prototyping platform and design flow suitable for the design of on-chip motion controllers and other SoCs with a need for analog interfacing. Section 2 describes the chosen prototyping platform and the methodology that supports embedded application software coupled with custom FPGA logic and analog interfacing. Section 3 presents the strategy for simulating and prototyping any control algorithm using Xilinx system Generator (XSG) along with Matlab/Simulink. A vector control for induction motor is taken as a running example to explain some features related to the cosimulation. Section 4 describes the process of integrating the designed controller, once completely debugged, within an SoC architecture using Xilinx Platform Studio (XPS) and targeting the chosen FPGA-based platform. Section 5 discusses the complex task of PCI initialization of the analog I/O card and controller setup by software under embedded Linux operating system. Section 6 takes the induction motor vector control algorithm as an application basis to demonstrate the usefulness of the chosen FPGA-based SoC platform to design/verify on-chip motion controllers. The last section concludes the paper.

2. THE FPGA-BASED PROTOTYPING PLATFORM FOR ON-CHIP MOTION CONTROLLERS

With the advent of a new generation of high-performance and high-density FPGAs offering speeds in the 100 seconds of MHz and complexities of up to 2 megagates, the FPGA-based prototyping becomes appropriate for verification of SoC and ASIC designs. Consequently the increasing design complexities and the availability of high-capacity FPGAs in high-pin-count packages are motivating the need for sophisticated boards. Board development has become a task that demands unique expertise. That is one reason why commercial off-the-shelf (COTS) boards are quickly becoming the solution of choice because they are closely related to the implementation and debugging tools. During many years, and under its System-on-Chip Research Network (SOCRN) program, CMC Microsystems provided canadian universities with development tools, various DSP/Embedded Systems/multimedia boards, and SoC prototyping boards such as Amirix AP1000 PCI FPGA development platform. In order to support our research on on-chip motion controllers, we have managed the former plateform, a host PC (3.4 GHz Xeon CPU with 2.75 GB of RAM) equiped with the Amirix AP1000 PCI FPGA development board, to support a multichannel analog I/O PMC daughter card (Figure 1) to communicate with exterior world.

The AP1000 has lots of features to support complex system prototyping, including test access and expansion capabilities. The PCB is a 64-bit PCI card that can be inserted in a standard expansion slot on a PC motherboard or PCI backplane. Use of the PMC site requires a second chassis slot on the backside of the board and an optional extender card to provide access to the board I/O. The AP1000 platform includes a Xilinx Virtex-II Pro XC2VP100 FPGA and is connected to dual banks of DDR SDRAM (64 MB) and SRAM (2 MB), Flash Memory (16 MB), Ethernet and other interfaces. It is configured as a single board computer based on two embedded IBM PowerPC processors, and it is providing an advanced design starting point for the designer to improve time-to-market and reduce development costs.

Figure 1. Rapid prototyping station equiped with FPGA board and multichannel analog I/O daughter card.

The analog electronics are considered modular, and can either be external or included on the same chip (e.g., when fabricated into an ASIC). On the prototyping platform, of course, they are supplied by the PMC daughter card. It is a General Standards PMC66-16AISS8A04 analog I/O board featuring twelve 16-bit channels: eight simultaneously sampled analog inputs, and four analog outputs, with input sampling rates up to 2.0 MSPS per channel. It acts as a two-way analog interface between the FPGA and lab equipment, connected through an 80-pin ribbon cable and a breakeout board to the appropriate ports of the power module.

The application software is compiled with the free Embedded Linux Development Kit (ELDK) from DENX Software Engineering. Since it runs under such a complete operating system as Linux, it can perform elaborated functions, including user interface management (via a serial link or through networking), and real-time supervision and adaptation of a process such as adaptive control.

The overall platform is very well suited to FPGA-in-the-loop control and SoC controller prototyping (Figure2). The controller can either be implemented completely in digital hardware, or executed on an application-specific instruction set processor (ASIP). The hardware approach has a familiar design flow, using the Xilinx System Generator (XSG) blockset and hardware/software cosimulation features in Matlab/Simulink. An ASIP specially devised for advanced control applications is currently under development within our laboratory.

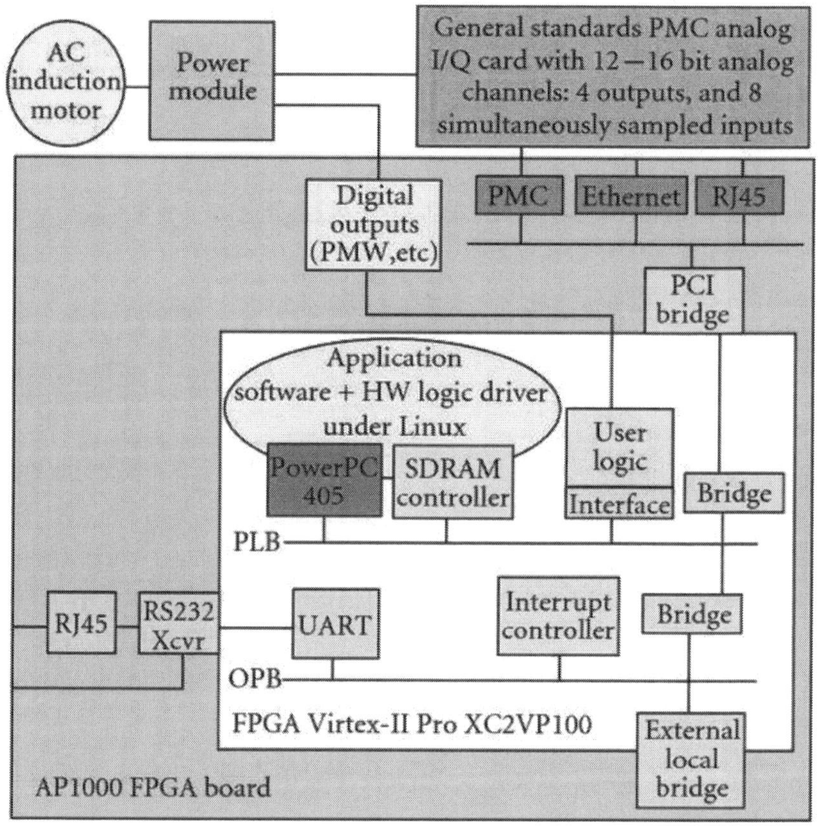

Figure 2. Architecture of the embedded platform driving a power system (schematic not to scale**).**

3. MATLAB/SIMULINK/XSG CONTROLLER DESIGN

It is well known that simulation of large systems within system analysis and modelling software environments takes a prohibitive amount of time. The main advantage of a rapid prototyping design flow with hardware/software cosimulation is that it provides the best of a system analysis and modelling environment while offering adequate hardware acceleration.

Hardware/software cosimulation has been introduced by major EDA vendors around year 2000, combining Matlab/Simulink, the computing, and Model-Based Design software, with synthesizable blocksets and automated hardware synthesis software such as *DSP Builder* from Altera, and *System Generator* from Xilinx (XSG). Such a design flow reduces the learning time and development risk for DSP developers, shortens the path from design concept to working hardware, and enables engineers to rapidly create and implement innovative, high-performance DSP designs.

The XSG cosimulation feature allows the user to run a design on the FPGA found on a certain platform. An important advantage of XSG is that it allows for quick evaluation of system response when making changes (e.g., changing coefficient and data widths). As the AP1000 is not supported by XSG among the preprogrammed cosimulation targets, we use the Virtex-4 ML402 SX XtremeDSP Evaluation Platform instead (Figure 3). The AP1000 is only targetted at the SoC integration step (see Section 4).

We begin with a conventional, floating-point, simulated control system model, and corresponding fixed-point hardware representation is then constructed using the XSG blockset, leading to a bit-accurate FPGA hardware model (Figure 4), and XSG generates synthesizable HDL targetting Xilinx FPGAs. The XSG design, simulation, and test procedure is briefly outlined below. Power systems including motor drives can be simulated using the SimPowerSystems (SPS) blockset in Simulink.

1 Start by coding each system module individually with the XSG blockset.

2 Import any user-designed HDL cores.

3 Adjust the fixed-point bit precisions (including bit widths and binary point position) for each XSG block of the system.

4 Use the Xilinx Gateway blocks to interface a floating-point Simulink model with a fixed-point XSG design. The Gateway-in and Gateway-out blocks, respectively, convert inputs from Simulink to XSG and outputs from XSG to Simulink.

5 Test system response using the same input stimuli for an equivalent XSG design and Simulink model with automatic comparision of their respective outputs.

Figure 3. Virtex-4 ML402 SX XtremeDSP evaluation platform.

Commonly, software simulation of a complete drive model, for a few seconds of results, could take a couple of days of computer time. Hardware/software cosimulation can be used to accelerate the process of controller simulation, thus reducing the computing time to about a couple of hours. It also ensures that the design will respond correctly once implemented in hardware.

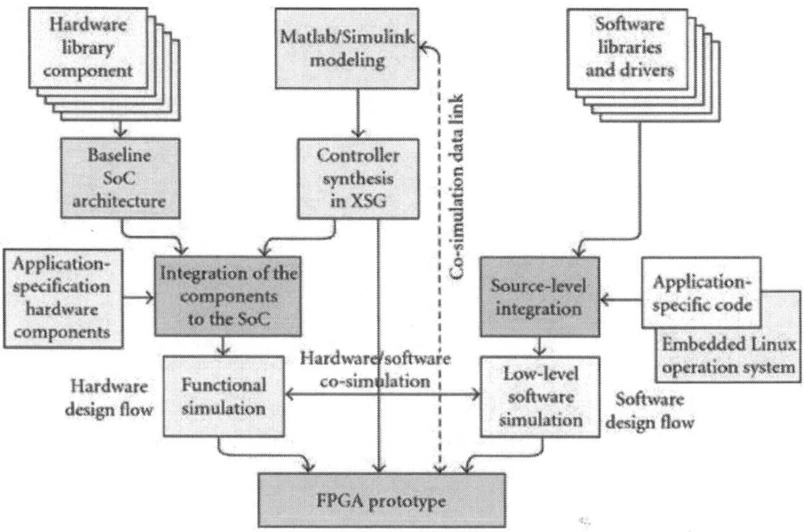

Figure 4. Controller-on-chip design flow.

4. SYSTEM-ON-CHIP INTEGRATION IN XILINX PLATFORM STUDIO

FPGA design and the SoC architecture are managed with Xilinx Platform Studio (XPS), targetting the AP1000. We have customized the CMC-modified Amirix baseline design to support analog interfacing, user logic on the Processor Local Bus (PLB), and communication with application software under embedded Linux. XPS generates the corresponding .bin file, which is then transferred to the Flash configuration memory on the AP1000. The contents of this memory is used to reconfigure the FPGA. We have found an undocumented fact that, on the AP1000, this approach is the only practicable way to program the FPGA. JTAG programming is proved inconvenient, because it suppresses the embedded Linux, which is essential to us for PCI initialization. Once programmed, user logic awaits a start signal from our application software following analog I/O card initialization.

To accelerate the logic synthesis process, the *mapper* and *place and route* options are set to STD (standard) in the implementation options file (etc/fast_runtime.opt), found in the *Project Files* menu. If the user wants a more aggressive effort, these options should be changed to HIGH, which requires much more time. Our experiments have shown that it typically amounts to several hours.

4.1. Bus Interfacing

The busses implemented in FPGA logic follow the IBM CoreConnect standard. It provides master and slave operation modes for any instanciated hardware module. The most important system busses are the Processor Local Bus (PLB), and the On-chip Peripheral Bus (OPB).

The implementation of the vector control scheme requires much less of generality, and deletes some communication stages that might be used in other applications. It is easier to start from such a generic design, dropping unneeded features, than to start from scratch. This way, one can quickly progress from SoC architecture in XPS down to a working controller on the AP1000.

4.1.1. Slave Model Register Read Mux

The baseline XPS design provides the developer with a slave model register read multiplexer. This allows to decide which data is provided when a read request is sent to the user logic peripheral by another peripheral in the system. While a greater number may be used, our pilot application, the vector control, only use four slave registers. The user logic peripheral has a specific base address (C_BASEADDR), and the four 32-bit registers are accessed through C_BASEADDR + register offset. In this example, C_BASEADDR + 0x0 corresponds to the control and status register, which is composed of the following bits:

0–7: the DIP switches on the AP1000 for debugging purposes,

8: used by user software to reset, start, or stop the controller,

9–31 : reserved.

As for the other 3 registers, they correspond to

C_BASEADDR + 0x4: Output to analog

channel 1

C_BASEADDR + 0x8: Output to analog

channel 2

C_BASEADDR + 0xC: Reserved (often used for debugging purposes)

4.1.2. Master Model Control

The master model control state machine is used to control the requests and responses between the user logic peripheral and the analog I/O card. The latter is used to read the input currents and voltages for vector control operation. The start signal previously mentioned in slave register 0 is what gets the state machine out of IDLE mode, and thus starts the data acquisition process. In this specific example, the I/O card is previously initialized by the embedded application software, relieving the state machine of any initialization code. Analog I/O initialization sets a lot of parameters, including how many active channels are to be read.

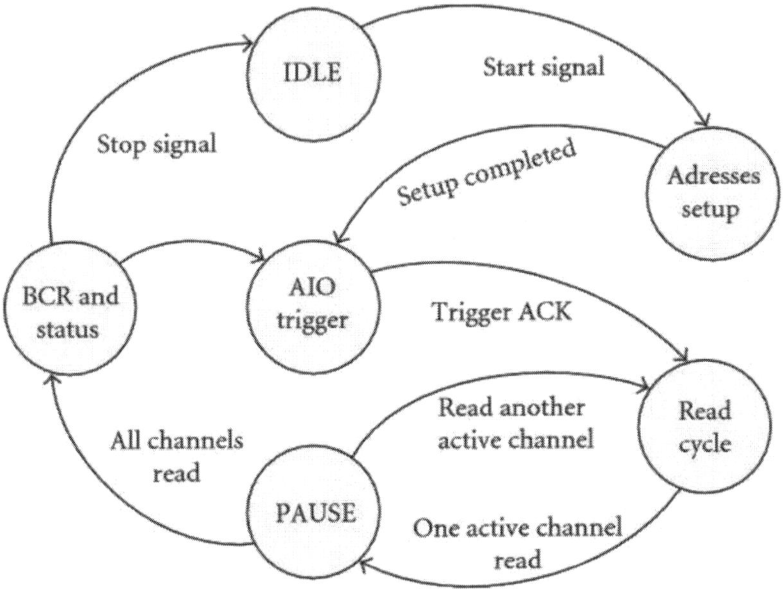

Figure 5. Master model state machine.

The state machine operates in the following way (Figure 5).

1 The user logic waits for a start signal from the user through slave register 0.

2 The different addresses to access the right AIO card fields are set up, namely, the BCR and read buffer.

3 A trigger is sent to the AIO card to buffer the values of all desired analog channels.

4 A read cycle is repeated for the number of active channels previously defined.

5 Once all channels have been read, the state machine falls back to trigger state, unless the user chooses to stop the process using slave register 0.

4.2. Creating or Importing User Cores

User-designed logic and other IPs can be created or imported into the XPS design following this procedure.

1 Select Create or Import Peripheral from the Hardware menu, and follow the wizard (unless otherwise stated below, the default options should be accepted).

2 Choose the preferred bus. In the case of our vector controller, it is connected to the PLB.

3 For PLB interfacing, select the following IPIF services:

   a. burst and cacheline transaction support,

   b. master support,

   c. S/W register support.

4 The User S/W Regitser data width should be 32.

5 Accept the other wizard options as default, then click Finish.

6 You should find your newly created/imported core in the Project Repository of the IP Catalog; right click on it, and select Add IP.

7 Finally go to the Assembly tab in the main System Assembly View, and set the base address (e.g., 0x2a001000), the memory size (e.g., 512), and the bus connection (e.g., plb_bus).

4.3. Instantiating a Netlist Core

Using HDL generated by System Generator may be inconvenient for large control systems described with the XSG blockset, as it can require a couple of days of synthesis time. System Generator can be asked to produce a corresponding NGC binary netlist file instead, which is then treated as a black box to be imported and integrated into an XPS project. This considerably reduces the synthesis time needed. The process of instantiating a Netlist Core in a custom peripheral (e.g., user_logic.vhd), performed following the steps documented in XPS user guide.

4.4. BIN File Generation and FPGA Configuration

To configure the FPGA, a BIN file must be generated from the XSG project. Since JTAG programming disables the embedded Linux, the BIN file must be downloaded directly to onboard Flash memory. There are two Intel Strataflash Flash memory devices on the AP1000, one for the configuration, and one for the U-boot bootstrap code (which should not be crushed) (Table 1).

Table 1. The Two Intel StrataFlash Flash memory devices.

Bank	Address	Size	Mode	Description
1	0x20000000	0x1000000 (16 MB)	16	Program Flash
2	0x24000000	0x1000000 (16 MB)	8	Config. Flash

The configuration memory (Table 2) is divided into three sections. Section 2 is the default Amirix configuration, and should not be crushed. Downloading the BIN file to memory is done through a network cable using the TFTP protocol. For this purpose, a TFTP server must be set up on the host PC. The remote side of the protocol is managed by U-boot on the AP1000. Commands to U-boot to initiate the transfer and to trigger FPGA reconfiguration from a designated region are entered by the user through a serial link terminal program. Here is the complete U-boot command sequence:

```
setenv serverip 132.212.202.166
setenv ipaddr 132.212.201.223
erase 2 : 0–39
Send tftp 00100000 download.bin
Send cp.b 00100000 24000000 00500000
Send swrecon
```

Table 2. AP1000 flash configurations.

Region	Bank	Sectors	Description
0	2	0–39	Configuration 0
1	2	40–79	Configuration 1
2	2	80–127	Configuration 2 (Default Config.)

5. APPLICATION SOFTWARE AND DRIVERS

One of the main advantages of using an embedded Linux system is the ability to perform the complex task of PCI initialization. In addition, it allows for application software to provide elaborated interfacing and user monitoring through appropriate software drivers. Initialization of the analog I/O card on the PMC site and controller setup are among such tasks that are best performed by software.

5.1. Linux Device Drivers Essentials

Appropriate device drivers have to be written in order to use daughter cards (such as an analog I/O board) or custom hardware components on a bus internal to the SoC, and be able to communicate with them from the embedded Linux. Drivers and application software for the AP1000 can be developed with the free Embedded Linux Development Kit (ELDK) from DENX Software Engineering, Germany. The ELDK includes the GNU cross development tools, along with prebuilt target tools and libraries to support the target system. It comes with full source code, including all patches, extensions, programs, and scripts used to build the tools. A complete discussion on writing Linux device drivers is beyond the scope of this paper, and this information may be found elsewhere, such as in [8]. Here, we only mention a few important issues relevant to the pilot application.

To support all the required functions when creating a Linux device driver, the following includes are needed:

```
#include<linux/config.h>
#include<linux/module.h>
#include<linux/pci.h>
#include<linux/init.h>
#include<linux/kernel.h>
#include<linux/slab.h>
#include<linux/fs.h>
#include<linux/ioport.h>
#include<linux/ioctl.h>
#include<linux/byteorder/
         big_endian.h>
#include<asm/io.h>
#include<asm/system.h>
#include<asm/uaccess.h>
```

5.2. PCI Access to the Analog I/O Board

The pci_find_device() function begins or continues searching for a PCI device by vendor/device ID. It iterates through the list of known PCI devices, and if a PCI device is found with a matching vendor and device, a pointer to its device structure is returned. Otherwise, NULL is returned. For the PMC66-16AISS8A04, the vendor ID is 0x10e3, and the device ID is 0x8260. The device must then be initialized with pci_initialize_device() before it can be used by the driver. The start address of the base address registers (BARs) can be obtained using pci_resource_start(). In the example, we get BAR 2 which gives access to the main control registers of the PMC66-16AISS8A04.

```
volatile u32 *base_addr;
struct pci_dev *dev;
struc resource *ctrl_res;

dev = pci_find_device(VENDORID,
      DEVICEID, NULL);
.
.
.
pci_enable_device (dev);
get_revision (dev);
base_addr = (volatile u32 *)
    pci_resource_start (dev, 2);
ctrl_res = request_mem_region (
    (unsigned long)base_addr,
    0x80L,"control");
bcr = (u32 *) ioremap_nocache (
    (unsigned long)base_addr,
    0x80L);
```

The readl () and writel() functions are defined to access PCI memory space in units of 32 bits. Since the PowerPC is big-endian while the PCI bus is by definition little-endian, a byte swap occurs when reading and writing PCI data. To ensure correct byte order, the le32_to_cpu () and cpu_to_le32() functions are used on incoming and outgoing data. The following code example defines some macros to read and write the Board Control Register, to read data from the analog input buffer, and to write to one of the four analog output channels.

```
volatile u32 *bcr;

#define GET_BCR() (le32_to_cpu(\\
    readl (bcr)))
#define SET_BCR(x) writel(\\
    cpu_to_le32(x), bcr)
#define ANALOG_IN()le32_to_cpu(\\
    readl (&bcr[ANALOG_INPUT_BUF]))
#define ANALOG_OUT(x,c) writel(\\
    cpu_to_le32(x), \\
    &bcr[ANALOG_OUTPUT_CHAN_00+c])
```

5.3. Cross-Compilation with the ELDK

To properly compile with the ELDK, a makefile is required. Kernel source code should be available in KERNELDIR to provide for essential includes. The version of the preinstalled kernel on the AP1000 is Linux 1.4. Example of a minimal makefile:

```
TARGET= thetarget
OBJS= myobj.o

#EDIT THE FOLLOWING TO POINT TO
#THE TOP OF THE KERNEL SOURCE TREE
KERNELDIR = ~/kernel-sw-003996-01

CC = ppc_4xx-gcc
LD = ppc_4xx-ld
DEFINES = -D__KERNEL__-DMODULE\\
          -DEXPORT_SYMTAB
INCLUDES= -I$(KERNELDIR)/include\\
    -I$(KERNELDIR)/include/Linux\\
          -I$(KERNELDIR)/include/asm
FLAGS =-fno-strict-aliasing \\
        -fno-common\\
        -fomit-frame-pointer\\
        -fsigned-char
CFLAGS = $(DEFINES) $(WARNINGS)\\
         $(INCLUDES) $(SWITCHES)\\
         $(FLAGS)
all: $(TARGET).o Makefile

$(TARGET).o: $(OBJS)
         $(LD) -r -o $@$^
```

5.4. Software and Driver Installation on the AP1000

For ease of manipulation, user software and drivers are best carried on a CompactFlash card, which is then inserted in the back slot of the AP1000 and mounted into the Linux file system. The drivers are then intalled, and the application software started, as follows:

```
mount /dev/discs/disc0/part1  /mnt
insmod  /mnt/logic2/hwlogic.o
insmo /mnt/aio.o
cd /dev
mknod hwlogic c 254 0
mknod aio c 253 0
 /mnt/cvecapp
```

6. APPLICATION: AC INDUCTION MOTOR CONTROL

Given their well-known qualities of being cheap, highly robust, efficient, and reliable, AC induction motors currently constitute the bulk of the motion industry park. From the control point of view, however, these motors have highly nonlinear behavior.

6.1. FPGA-Based Induction Motor Vector Control

The selected control algorithm for our pilot application is the rotor-flux oriented vector control of a three-phase AC induction motor of the squirrel-cage type. It is the first method which makes it possible to artificially give some linearity to the torque control of induction motors [9].

RFOC algorithm consists in partial linearization of the physical model of the induction motor by breaking up the stator current i_s into its components in a suitable reference frame (d,q). This frame is synchronously revolving along with the rotor flux space vector in order to get a separate control of the torque and rotor flux. The overall strategy then consists in regulating the speed while maintaining the rotor flux constant (e.g., 1 Wb). The RFOC algorithm is directly derived from the electromechanical model of a three-phase, Y-connected, squirrel-cage induction motor. This is described by equations in the synchronously rotating reference frame (d, q) as

$$u_{sd} = R_s i_{sd} + \sigma L_s \frac{\mathrm{d}}{\mathrm{d}t} i_{sd} \underbrace{- \sigma L_s \omega i_{sq} + \frac{M}{L_r}\frac{\mathrm{d}}{\mathrm{d}t}\Psi_r}_{D_d},$$

$$u_{sq} = R_s i_{sq} + \sigma L_s \frac{\mathrm{d}}{\mathrm{d}t} i_{sq} \underbrace{+ \sigma L_s \omega i_{sd} + \frac{M}{L_r}\omega\Psi_r}_{D_q},$$

$$\frac{\mathrm{d}}{\mathrm{d}t}\Psi_r = \frac{R_r}{L_r}(M i_{sd} - \Psi_r),$$

$$\omega = P_p \omega_r + \frac{M R_r}{\Psi_r L_r} i_{sq},$$

$$\frac{\mathrm{d}\omega_r}{\mathrm{d}t} = \frac{3}{2} P_p \frac{M}{J L_r} \Psi_r i_{sq} - \frac{D}{J}\omega_r - \frac{T_l}{J}, \tag{1}$$

where u_{sd} and u_{sq} are d and q components of stator voltage u_s, i_{sd}, and i_{sq} are d and q components of stator current i_s, Ψ_r is the modulus of rotor flux modulus, and θ is the angular position of rotor flux, ω is the synchronous angular speed of the (d, q) reference frame $(\omega = d\theta / dt)$, and L_s, L_r, and M are stator, rotor, and mutual inductances, R_s, R_r are stator and rotor resistances, σ is the leakage coefficient of the motor, and P_p is the number of pole pairs, ω_r is the mechanical rotor speed, D is damping coefficient, J is the inertial momentum, and T_l is torque load.

6.2. RFOC Algorithm

The derived expressions for each block composing the induction motor RFOC scheme, as shown in Figure 6, are given as follows:

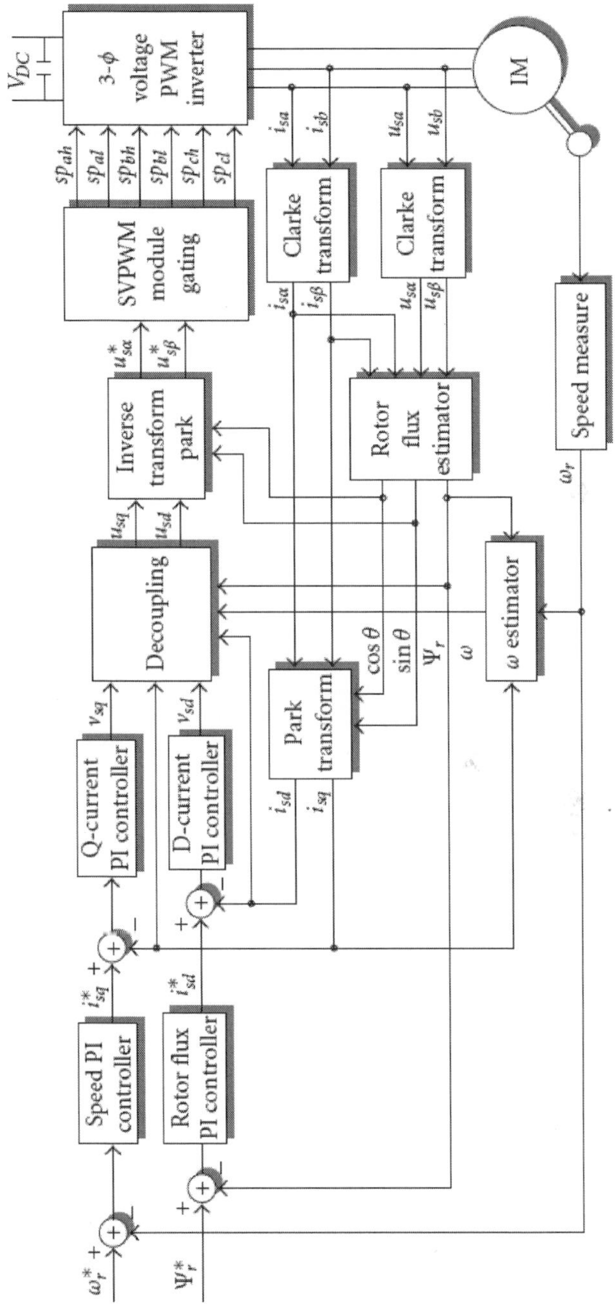

Figure 6. Conceptual block diagram of the system.

Speed PI Controller:

$$i_{sq}^* = k_{p_v}\epsilon_v + k_{i_v}\int \epsilon_v \, dt; \quad \epsilon_v = \omega_r^* - \omega_r. \tag{2}$$

Rotor Flux PI Controller:

$$i_{sd}^* = k_{p_f}\epsilon_f + k_{i_f}\int \epsilon_f \, dt; \quad \epsilon_f = \Psi_r^* - \Psi_r. \tag{3}$$

Rotor Flux Estimator:

$$\Psi_r = \sqrt{\Psi_{r\alpha}^2 + \Psi_{r\beta}^2}, \tag{4}$$

$$\cos\theta = \frac{\Psi_{r\alpha}}{\Psi_r}, \qquad \sin\theta = \frac{\Psi_{r\beta}}{\Psi_r}, \tag{5}$$

with

$$\Psi_{r\alpha} = \frac{L_r}{M}(\Psi_{s\alpha} - \sigma L_s i_{s\alpha}), \qquad \Psi_{r\beta} = \frac{L_r}{M}\left(\Psi_{s\beta} - \sigma L_s i_{s\beta}\right), \tag{6}$$

$$\Psi_{s\alpha} = \int (u_{s\alpha} - R_s i_{s\alpha}), \qquad \Psi_{s\beta} = \int \left(u_{s\beta} - R_s i_{s\beta}\right), \tag{7}$$

and using Clarke transformation

$$i_{s\alpha} = i_{sa}, \qquad i_{s\beta} = \frac{1}{\sqrt{3}} i_{sa} + \frac{2}{\sqrt{3}} i_{sb}, \tag{8}$$

$$u_{s\alpha} = u_{sa}, \qquad u_{s\beta} = \frac{1}{\sqrt{3}} u_{sa} + \frac{2}{\sqrt{3}} u_{sb}. \tag{9}$$

To be noticed that sine and cosine, of (5), sum up to a division, and therefore do not have to be directly calculated.

Current PI Controller:

$$v_{sd} = k_{p_i}\epsilon_{i_{sd}} + k_{i_i}\int \epsilon_{i_{sd}}\,\mathrm{d}t; \quad \epsilon_{i_{sd}} = i_{sd}^{*} - i_{sd}, \tag{10}$$

$$v_{sq} = k_{p_i}\epsilon_{i_{sq}} + k_{i_i}\int \epsilon_{i_{sq}}\,\mathrm{d}t; \quad \epsilon_{i_{sq}} = i_{sq}^{*} - i_{sq}. \tag{11}$$

Decoupling:

$$u_{sd} = \sigma L_s v_{sd} + D_d; \quad u_{sq} = \sigma L_s v_{sq} + D_q, \tag{12}$$

with

$$D_d = -\sigma L_s \omega i_{sq} + \frac{M}{L_r}\frac{\mathrm{d}}{\mathrm{d}t}\Psi_r, \qquad D_q = +\sigma L_s \omega i_{sd} + \frac{M}{L_r}\omega\Psi_r. \tag{13}$$

Omega (ω) Estimator:

$$\omega = P_p\omega_r + \frac{MR_r}{\Psi_r L_r} i_{sq}. \tag{14}$$

Park Transformation:

$$\begin{bmatrix} i_{s_d} \\ i_{s_q} \end{bmatrix} = \begin{bmatrix} \cos\theta & \sin\theta \\ -\sin\theta & \cos\theta \end{bmatrix} \begin{bmatrix} i_{s_\alpha} \\ i_{s_\beta} \end{bmatrix}. \tag{15}$$

Inverse Park Transformation:

$$\begin{bmatrix} u_{s_\alpha}^* \\ u_{s_\beta}^* \end{bmatrix} = \begin{bmatrix} \cos\theta & -\sin\theta \\ \sin\theta & \cos\theta \end{bmatrix} \begin{bmatrix} u_{s_d} \\ u_{s_q} \end{bmatrix}. \tag{16}$$

In the above equations, for x standing for any variable such as voltage u_s, current i_s or rotor flux Ψ_r, we have the following.

($x*$) Input reference corresponding to *x*.

(ϵ_x) Error signal corresponding to *x*.

(*kpx* , *kix*) Proportional and integral parameters corresponding to the PI controller of *x*.

(x_a, x_b, x_c) a, b, and c three-phase components of *x* in the stationary reference frame.

(x_α, x_β) α and β two-phase components of *x* in the stationary reference frame.

(x_d, x_q) d and q components of *x* in the synchronously rotating frame.

The RFOC scheme features vector transformations (Clarke and Park), 4 IP regulators, and space-vector PWM generator (SVPWM). This algorithm is of interest for its good performances, and because it has a fair level of complexity which benefits from a very-high-performance FPGA implementation. In fact, FPGAs make it possible to execute the loop of a complicated control algorithm in a matter of a few microseconds. The first prototype of such a controller has been developed using the method and platform described here, and has been implemented entirely in FPGA logic [10].

Commonly used mediums prior to the advent of today's large FPGAs, including the use of DSPs alone and/or specialized microcontrollers, led to a total cycle time of more than 100 μs for vector control. This lead to switching frequencies in the range of 1–5 kHz, which produced disturbing noise in the audible band. With today's FPGAs, it becomes possible to fit a very large control system on a single chip, and to support very high switching frequencies.

6.3. Validation of RFOC Using Cosimulation with XSG

A strong hardware/software cosimulation environment and methodology is necessary to allow validation of the hardware design against a theoretical control system model.

As mentioned is Section 3, the design flow which has been adopted in this research uses the XSG blockset in Matlab/Simulink. XSG model of RFOC block is built up from (2) to (16) and the global system architecture is shown in Figure 8 where Gateway-in and Gateway-out blocks provide the necessary interface between the fixed-point FPGA hardware that include the RFOC and Space Vector Pulse Width Modulation (SVPWM) algorithms and the floating-point Simulink blocksets mainly the SimPowerSystems (SPS) models. In fact to make the simulations more realistic, the three-phase AC induction motor and the corresponding Voltage Source Inverter were modelled in Simulink using the SPS blockset, which is robust and well proven. To be noticed that SVPWM is a widely used technique for three-phase voltage-source inverters (VSI), and is well suited for AC induction motors.

At runtime, the hardware design (RFOC and SVPWM) is automatically downloaded into the actual FPGA device, and its response can then be verified in real-time against that of the theoretical model simulation done with floating-point Simulink blocksets. An arbitrary load is induced by varying the torque load variable T_l as a time function. SPS receives a reference voltage from the control through the inverse Park transformation module. This voltage consists of two quadrature voltages ($u^*_{s\alpha}$, $u^*_{s\beta}$), plus the angle (sine/cosine) of the voltage phasor u_{sd} corresponding to the rotor flux orientation (Figure 6).

6.4. Reducing Cosimulation Times

In a closed loop setting, such as RFOC, hardware acceleration is only possible as long as the replaced block does not require a lot of steps for completion. If the XSG design requires more steps to process the data which is sent than what is necessary for the next data to be ready for processing, a costly (time wise) adjustment has to be made. The Simulink period for a given simulated FPGA clock (one XSG design step) must be reduced, while the rest of the Simulink system runs at the same speed as before. In a fixed step Simulink simulation environment, this means that the fixed step size must be reduced enough so that the XSG system has plenty of time to complete between two data acquisitions. Obviously, such lenghty simulations should only be launched once the debugging process is finished and the controller is ready to be thouroughly tested.

Once the control algorithm is designed with XSG, the HW/SW cosimulation procedure consists of the following.

1 Building the interface between Simulink and FPGA-Based Cosimulation board.

2 Making a hardware cosimulation design.

3 Executing hardware cosimulation.

When using Simulink environment for cosimulation, one should distinguish between the single-step and free-running modes, in order for debugging purposes, to get much shorter simulations times.

Single-step cosimulation can improve simulation time when replacing one part of a bigger system. This is especially true when replacing blocks that cannot be natively accelerated by Simulink, like embedded Matlab functions. Replacing a block with an XSG cosimulated design shifts the burden from Matlab to the FPGA, and the block no longer remains the simulation's bottleneck.

Free-running cosimulation means that the FPGA will always be running at full speed. Simulink will no longer be dictating the speed of an XSG step as was the case in single-step cosimulation. With the Virtex-4 ML402 SX XtremeDSP Evaluation Platform, that step will now be a fixed 10 nanoseconds. Therefore, even a very complicated system requiring many steps for completion should have ample time to process its data before the rest of the Simulink system does its work. Nevertheless, a synchronization mechanism should always be used for linking the free-running cosimulation block with the rest of the design to ensure an exterior start signal will not be mistakenly interpreted as more than one start pulse. Table 3 shows the decrease of simulation time afforded by the free-running mode for the induction motor vector control. This has been implemented using XSG with the motor and its SVPWM-based drive being modeled using SPS blockset from Simulink. For the same precision and the same amount of data to be simulated (speed variations over a period of 7 seconds), a single-step approach would require 100.7 times longer to complete, thus being an ineffective approach. A more complete discussion of our methodology for rapid testing of an XSG-based controller using free-running cosimulation and SPS, has been given in [11].

Table 3. Simulation times and methods

Type of simulation	Simulation time
Free-running cosimulation	1734 s
Single-step cosimulation	174610 s (48 hours)

6.5. Timing Analysis

Before actually generating a BIT file to reconfigure the FPGA, and whether the cosimulation is done through JTAG or Ethernet, the design must be able to run at 100 MHz (10 nanoseconds step time). As long as the design is running inside Simulink, there are never any issues with meeting timing requirements for the XSG model. Once completed, the design will be synthesized, and simulated on FPGA. If the user launches the cosimulation block generation process, the timing errors will be mentioned quite far into the operation. This means that, after waiting for a relatively long delay (sometimes 20–30 minutes depending on the complexity of a design and the speed of the host computer), the user notices the failure to meet timing requirements with no extra information to quickly identify the problem. This is why the timing analysis tool must always be run prior to cosimulation. While it might seem a bit time-consuming, this tool will not simply tell you that your design does not meet requirements, but it will give you the insight required to fix the timing problems. The control algorithm once being fully designed, analysed (timing wise), and debugged through the aforementioned *FPGA-in-the-loop* simulation platform, the corresponding NGC binary netlist file or VHDL/Verilog code are automatically generated. These could then be integrated within the SoC architecture using Xilinx Platform Studio (XPS) and targetting the AP1000 platform. Next section describes the related steps.

6.6. Experimental Setup

Figure 7 shows the experimental setup with power electronics, induction motor, and loads. The power supply is taken from a 220 V outlet. The high voltage power module, from Microchip, is connected to the analog I/O card through the rainbow flex cable, and to the expansion digital I/Os of the AP1000 through another parallel cable. Signals from a 1000-line optical speed encoder are among the digital signals fed to the FPGA. As for the loads, there is both a manually-controlled resistive load box, and a dynamo coupled to the motor shaft.

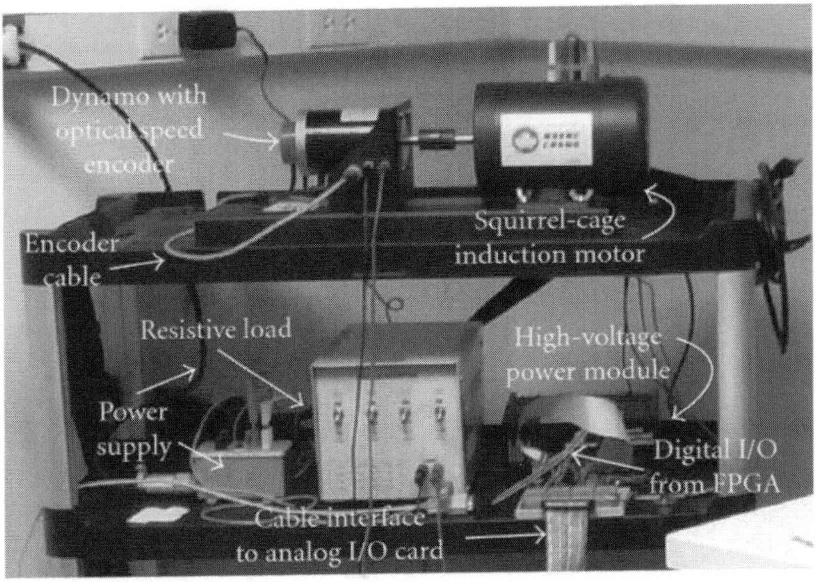

Figure 7. Experimental setup with power electronics, induction motor, and loads.

From the three motor phases, three currents and three voltages (all prefiltered and prescaled) are fed to the analog I/O board to be sampled. Samples are stored in an internal input buffer until fetched by the controller on FPGA. Data exchange between the FPGA and the I/O board proceeds through the PLB and the Dual Processor PCI Bus Bridge to and from the PMC site.

The process of generating SVPWM signals continuously runs in parallel with controller logic, but the speed at which these signals are generated is greater than the speed required for the vector control processing. As a consequence, these two processes are designed and tested separately before being assembled and tested together.

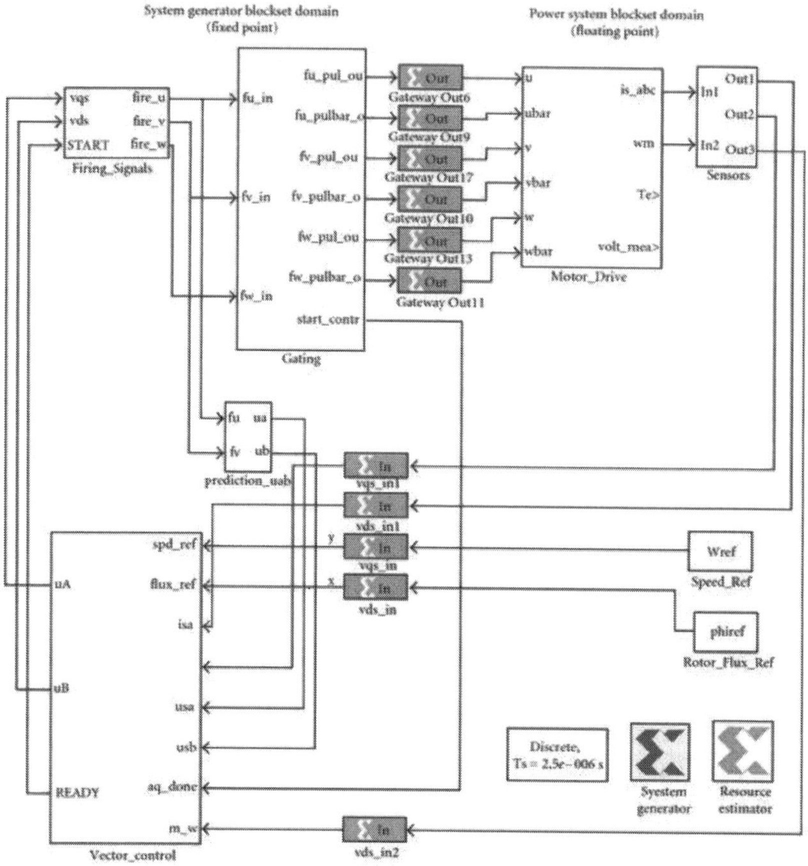

Figure 8. Indcution motor RFOC drive, as modelled with XSG and SPS blocksets.

Power gating and motor speed decoding are continuous processes that have critical clocking constraints beyond the capabilities of bus operation to and from the I/O board. Therefore, even though the PMC66-16AISS8A04 board also provides digital I/O, both the PWM gating signals and the input pulses from the optical speed encoder are directly passed through FPGA pins to be processed by dedicated hardware logic. This is done by plugging a custom-made adapter card with Samtec CON 0.8 mm connectors into the expansion site on the AP1000. While the vector control uses data acquired from the AIO card through a state machine, the PWM signals are constantly fed to the power module (Figure 6). Those signals are sent directly through the general purpose digital outputs on the AP1000 itself instead of going through the AIO card. This ensures complete control over the speed at which these signals are generated and sent while targeting a specific operating frequency (16 kHz in our example). This way, the speed calculations required for the vector control algorithm are done using precise clocking without adding to the burden of the state machine which dictates the communications between FPGA and the AIO card. The number of transitions found on the signal lines between the FPGA and speed encoder are used to evaluate the speed at which the motor is operating.

6.7. Timing Issues

Completion of one loop cycle of our vector control design, takes 122 steps leading to a computation time of less than 1.5 μs. To be noticed that for a sampling rate of 32 kHz, the SVPWM signal has 100 divisions (two zones divided by 50), which has been chosen as a good compromise between precision and simulation time. The simulation fixed-step size is then 625 nanoseconds, which is already small enough to hinder the performance of simulating the SPS model. Since PWM signal generation is divided into two zones, for every 50 steps of Simulink operations (PWM signal generation and SPS model simulation), the 122 vector control steps must complete. The period of the XSG—Simulink system must be adjusted in order for the XSG model to run 2.44 times faster than the other Simulink components. The simulation fixed-step size becomes 2.56 nanoseconds, thus prolonging simulation time. In other words, since the SPS model and PWM signals generation take little time (in terms of steps) to complete whereas the vector control scheme requires numerous steps, the coupling of the two forces the use of a very small simulation fixedstep size.

7. CONCLUSION

In this paper, we have discussed our choice, adaptation, and use of a rapid prototyping platform and design flow suitable for the design of on-chip motion controllers and other SoCs with a need for analog interfacing. It supports embedded application software coupled with custom FPGA logic and analog interfacing, and is very well suited to FPGA-in-the-loop control and SoC controller prototyping. Such platform is suitable for academia and research communauty that cannot afford the expensive commercial solutions for FPGA-in-the-loop simulation [12, 13].

A convenient FPGA design, simulation, and test procedure, suitable for advanced feedback controllers, has been outlined. It uses the Xilinx System Generator blockset in Matlab/Simulink and a simulated motor drive described with the SPS blockset. SoC integration of the resulting controller is done in Xilinx Platform Studio. Our custom SoC design has been described, with highlights on the state machine for bus interfacing, NGC file integration, BIN file generation, and FPGA configuration.

Application software and drivers development for embedded Linux are often needed to provide for PCI and analog I/O card initialization, interfacing, and monitoring. We have provided here some pointers along with essential information not easily found elsewhere. The proposed design flow and prototyping platform have been applied to the analysis, design, and hardware implementation of a vector controller for three-phase AC induction motors, with very good performance results. The resulting computation times, of about 1.5 μs, can in fact be considered record-breaking for such a controller.

ACKNOWLEDGMENTS

This research is funded by a Grant from the National Sciences and Engineering Research Council of Canada (NSERC). CMC Microsystems provided development tools and support through the System-on-Chip Research Network (SOCRN) program.

REFERENCES

1. *Accelerating Canadian competitiveness through microsystems: strategic plan 2005–2010* CMC Microsystems, Kingston, Canada; 2004.

2. Rodriguez-Andina JJ, Moure MJ, Valdes MD: **Features, design tools, and application domains of FPGAs.***IEEE Transactions on Industrial Electronics* 2007,**54**(4):1810-1823.

3. Dubey R, Agarwal P, Vasantha MK: **Programmable logic devices for motion control—a review.** *IEEE Transactions on Industrial Electronics* 2007,**54**(1):559-566.

4. Monmasson E, Cirstea MN: **FPGA design methodology for industrial control systems—a review.** *IEEE Transactions on Industrial Electronics* 2007,**54**(4):1824-1842.

5. Zhang D: *A stochastic approach to digital control design and implementation in power electronics, Ph.D. thesis*. Florida State University College of Engineering, Tallahassee, Fla, USA; 2006.

6. Tzou Y-Y, Hsu H-J: **FPGA realization of space-vector PWM control IC for three-phase PWM inverters.** *IEEE Transactions on Power Electronics* 1997,**12**(6):953-963.

7. de Castro A, Zumel P, García O, Riesgo T, Uceda J: **Concurrent and simple digital controller of an AC/DC converter with power factor correction based on an FPGA.** *IEEE Transactions on Power Electronics*2003,**18**(1, part 2):334-343.

8. *Developing device drivers for Linux Kernel 1.4* CMC Microsystems, Kingston, Canada; 2006.

9. Bose BK: *Power Electronics and Variable-Frequency Drives: Technology and Applications*. IEEE Press, New York, NY, USA; 1996.

10. Mailloux J-G: *Prototypage rapide de la commande vectorielle sur FPGA à l'aide des outils Simulink—System Generator, M.S. thesis*. Université du Québec à Chicoutimi, Quebec, Canada; January 2008.

11. Mailloux J-G, Simard S, Beguenane R: **Rapid testing of XSG-based induction motor vector controller using free-running hardware co-simulation and SimPowerSystems.** *Proceedings of the 5th International*

Conference on Computing, Communications and Control Technologies (CCCT '07), July 2007, Orlando, Fla, USA

12. Dufour C, Abourida S, Bélanger J, Lapointe V: **Real-time simulation of permanent magnet motor drive on FPGA chip for high-bandwidth controller tests and validation.** *Proceedings of the 32nd Annual Conference on IEEE Industrial Electronics (IECON '06), November 2006, Paris, France* 4581-4586.

13. National Instruments : **Creating Custom Motion Control and Drive Electronics with an FPGA-based COTS System.** 2006.

Chapter 8

State-of-The-Art and Applications of 3D Imaging Sensors in Industry, Cultural Heritage, Medicine, and Criminal Investigation

Giovanna Sansoni *, **Marco Trebeschi and Franco Docchio**

Laboratory of Optoelectronics, University of Brescia / via Branze 38, Brescia I-25123, Italy

ABSTRACT

3D imaging sensors for the acquisition of three dimensional (3D) shapes have created, in recent years, a considerable degree of interest for a number of applications. The miniaturization and integration of the optical and electronic components used to build them have played a crucial role in the achievement of compactness, robustness and flexibility of the sensors. Today, several 3D sensors are available on the market, even in combination with other sensors in a "sensor fusion" approach. An importance equal to that of physical miniaturization has the portability of the measurements, via suitable interfaces, into software environments designed for their elaboration, e.g., CAD-CAM systems, virtual renders, and rapid prototyping tools. In this paper, following an overview of the state-of-art of 3D imaging sensors, a number of significant examples of their use are presented, with particular reference to industry, heritage, medicine, and criminal investigation applications.

KEYWORDS

3D sensors; surface quality control; reverse engineering; optical triangulation; crime scene investigation; heritage restoration; virtual reality

1. INTRODUCTION

In recent years, demand for optical 3D imaging sensors has become increasingly relevant, and has led to the development of instruments that are now commercially available [1]. During the 1970s and 1980s their development was mainly performed in research laboratories, and was aimed at designing new techniques exploiting the use of light beams (both coherent and incoherent) instead of contact probes, in view of their application in the mechanical manufacturing industry, for measurement and quality control applications. Novel measurement principles were proposed, and suitable prototypes were developed and characterized to prove their performances [2–9].

In parallel, we participated in a considerable effort directed towards the miniaturization and integration of optical light sources, detectors and components, in the electronic equipment and the mechanical structure of the sensors. In the last decade, the availability of techniques and components has led to the production of a wide spectrum of commercially available devices, with measurement resolution from a few nanometers to fractions of a meter, and ranges from microns to a few kilometers. In recent times, the trend has been to produce devices at decreased costs and with increased ruggedness and portability.

The problem of manipulating, editing, and storing the measured data was approached at the software level, by developing a very powerful suite of programs that import and manipulate the data files, and output them in popular and well-standardized formats, such as the DXF and IGES formats for CAD applications, the STL format for rapid prototyping machines, and the VRML and 3D formats for visualization.

As a result, the interest in the use of 3D imaging sensors has increased. In the mechanical and manufacturing industry, surface quality control, microprofiling and macroprofiling are often carried out on a contactless, optical basis. Optical probes and contact probes are used in combination: this occurs whenever both the accuracy of the measurement and the efficiency of the process are the critical points [10]. It is significant that, today, one of the input requirements in the design of Coordinate Measuring Machines (CMMs) is represented by the possibility of mounting optical 3D measurement sensors *and* contact probes.

In addition, 3D imaging sensors are becoming of interest in combination with two dimensional (2D) vision sensors, especially in robotic applications, for collision avoidance, and to solve 'removing-from-heap' and assembling problems [11]. As a result, those companies traditionally focused on the development of 2D vision systems, are now enlarging their product spectrum by including 3D range sensors.

The use of optical depth sensors has gone beyond the mechanical field for which they were originally intended. Examples of application fields are geology, civil engineering, archaeology, reverse engineering, medicine, and virtual reality [12–16].

The aim of this paper is to briefly review the state of the art concerning 3D sensing techniques and devices, and to present their applications in industry, cultural heritage, medicine and forensics. It focuses in part on the research carried out at our Laboratory, and briefly describes related approaches developed by other groups.

The paper has the following structure: Section 2 overviews 3D imaging techniques, and evaluates the different approaches to highlight which method can be used and what are the main applications. Section 3 gives an insight of the results achieved in the mentioned applications. As far as the industrial field is concerned, the topics of surface quality control, dimensional measurement and reverse engineering are covered. Significant results in the cultural heritage field, both achieved by us and by other research groups are shown. The approaches developed in the medical field are briefly reviewed, and the *post mortem* analysis of lesions is cited as an example of the latest applications in this area. The last section is dedicated to the use of 3D imaging techniques for the accurate, fast and non-invasive measurement and modeling of crime scenes.

2. OVERVIEW OF 3D IMAGING TECHNIQUES

3D imaging sensors generally operate by projecting (in the active form) or acquiring (in the passive form) electromagnetic energy onto/from an object followed by recording the transmitted or reflected energy. The most important example of transmission gauging is the industrial computer tomography (CT), which uses high-energy x-rays and measures the radiation transmitted through the object.

Reflection sensors for shape acquisition can be subdivided into non-optical and optical sensing. Non-optical sensing includes acoustic sensors (ultrasonic, seismic), electromagnetic (infrared, ultraviolet, microwave radar, etc...) and others. These techniques typically measure distances to objects by measuring the time required for a pulse of sound or microwave energy to bounce back from an object.

In reflection optical sensing, light carries the measurement information. There is a remarkable variety of 3D optical techniques, and their classification is not unique. In this section, we mention the more prominent approaches, and we classify them as shown in Table 1.

The 3D techniques are based on optical triangulation, on time delay, and on the use of monocular images. They are classified into passive and active methods. In passive methods, the reflectance of the object and the illumination of the scene are used to derive the shape information: no active device is necessary. In the active form, suitable light sources are used as the internal vector of information. A distinction is also made between direct and indirect measurements. Direct techniques result in range data, i.e., into a set of distances between the unknown surface and the range sensor. Indirect measurements are inferred from monocular images and from prior knowledge of the target properties. They result either in range data or in surface orientation.

Table 1. Classification of 3D imaging techniques.

	Triangulation	Time delay	Monocular Images	Passive	Active	Direct	Indirect	Range	Surface Orientation
Laser triangulators	X				X	X		X	
Structured light	X				X	X		X	
Stereo vision	X			X		X		X	
Photogrammetry	X			X		X		X	
Time of Flight		X			X	X		X	
Interferometry		X			X	X		X	
Moiré fringe range contours			X		X		X	X	
Shape from focusing			X	X	X		X	X	
Shape from shadows			X		X		X	X	
Texture gradients			X	X			X		X
Shape from shading			X		X		X		X
Shape from photometry			X		X		X		X

Excellent reviews of optical methods and range sensors for 3D measurement are presented in references [1–7]. In [1] a review of 20 years of development in the field of 3D laser imaging with emphasis on commercial systems available in 2004 is given. Comprehensive summaries of earlier techniques and systems are provided in the other publications. A survey of 3D imaging techniques is also given in [8] and in [9], in the wider context of both contact and contactless 3D measurement techniques for the reverse engineering of shapes.

2.1 Laser triangulators

Both single-point triangulators and laser stripes belong to this category. They are all based on the active triangulation principle [17]. Figure 1 shows a typical system configuration. Points O_P and O_C are the exit and the entrance pupils of a laser source and of a camera. Their mutual distance is the baseline d. The optical axes z_P and z_C of the laser and the camera form an angle of α degrees.

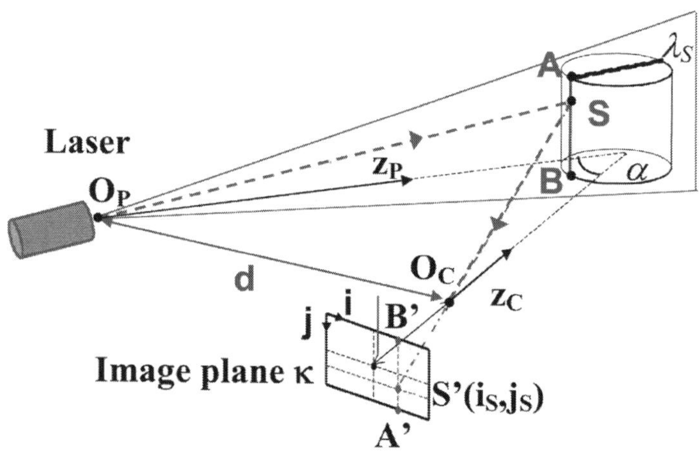

Figure 1. Schematics of the triangulation principle.

The laser source generates a narrow beam, impinging the object at point S (single-point triangulators). The back scattered beam is imaged at point S' at image plane κ. The measurement of the location (i_S, j_S) of image point S' defines the line of sight $\overline{S'O_C}$, and, by means of simple geometry, yields the position of S. The measurement of the surface is achieved by scanning. In a conventional triangulation configuration, a compromise is necessary between the Field of View (FOV), the measurement resolution and uncertainty, and the shadow effects due to large values of angle α.

To overcome this limitation, a method called 'synchronized scanning' has been proposed. Using the approach illustrated in [18, 19], a large field of view can be achieved with a small angle α, without sacrificing range measurement precision.

Laser stripes exploit the optical triangulation principle shown in Figure 1. However, in this case, the laser is equipped with a cylindrical lens, which expands the light beam along one direction. Hence, a plane of light is generated, and multiple points of the object are illuminated at the same time. In the figure, the light plane is denoted by λ_S, and the illuminated points belong to the intersection between the plane and the unknown object $(\text{line } \overline{AB})$. The measurement of the location of all the image points from A′ to B′ at plane κ allows the determination of the 3D shape of the object in correspondence with the illuminated points. For dense reconstruction, the plane of light must scan the scene [20–22]. An interesting enhancement of the basic principle exploits the Biris principle [23]. A laser source produces two stripes by passing through the Bi-Iris component (a mask with two apertures). The measurement of the point location at the image plane can be carried out on a differential basis, and shows decreased dependence on the object reflectivity and on the laser speckles.

One of the most significant advantages of laser triangulators is their accuracy, and their relative insensitivity to illumination conditions and surface texture effects. Single-point laser triangulators are widely used in the industrial field, for the measurement of distances, diameters, thicknesses, as well as in surface quality control applications. Laser stripes are becoming popular for quality control, reverse engineering, and modeling of heritage. Examples are the Vivid 910 system (Konica Minolta, Inc.), the sensors of the SmartRay series (SmartRay GmbH, Germany) and the ShapeGrabber systems (ShapeGrabber Inc., CA, USA). 3D sensors are designed for integration with robot arms, to implement "pick and place" operations in de-palletizing stations. An example is the Ranger system (Sick, Inc.). The NextEngine system (NextEngine, Inc., CA, USA) and the TriAngles scanner (ComTronics, Inc., USA) device deserve particular attention, since they show how the field is progressing. These two systems, in fact, break the price barrier of laser-based systems, which is a limiting factor in their diffusion.

2.2 Structured light

Structured light based sensors share the active triangulation approach above mentioned. However, instead of scanning the surface, they project bi-dimensional patterns of non-coherent light, and elaborate them to obtain the range information for each viewed point simultaneously. A single pattern as well as multiple patterns can be projected. In both cases, the single light plane $\lambda_S$shown in Figure 1 is replaced by a bundle of geometrical planes, schematically shown in Figure 2. The planes are indexed along the LP coordinate at the projector plane. The depth information at object point S is obtained as the intersection between line sight SS′ and the plane indexed by $LP=LP_S$ [25]. The critical point is to guarantee that different object points are assigned to different indexes along the LP coordinate. To this aim, a large number of projection strategies have been developed. The projection of grid patterns [26, 27], of dot patterns [28], of multiple vertical slits [29] and of multi-color projection patterns [30] have been extensively studied. Particular research has been carried out on the projection of fringe patterns [31, 32], that are particularly suitable to maximize the measurement resolution.

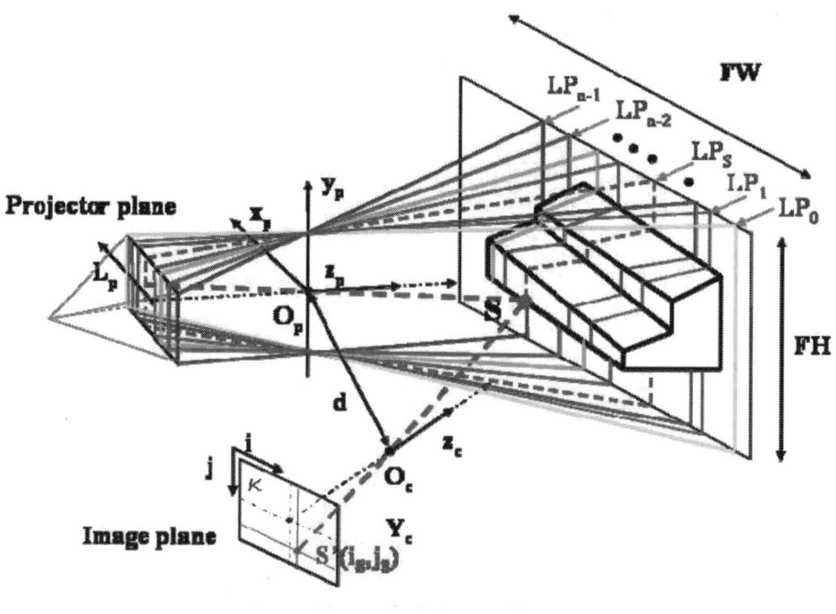

Figure 2. Principle of measurement in structured light systems.

As an example, in Figure 3, three fringe patterns are shown. The first one is formed by fringes of sinusoidal profile, the second one is obtained by using the superposition of two patterns with sinusoidal fringes at different frequencies [33], and the last one is formed by fringes of rectangular profile [34].

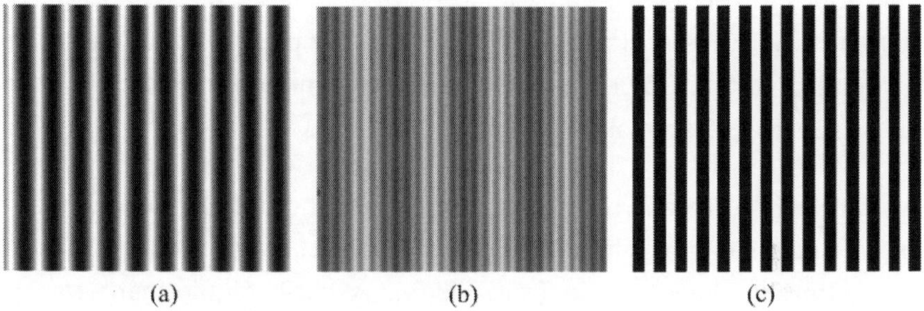

Figure 3. Example of fringe projection schemes. (a) Fringe pattern of sinusoidal fringes. (b) Superposition of two sinusoidal fringe patterns at different frequencies. (c) Projection of fringes of rectangular profile.

Recent trends in the development of structured light systems are aimed at increasing the speed of projection of multiple patterns, in order to allow the real-time acquisition of the surfaces, especially for motion planning and human body acquisitions. The MobilCam 3D system (ViaLUX GmbH, Germany), and the Broadway scanner (Artec Group, Inc., CA, USA) belong to this category.

2.3 Stereo vision

The stereo vision method represents the passive version of structured light techniques. Here, two (or more) cameras concurrently capture the same scene. In principle, the reconstruction by stereo approach uses the following sequence of processing steps: (i) image acquisition, (ii) camera modeling, (iii) feature extractions, (iv) correspondence analysis and (v), triangulation. No further equipment (e.g. specific light sources) and no special projections are required. The remarkable advantages of the stereo approach are the simplicity and the low cost; the major problem is the identification of common points within the image pairs, i.e., the solution of the well-known correspondence problem. Moreover, the quality of the shape extraction depends on the sharpness of the surface texture (affected by variations in surface reflectance). Stereo vision has significant applications in robotics and in computer vision, where the essence of the problem is not the accurate acquisition of highly quality data, but, rather, their interpretation (for example for motion planning, collision avoidance and grasping applications).

A variant of the stereo vision approach implies the use of multiple images from a single camera, which captures the object in a sequence of images from different views (shape from video). A basic requirement for this technique is that the scene does not contain moving parts. 3D urban modeling and object detection are typical applications [35–38].

Stereo vision based on the detection of the object silhouette has recently become very popular. The Stereo approach is exploited, but the 3D geometry of the object is retrieved by using the object contours under different viewing directions. One of the most prominent applications of this method is the modeling of 3D shapes for heritage, especially when the texture information is captured together with the range [39]. Among the devices on the market, the PrOMT.stereo system (SOLVing3D GmbH, Germany) shows high performance and simplicity of use.

2.4 Photogrammetry

Photogrammetry obtains reliable 3D models by means of photographs. In digital photogrammetry digital images are used. The elaboration pipeline consists basically of the following steps: camera calibration and orientation, image point measurements, 3D point cloud generation, surface generation and texture mapping. Camera calibration is crucial in view of obtaining accurate models. Image measurement can be performed by means of automatic or semi-automatic procedures. In the first case, very dense point clouds are obtained, even if at the expense of inaccuracy and missing parts. In the second case, very accurate measurements are obtained, over a significantly smaller number of points, and at increased elaboration and operator times [40–42]. Typical applications of photogrammetry, besides the aerial photogrammetry, are in close range photogrammetry, for city modeling, medical imaging and heritage [48–43].

Reliable packages are now commercially available for complete scene modeling or sensor calibration and orientation. Examples are the Australis software (Photometrics, Australia), Photomodeler (Eos Systems, Inc., Canada), Leica Photogrammetry Suite (Leica Geosystems GIS & Mapping), and Menci (Menci Software srl, Italy).

Both stereo vision and photogrammetry share the objective of obtaining 3D models from images and are currently used in computer vision applications. The methods rely on the use of camera calibration techniques. The elaboration chain is basically the same, even if linear models for camera calibration and simplified point measurement procedures are used in computer vision applications. In fact, in computer vision the automation level of the overall process is more important with respect to the accuracy of the models [44].

In recent times, the photogrammetric and computer vision communities have proposed combined procedures, for increasing both the measurement performance and the automation levels. Examples are in the use of laser scanning and photogrammetry [45–47] and in the use of stereo vision and photogrammetry for facade reconstruction and object tracking [48, 50]. On the market, combinations of structured light projection with photogrammetry are available (Atos II scanner, Gom GmbH, Germany) for improved measurement performance.

2.5 Time of Flight

Surface range measurement can be made directly using the radar time-of-flight principle. The emitter unit generates a laser pulse, which impinges onto the target surface. A receiver detects the reflected pulse, and suitable electronics measures the roundtrip travel time of the returning signal and its intensity. Single point sensors perform point-to-point distance measurement, and scanning devices are combined to the optical head to cover large bi-dimensional scenes. Large range sensors allow measurement ranges from 15 m to 100 m (reflective markers must be put on the target surfaces). Medium range sensors can acquire 3D data in shorter ranges. The measurement resolutions vary with the range. For large measuring ranges, time-of flight sensors give excellent results. On the other side, for smaller objects, about one meter in size, attaining 1 part per 1,000 accuracy with time-of-flight radar requires very high speed timing circuitry, because the time differences are in the pico-second range. A few amplitude and frequency modulated radars have shown promise for close range distance measurement [37, 51, 52].

In many applications, the technique is range-limited by allowable power levels of laser radiation, determined by laser safety considerations. Additionally, time-of-flight sensors face difficulties with shiny surfaces, which reflect little back-scattered light energy except when oriented perpendicularly to the line of sight.

2.6 Interferometry

Interferometric methods operate by projecting a spatially or temporally varying periodic pattern onto a surface, followed by mixing the reflected light with a reference pattern. The reference pattern demodulates the signal to reveal the variation in surface geometry. The measurement resolution is very high, since it is a fraction of the wavelength of the laser radiation. For this reason, surface quality control and microprofilometry are the most explored applications. Use of multiple wavelengths and of double heterodyne detection lengthens the non-ambiguity range. Systems based on this principle are successfully used to calibrate CMMs. Holographic interferometry relies on mixing coherent illumination with different wave vectors. Holographic methods typically yield range accuracy of a fraction of the light wavelength over microscopic fields of view [5, 53].

2.7 Moiré fringe range contours

Moiré fringe range contours are obtained by illuminating the scene with a light source passing through a grating, and viewing the scene with a laterally displaced camera through an identical second grating. The resulting interference pattern shows equidistant contour lines, but there is no information about the corresponding depth values. In addition, it is impossible to have direct information about the sign of the concavities. Moirè methods can have phase discrimination problems when the surface does not exhibit smooth shape variations [54].

2.8 Shape from focusing

Depth and range can be determined by exploiting the focal properties of a lens. A camera lens can be used as a range finder by exploiting the "depth of view" phenomena. In fact, the target image is blurred by an amount proportional to the distance between points on the object and the in-focus object plane. This technique has evolved from the passive approach to an active sensing strategy. In the passive case, surface texture is used to determine the amount of blurring. Thus, the object must have surface texture covering the whole surface in order to extract shape. The active version of the method operates by projecting light onto the object to avoid difficulties in discerning surface texture. Most prior work in active depth from focus has yielded moderate accuracy up to one part per 400 over the field of view [55]. There is a direct trade-of between depth of view and field of view; satisfactory depth resolution is achieved at the expense of a sub-sampling the scene, which in turn requires some form of mechanical scanning to acquire range measurement over the whole scene. Moreover, spatial resolution is non-uniform. Specifically, depth resolution is substantially less than resolution perpendicular to the observation axis. Finally, objects not aligned perpendicularly to the optical axis and having a depth dimension greater than the depth of view will come in to focus at different ranges, complicating the scene analysis and interpretation [56].

2.9 Shape from shadows

This technique is a variant of the structured light approach. The 3D model of the unknown object is rebuilt by capturing the shadow of a known object projected onto the target when the light is moving. Low cost and simple hardware are the main advantages of this approach, even if at the expense of low accuracy [57].

2.10 Shape from texture

The idea is to find possible transformations of texture elements (texels) to reproduce the object surface orientation. For example, given a planar surface, the image of a circular texel is an ellipse with varying values of its axes depending on its orientation [58]. A review of the techniques developed in this area is in reference [37]. These methods yield simple, low cost hardware. However, the measurement quality is low.

2.11 Shape from shading

Shape-from-shading requires the acquisition of the object from one viewing angle and varying the position of the light source, which results in varying the shading on the target surface. A variant of this method implies the variation of the lighting conditions. A review of the algorithms able to extract the shape information, starting from the reflectance map of the image, is in reference [59]. The acquisition hardware is very simple, and low cost. However, low accuracy is obtained, especially in the presence of external factors influencing the object reflectance. The measurement software is rather complex.

2.12 Strengths and weaknesses of 3D imaging techniques

The main characteristics of optical range imaging techniques are summarized in Table 2. The comments on the table are quite general in nature, and a number of exceptions are known. Strengths and weaknesses of the different techniques are strongly application-dependent. The common attribute of being non-contact is an important consideration in those applications characterized by either fragile, deformable objects, or on-line measurements or hostile environments. Acquisition time is another important aspect, when the overall cost of the measurement process suggests the reduction of the operator time even at the expense of deteriorating the quality of the data. On the other hand, active vision systems using a laser beam that illuminates the object inherently involve safety considerations, and possible surface interaction effects. In addition, the speckle effect introduces disturbances that represent a serious limit to the accuracy of the measurements [60]. Fortunately, recent advances in LEDs technology yield a valuable solution to this problem, since they are suitable candidates as light projectors in active triangulation systems.

The dramatic evolution of CPUs and memories has led in the last three years to elaboration performances that were by far impossible before, at low costs. For this reasons, techniques that are computation demanding (e.g., passive stereo vision) are now more reliable and efficient.

The selection of which sensor type should be used to solve a given depth measurement problem is a very complex task, that must consider (i) the measurement time, (ii) the budget, and (iii) the quality expected from the measurement. In this respect, 3D imaging sensors may be affected by missing or bad quality data. Reasons are related to the optical geometry of the system, the type of projector and/or acquisition optical device, the measurement technique and the characteristics of the target objects. The sensor performance may depend on the dimension, the shape, the texture, the temperature and the accessibility of the object. Relevant factors that influence the choice are also the ruggedness, the portability, and the adaptiveness of the sensor to the measurement problem, the easiness of the data handling, and the simplicity of use of the sensor.

Table 2. Comparison of optical range imaging techniques.

TECHNOLOGY	STRENGTH	WEAKNESS
Laser triangulators	Relative simplicity Performance generally independent of ambient light High data acquisition rate	Safety constraint associated with the use of laser source Limited range and measurement volume Missing data in correspondence with occlusions and shadows Cost
Structured Light	High data acquisition rate Intermediate measurement volume Performance generally dependent of ambient light	Safety constraints, if laser based Computationally middle-complex Missing data in correspondence with occlusions and shadows Cost
Stereo Vision	Simple and inexpensive High accuracy on well-defined targets	Computation demanding Sparse data covering Limited to well defined scenes Low data acquisition rate
Photogrammetry	Simple and inexpensive High accuracy on well-defined targets	Computation demanding Sparse data covering Limited to well defined scenes Low data acquisition rate
Time-of-Flight	Medium to large measurement range Good data acquisition rate Performance generally independent of ambient light	Cost Accuracy is inferior to triangulation at close ranges
Interferometry	Sub-micron accuracy in micro-ranges	Measurement capability limited to quasi-flat surfaces Cost Limited applicability in industrial environment
Moiré fringe range contours	Simple and low cost Short ranges	Limited to the measurement of smooth surfaces
Shape from focusing	Simple and inexpensive Available sensors for surface inspection and microprofilometry	Limited fields of view Non-uniform spatial resolution Performance affected by ambient light (if passive)
Shape from shadows	Low cost Limited demand for computing power	Low accuracy
Texture gradients	Simple and low cost	Low accuracy
Shape from shading	Simple and low cost	Low accuracy

2.13 The software for the elaboration of 3D data

Besides the acquisition of 3d raw data, the construction of 3D models requires the following steps:

1 Registration of multiple images;

2 Integration of registered images into a fused single point cloud and determination of the tessel mesh that models the surface;

3 Acquisition of reflection data, for surface visualization.

The registration step consists of the alignment in a common reference frame of all the views captured to cover the whole surface. A relevant number of techniques have been proposed. ICP based algorithms, for example, allow the pair wise registration of adjacent views [61, 62]. Multi-view registration methods carry out the alignment of multiple views following a global approach [63].

The integration step has been widely studied by the computer graphics community, to develop efficient methods for the creation of meshes. Volumetric methods [64, 65], mesh stitching [66, 67], region growing techniques [68, 69], and sculpting based methods [70] are of outmost importance in this field.

The acquisition of reflectance data is required for the correct visualization of the 3D models. Typical applications are for constructing 3D models for virtual reality, animation, and cultural heritage. The research developed in this area has led to approaches based either on parametric reflectance models or on a set of colour images of the object [71, 72]. Excellent reviews of these methods are in references [73–75].

There are a number of commercial packages available for manipulation of 3D data. Examples are PolyWorks (InnovMetric, Inc., Canada), Geomagic (Raindrop Geomagic, Inc., USA), Rapidform (Inus Technology, Inc. & Rapidform, Inc.), Rinhoceros (Rino3D Inc., USA), Surfacer (Powershape, Inc., UK). They provide view importing, editing, alignment and fusion. Specific modules allow mesh-editing, compression, rendering, visualizing and inspecting. Some of them provide the tools for the construction of the CAD model from the mesh. It is worth noting that in general, the operations are performed in a semi-automatic way, i.e., the operator skill is crucial to optimize the various steps, and to keep under control the influence of the alignment errors and of the editing operations over the 3D models.

3. EXPERIENCE IN THE APPLICATION OF 3D IMAGING SENSORS

A wide range of applications is possible nowadays, thanks to the availability of engineered sensors, of laboratory prototypes, and of suitable software environments to elaborate the measurements. This section presents a brief insight of the most important fields where 3D imaging sensors can be fruitfully used. For each one, an application example that has been carried out in our Laboratory is presented.

3.1 Industrial applications

Typical measurement problems in the industrial field deal with (i) the control of machined surfaces, for the quantitative measure of roughness, waviness and form factor, (ii) the dimensional measurement and the quality control of products, and (iii) the reverse engineering of complex shapes.

3.1.1 Surface quality control

Microprofilometry techniques and sensors are the best suited to carry out the measurement processes in the surface control field. In this application, the objective is to gauge the 3D quantitative representation of the surfaces in measurement intervals from a few microns to tens of millimeters, with resolutions from a few tens of nanometers to tens of microns. A typical application is the measurement of roughness and of waviness and the gauging of the 3D topology of machined surfaces. Typical contactless probes are represented by interferometers, autofocus and triangulator sensors. Since these are single-point devices, the measurement must be accomplished by scanning suitable samples of the surfaces. Techniques have been proposed by various authors. Laser integrated measurement of surface roughness and micro-displacement is proposed in [76]. In [77], a multi-detector triangulation laser probe is developed and mounted on a CMM for very accurate surface inspection.

Whenever the control is off-line, a system like that shown in Figure 4 can represent a good solution. Two automatic micropositioning high-accuracy slits carry out bi-dimensional x and y scanning of the surface under test. Depending on the measurement range and the resolution, an active autofocus sensor or a triangulator are mounted as the measuring probes along the z direction.

Figure 4. The microprofilometer setup developed at the laboratory for off-line microprofilometry applications.

An example of the system performance is shown in Figure 5. The measured surface in Figure 5ais the 2 mm×2 mm portion of a thin-film sensor. The sampling step along the x and y coordinates is equal to 10 μm. Due to the extremely small height range of the target, an autofocus sensor (LNS 2.3/4.4 Dynavision, now LMI Inc) was selected as the measurement probe. The 3D topographic map of the surface is presented in Figure 5b. The measurement units are in μm.

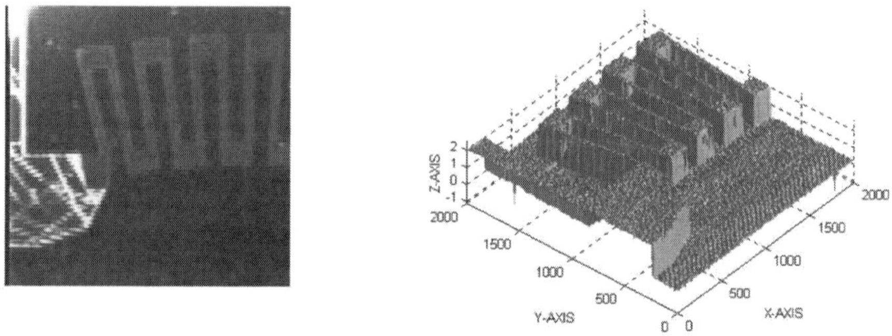

(a) (b)

Figure 5. 3D topography of a 2 mm×2 mm surface of a thin-film sensor. (a) Image of the measured surface. (b) 3D plot of the surface topography.

Another interesting example of the application of the setup in Figure 4 is the measurement of the turning machined surface shown in Figure 6a. In this case, a single-point triangulator (LTS 15/3, Dynavision) was used to capture the depth map shown in Figure 6b. Here, the dimension of the sample is equal to 5 mm × 5 mm, and the plotted range is from 0 to 600 μm.

For on-line measurements, our Laboratory has developed the sensor shown in Figure 7. The system works on typical grinding stations, used to recondition rolls for milling; it integrates a surface profiler and a light scattering unit in a compact setup suitable for industrial applications [81]. The optical profiler is the same triangulation sensor as in Figure 6, suitable for measuring the surface waviness. The scattering sensor is integrated on the triangulator for the detection of the surface roughness. Figure 8 shows a measurement example.

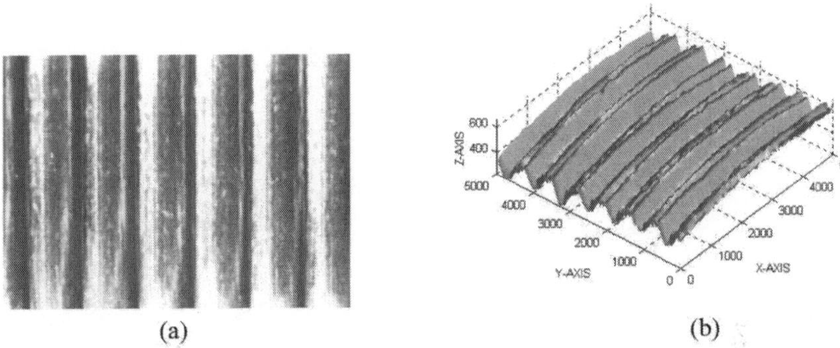

Figure 6. Example of the measurement by using the LTS 15/3 triangulator sensor. (a) The specimen. (b) The measured point cloud.

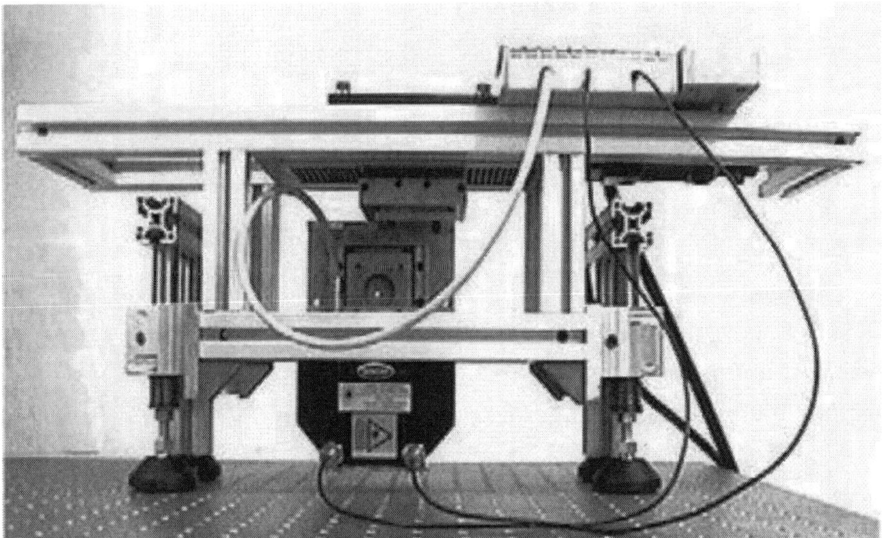

Figure 7. View of the mechanical frame that holds the sensor during industrial testing.

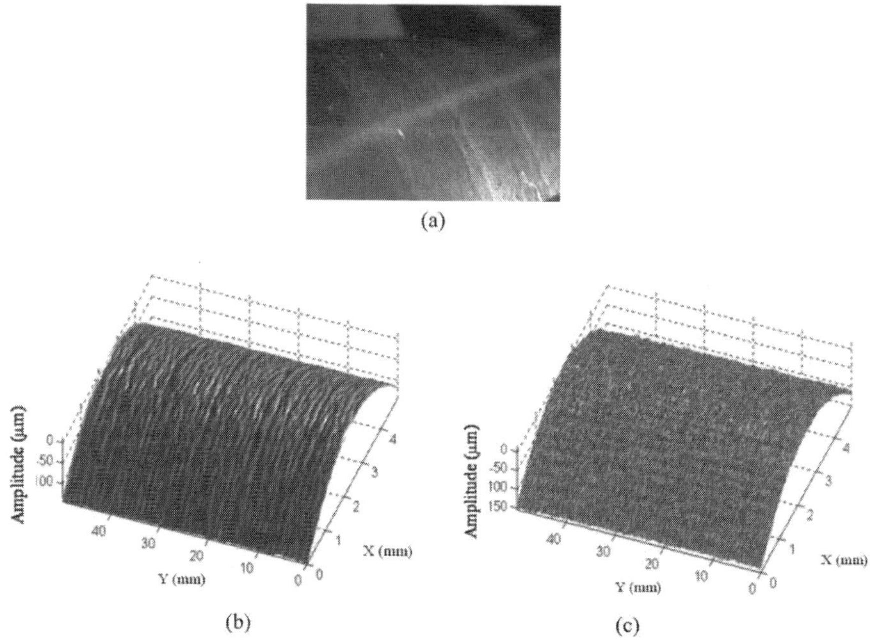

Figure 8. Example of 3D acquisition in the micro range. (a) The inspected surface. (b) 3D profile of the surface waviness. (c) 3D profile of the surface roughness.

3.1.2 Dimensional measurement and quality control

The dimensional measurement of complex surfaces is a really wide-range field of application, since it involves the 3D acquisition of shapes in the range from tens of millimetres to a few meters, with measurement resolution from one hundred microns to a few centimetres. The choice of the sensor depends on the object shape and dimension, on the environmental conditions, on the time available to perform the measurement, and, of course, on the measurement requirements.

An interesting application is the measurement of large, free-form objects, as that one shown inFigure 9. The complexity and the dimension of the target suggests the use of a 3D imaging sensor belonging to the class of stereo vision or structured light devices, and the acquisition of multiple point clouds, to cover the whole surface. In addition, to obtain measurement processes suitable for the industrial production field, the alignment of the views should be carried out automatically, keeping the operator intervention at minimum.

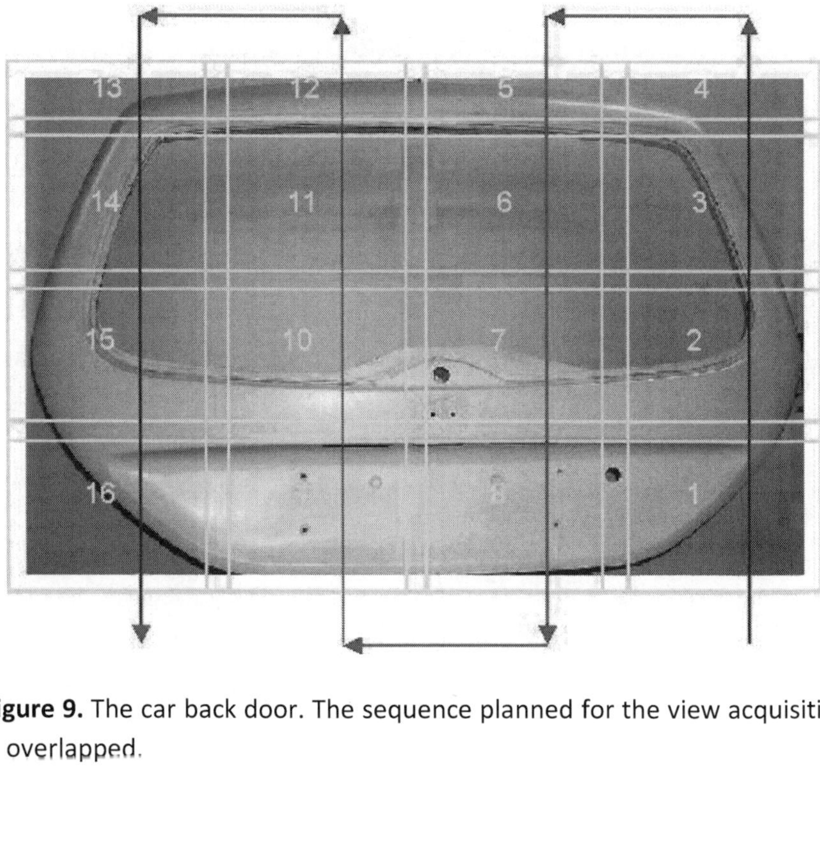

Figure 9. The car back door. The sequence planned for the view acquisition is overlapped.

The stereo vision based Ortigo 200 system (Cognitens, Inc) and the Romer Omega mobile scan arm, equipped with the laser stripe R Scan (Hexagon, Inc) are two examples of market available instruments specifically developed for quality control. Our Laboratory has designed and developed the system shown in Figure 10 [82]. The system layout is shown in Figure 10a.

The camera-projector pair that is configured following the triangulation geometry shown inFigure 1 represents the optical head. The light coding approach is based on the well known Gray-Code and Phase-Shift (GCPS) projection technique [83]. The geometry of the optical head can be varied depending on the resolution required by the measurement. In detail, both the orientation and the distance of the projector with respect to the video-camera can be varied respectively within the rotation interval 20°–50° (α is the angle of rotation) and the translation interval 400 mm–1 m (d is the mutual distance between the optical devices). The optical head is mounted on a moving stage, allowing its translation along directions X and Y; in this way, areas up to 2 m^2 can be scanned and larger surfaces can be measured by acquiring and aligning a number of separate patches. Moreover, objects presenting circular symmetry can be placed on a rotation stage: this enables the acquisition of patches at different values of the rotation angle, denoted by φ in the figure.

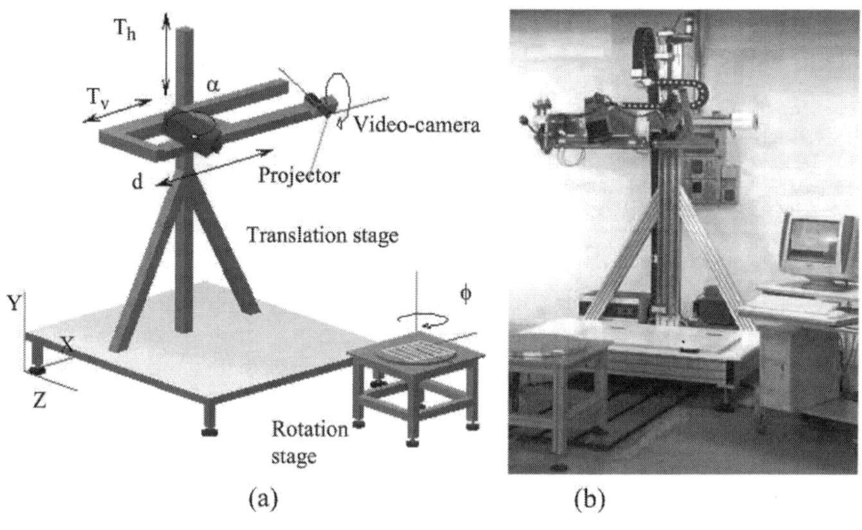

Figure 10. The 3D instrument developed at the laboratory. (a) Layout of the system. (b) Photograph of the device.

The system, shown in Figure 10b is equipped with stepped motors, to fully control the rotation and the translation of the optical head. The sequence of acquisition of the range images is decided on the basis of the dimension and the shape of the object. Objects characterized by predominant shapes along the X and the Y axes are acquired by moving the optical head horizontally and vertically, at steps depending on the field of view. In this case, only translation matrices are used to align the range images. In the general case of objects which can be completely measured by a combination of rotation and displacement of the optical head, the alignment is performed by using a combination of rotation and translation matrices.

The measurement of the car back door (1.20 m height by 1.60 m width) required the acquisition of the patches labeled from 1 to 13 in Figure 9, (the blue line represents the acquisition path); each patch was 400 mm large and 300 mm high. The time to acquire a single patch was 4sec. The variability of the measurement is ±30 µm, with a resolution of 70 µm. The whole point cloud is shown in Figure 11. The overall error is within 0.1 mm, taking into account the contribution of the matching between adjacent views.

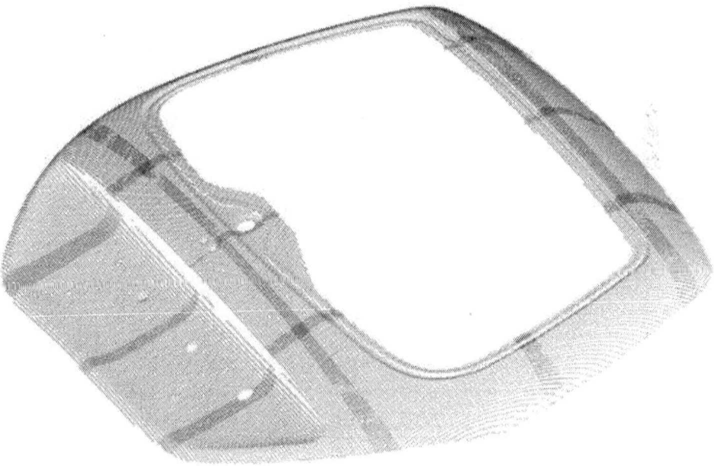

Figure 11. Whole point cloud of the car back door.

3.1.3 Reverse engineering of free-form shapes

Reverse engineering is the process of creating a set of engineering specifications and drawings directly from the inspection of an object, a geometric model of which is obtained from sensor data. For objects with geometric regularity, it is customary to generate them analytically, using one of several geometric model schemes. For free-form shapes that do not present regular geometric properties, it is necessary to measure them and to create the 3D model for their 3D features representation.

The current industrial technology for precise measurement of 3-D object involves contact scanning by Coordinate Measuring Machines (CMMs). This technique is precise and widely used for the creation of the surface model [9]. As already mentioned, however, the primary disadvantage of this approach is the time wasting nature of the work. On the other hand, the use of 3D imaging sensors allows the collection of large amount of dimensional data in reasonably short time. However, the metrological performance of contactless sensors is usually lower than that of the CMM. The combination of optical and mechanical probes is strategic, in view of obtaining high quality of the CAD description at a dramatically reduced time. A survey of techniques developed in this field is in publications [84–87]. Our Laboratory, in collaboration with other partners, developed a novel methodology for the reverse engineering of free-form surfaces based on the integration of the measurement information from the system in Figure 10 and a CMM [88]. Figure 12 shows the basic steps of the method. The optical system rapidly gauges the shape of the wheel rim, as shown in Figure 12a. The acquired point cloud, shown in Figure 12b is the starting information for the reconstruction of a 'rough' CAD model of the object.

To this aim, we used a suitably developed program, called Visual Point, which allows the manipulation of the point clouds in the pre-processing of raw data. The CAD model was then elaborated by the PRO/Engineer software (PTC Inc). This model presented an accuracy of 0.5mm, which was sufficient to generate a collision-free inspection path on the CMM. In this way, the CMM could work independently from the operator. It acquired automatically a very dense point cloud with 4 μm of uncertainty, at dramatically reduced time. Figure 12c shows the partial reconstruction of the wheel rim after the first initial digitization. The measured points allowed us to obtain the accurate CAD model of the wheel rim shown in Figure 12d.

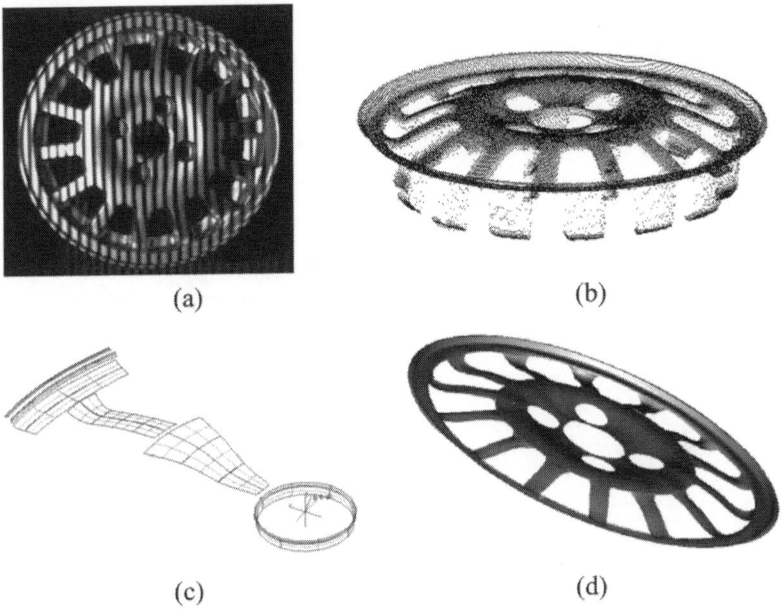

Figure panels: (a) (b) (c) (d)

Figure 12. Process to create the CAD model of a free-form surface. (a) Optical acquisition of the wheel rim used as the target. (b) Range image of the top side of the wheel rim. (c) Generation of the paths for the digitization by using the CMM. (d) CAD model of the target.

Reverse engineering processes can be accomplished even on a full-optical acquisition basis. In this case, 3D imaging sensors gauge the surfaces. This choice is optimal in Collaborative Design and Rapid Prototyping applications, which are typically involved in the design process of products that must have aesthetical appeal, such as the exterior of consumer products ranging from perfume bottles to automobiles. A considerable number of research projects have been carried out so far [89–92]. Among the projects developed at our Laboratory, we mention two examples.

The first is the development of the low-cost whole field structured light sensor shown in Figure 13. The optical head is composed by a market available, low-cost SVGA LCD projector, and the camera is a low-cost device at standard resolution. This sensor performs the measurement by projecting a single fringe pattern, similar to that shown in Figure 3c. The elaboration of the pattern is performed by means of a phase demodulation approach specifically designed to increase the measurement range [79]. The optical head is mounted on a bar, fixed on a robust tripod: special calibration allows us to adapt the system set-up dependently on the required input resolution and range. In contrast to the system shown in Figure 10, the full coverage of the shape is obtained by manually moving the instrument in the measurement scene, and by acquiring multiple point clouds. The procedure for their alignment exploits the correspondence between points in different adjacent views. The PolyWorks (InnovMetric Inc, Ca) suite of programs carries out this task. An application example is shown in Figure 14. The target object is a (135 × 60 × 45) mm^3 (height × width × depth) perfume bottle, reproducing the form of a female body.

Figure 13. The low-cost whole-field structured light sensor designed for modeling applications.

Figure 14a shows the projection of the fringe pattern during the measurement of a single point cloud. The acquisition of the target is accomplished by acquiring six views. These are aligned by using the ImAlign module of the PolyWorks suite. The accuracy of the 3D raw data is 233 μm, a reasonable value for the modeling process. This is carried out by using the ImMerge and the ImEdit modules of PolyWorks, for the creation and the optimization of the triangle mesh. The mesh is presented in Figure 14b.

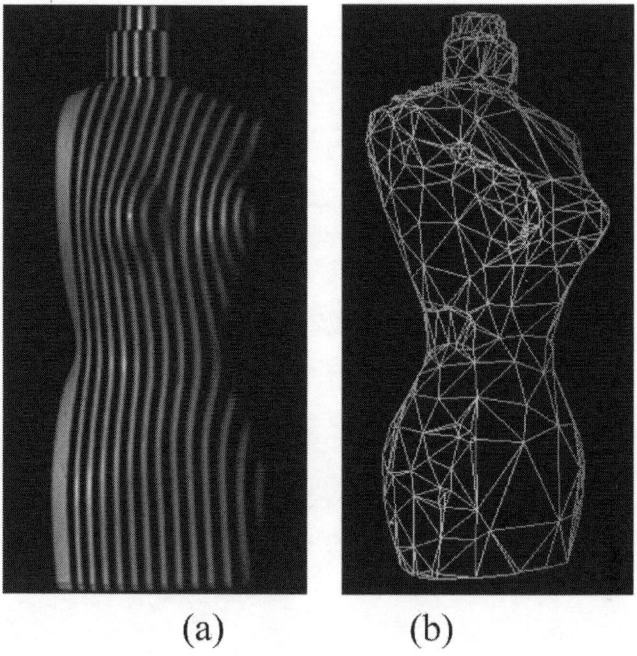

Figure 14. Example of the modeling of a perfume bottle. (a) Projection of the fringe pattern. (b) Triangle mesh that models the object shape.

The latter project is the development of the 3D imaging sensor shown in Figure 15. This system, called OPL-3D, is a whole-field structured light sensor that combines the GCPS coding procedure of the instrument in Figure 10 with a calibration approach similar to the one developed for the system in Figure 13 [25].

OPL-3D exhibits low-measurement uncertainty (120 μm) over large measurement areas (450 mm by 340 mm), linearly scalable in the case of smaller areas. It is portable and easy reconfigurable to be successfully used in different measurement conditions. It is now commercially available under the name of 3Dshape (OpenTechnologies s.r.l., Italy).

Figure 15. Photograph of OPL-3D.

This sensor is particularly suitable whenever the measurement problem requires high measurement performance and flexibility of reconfiguration. We fruitfully used it to carry out the complete acquisition of the car body of the Ferrari 250MM shown in Figure 16. The aim of this experiment was to assess the efficiency of the process from the acquisition to the modeling of the surfaces [93]. Figure 17 shows the performance of OPL-3D. The whole point cloud in Figure 17awas obtained by acquiring and merging 400 point clouds, at different resolution and dimension, depending on the details. The Geomagic suite of programs elaborated the 3D raw data. First, the triangle mesh was created (Figure 17b); then the CAD model was calculated starting from the mesh. The CAD model is shown in Figure 17c. The model was then exported in the STL format and input to a Rapid Prototyping machine, for the production of the 1:8 scaled copy, shown in Figure 17d.

Figure 16. The Ferrari 250MM historical racing car.

3.2 Cultural heritage applications

In the last years, the use of 3D imaging sensors for the contactless acquisition of cultural heritage has gained increased attention by museums and by the archaeological specialists [100]. A number of reasearch laboratories have worked on the modeling of statues [95–97], the 3D documentation and virtualizing of archaeological sites [98–100], the automated classification of pieces [101], and visualization applications [102]. The measurement and elaboration chain is still a reverse engineering process, similar to the one developed for the industrial field. Even the objectives are the same: acquisition, modeling and visualization are required in the cultural frame, to monitor the archaeological founds. In addition, the availability of 3D models opens the door to the virtual reproduction, for didactical and visualization purposes. Physical copies of the originals are produced by using Rapid Prototyping techniques: an example is the reproduction at full scale of the two meter high Winged Victory of Brescia, shown in Figure 18. Our Laboratory at the City Museum accomplished the acquisition in 2001 [103, 104]. The optical sensor was the OPL-3D.

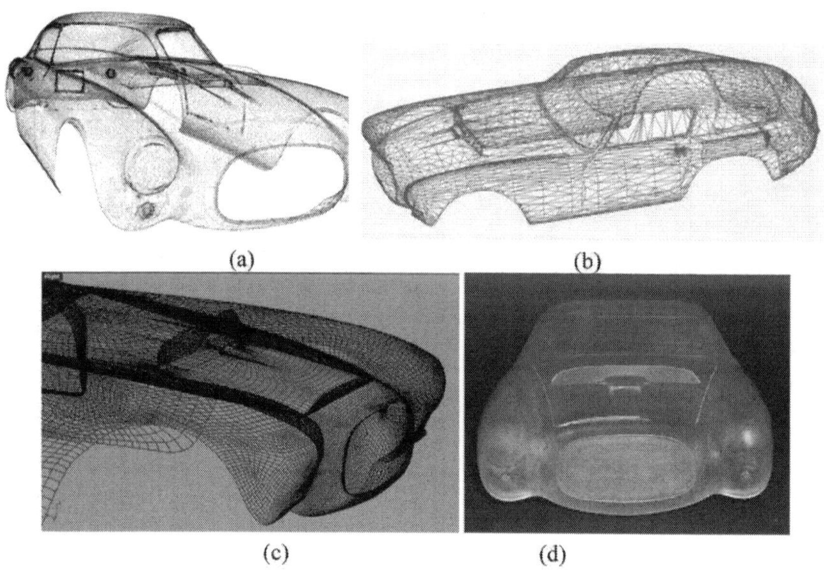

Figure 17. Example of full optical reverse engineering in the automotive domain by using OPL-3D. (a) Point cloud of the car body. (b) Triangle mesh. (c) CAD model. (d) Scaled prototype of the Ferrari.

One of the fields where 3D accurate acquisition is strategic is the documentation of finds. Traditional techniques require the use of contact probes and the hand-made drawing of the originals: this practice introduces (i) inaccuracies of the reproduction, (ii) loss of information, and (iii) subjectivity of the description. The most recent project we are working at focuses on the documentation of the so-called 'Tavolette enigmatiche', two examples of which are presented inFigure 19.

(a) (b)

Figure 18. The Winged Victory of Brescia. (a) The original statue. (b) The full scale copy of the statue.

The 'Tavolette enigmatiche' are small baked-clay objects of prevalently ovoid shape of the 2,100-1,400 B.C. periods, engraved with symbols and drilled holes whose meaning is still unknown. Their presence in Italy and in many countries in the northeast Europe represents an 'enigma' for the specialists, since the shape and the orientation of the signs is very similar among the objects, even if they have been found in different geographical sites. Hence, we have been required to accomplish an extensive measurement campaign in Europe, and to produce and collect the 3D models in a unique database of 3D models, in view of their future study by the specialists. To carry out the measurement, we used the Vivid 910 sensor (Konica Minolta Inc.). Besides the measurement performances, that well suit to the resolutions required in this application, the system is rugged, portable, and fast in the setup and the acquisition processes. So far, 30 specimens have been acquired, modeled and organized in a database.

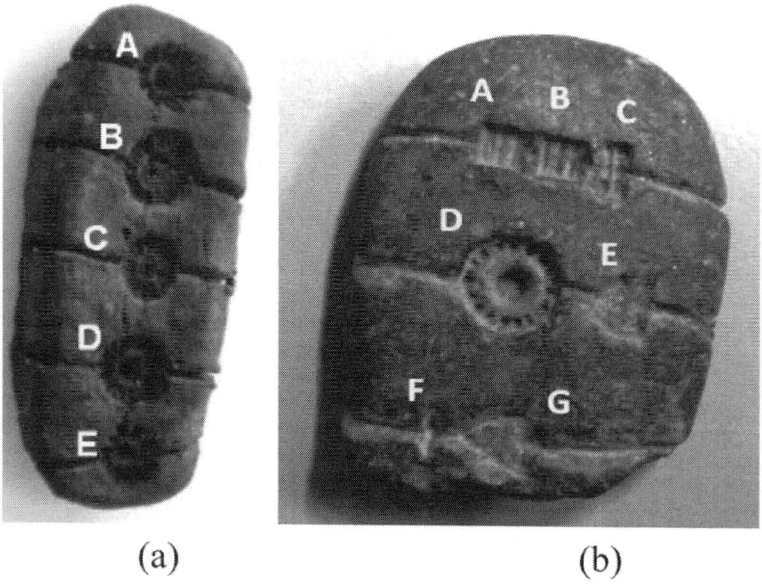

Figure 19. Examples of the 'Tavolette enigmatiche'. (a) The 'VESELE' piece, found in Slovenia. (b) The LOVERE piece, found in Northern Italy.

Figure 20 shows the 3D models of the objects in Figure 19. Their resolution is 120 μm. The snapshots in Figure 20c and in Figure 20d are the zoomed views of the signs denoted by letter 'A' in the model of Figure 20a, and by the letter 'D' in the model in Figure 20b. The availability of these representations is of outmost importance in view of carrying out the comparative analysis among the objects on a quantitative, objective basis. Figure 21 shows an example: the two signs are overlapped in the same reference frame, and can be compared. The work is still in progress: we are now developing the algorithms dedicated at automatically retrieving and correlating similar symbols among different founds [105].

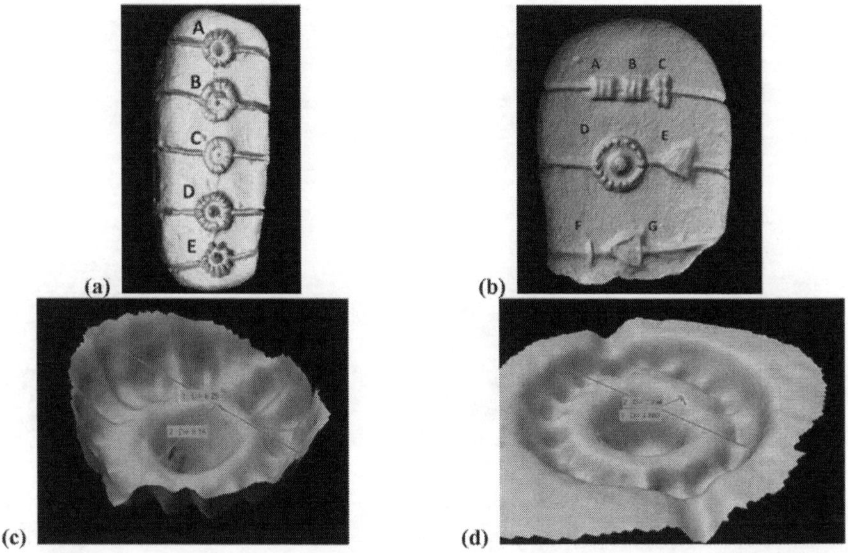

Figure 20. Modeling of the 'Tavolette enigmatiche'. (a) 3D mesh of the 'VESELE' specimen. (b) 3D mesh of the 'LOVERE' specimen. (c) Zoom of the detail labeled by letter 'A' in the 3D model of Figure 19a. (d) Zoom of the detail labeled by letter 'D' in the 3D model of Figure 19b.

3.3 Medical applications

3D imaging sensors designed specifically for the living human body are becoming increasingly available, providing high-resolution surface data with capability to build numerically and perceptually accurate digital body models [106–108]. 3D data are used in prosthetics design, plastic surgery, orthopaedy, prothetic orthodontics, surgery and dermatology [16, 109]. An intense research activity focuses onto the construction of dynamic 3D digital models for the study of pose and walking, and for real time surgical applications [110, 111]. Very recently, uses of 3D imaging sensors have been proposed in forensic medicine, even in combination with radiological data, for the complete documentation of injuries [112–116].

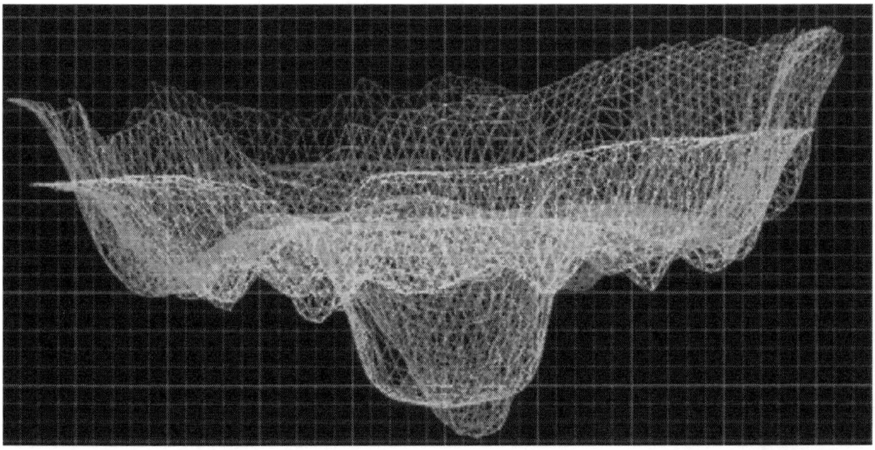

Figure 21. Superposition of the signs in Figure 20c and Figure 20d, to quantitatively evaluate their similarities.

A research activity dealing with the *post mortem* analysis of lesions on soft tissues and bones was developed at our Laboratory, in collaboration with the Institute of Legal Medicine of Milan. The aim was to study the feasibility of using 3D imaging sensors in order to assess a unique, precise and reliable method of investigation, providing accurate information about the origin of lesions and the modality of the event [117, 118]. In this project, we used the Vivid 910 system to perform the measurements during the autopsy. One example of the tests performed so far is shown inFigure 22.

This case refers to a woman killed by a blow with a metal pipe. The face of the victim, shown inFigure 22a, presented numerous lacerated and contused lesions. The optical acquisition resulted into the 3D model in Figure 22b (the elaboration was performed in the PolyWorks software environment). This model presents a high degree of fidelity with respect to the original surfaces, since the 3D raw data showed a resolution of 150 μm. Figure 22c shows the wireframe representation of the lesion framed in Figure 22b, and highlights the quality of the representation.

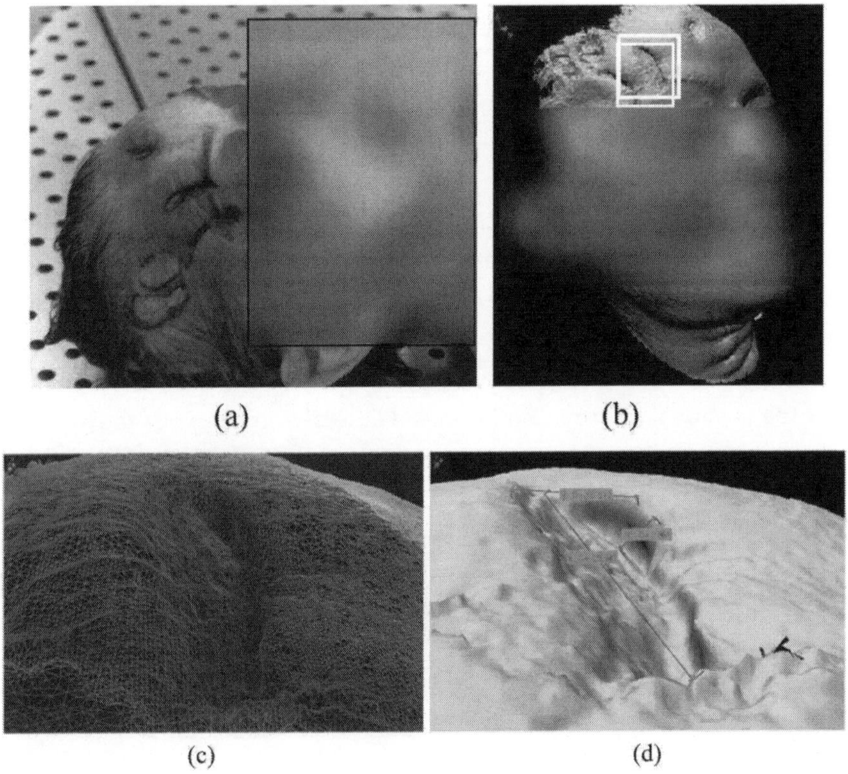

Figure 22. Example of post mortem analysis. (a) The victim. (b) 3D model of the face. (c) Zoom of the framed lesion (color wireframe). (d) Example of the measurements (the measurement unit is mm).

In Figure 22d, an example of the measurements that can be carried out is presented. The 3D model represents a quantitative, objective database of measurements, which different operators can share for subsequent analysis. The sensor proved to be adequate to this application, both in terms of the measurement quality and of the speed of acquisition.

3.4 Crime scene documentation

Crime scene investigation represents one of the fields where the use of contactless, accurate, fast acquisition systems would be of great advantage. This activity indeed requires the complete, accurate and objective description of a very complex and intrinsically three-dimensional scene, which should be documented at minimum invasiveness and time.

Traditional techniques, based on the use of contact rulers and on the two-dimensional acquisition of the scenes, do not match all these requirements: hence, in recent times, investigation techniques have moved toward more advanced methods, such as photograph stitching, virtual reality and photogrammetry [113]. These methods have partially fulfilled the lacks of the traditional approaches. However, neither they intrinsically produce three-dimensional information (as in the case of stitching) nor they provide full contactless measurement (as in the case of photogrammetry).

3D imaging sensors show promising to overcome the previously described limitations. Previous research was aimed at assessing the feasibility of using laser structured light sustems and video pairs for the documentation and 3D rendering of crime scenes [119, 120] The activity developed at our Laboratory in this field began in 2004, in collaboration with the UACV (Violent Crime Analysis Unit), a special unit of the Italian State Police.

The main goal was to assess the feasibility of using long-range three-dimensional sensors for the accurate, digital storing of crime scenes. In this research, the commercial HDS3000 laser scanner was used for data acquisition. This device is a Time-of-Flight system, originally developed for geology and civil engineering applications. It allows the 3D gauging of the surfaces up to 15 m, with resolution of 20 mm, and the acquisition up to 2 m with resolution of 2 mm.

The system was used to acquire a simulated crime scene. The victim was simulated by using the dummy shown in Figure 23a. The photograph in Figure 23b presents the whole scene: the area inFigure 23a in highlighted by the oval. The 'victim' area was acquired at the highest resolution, and the 3D model shown in Figure 24 was created.

(a) (b)

Figure 23. The simulated crime scene.

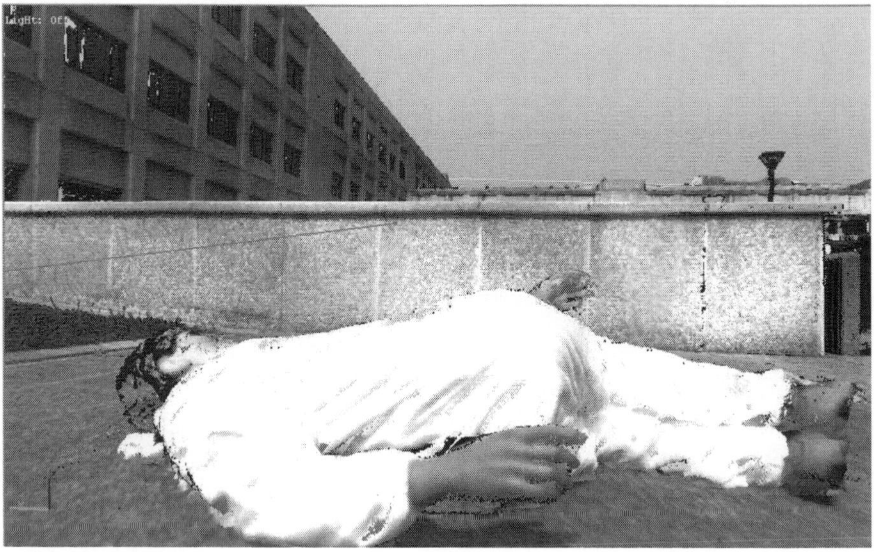

Figure 24. 3D model of the victim area.

The surroundings were captured by using the sensor at the lowest resolution, over a 15 meters long range. The resulting 3D model was then merged to the one corresponding to the victim, and the scene was modeled as in Figure 25. The combination of the models in a multi-resolution approach was strategic to maintain the level of details and, at the same time, to reduce the data amount. The availability of this whole model turned out to be crucial for subsequent analysis and visualization. The model is metrically traceable, and a large variety of measurement could be accomplished. Some examples are the measurement of areas, of sections, and of distances among the details of the scene. In the figure, one of the elaborations allowed by this representation is shown: it deals with the study of the possible directions of projectiles [121].

Figure 25. 3D model of the crime scene.

4. CONCLUSIONS

In this paper, a review of the most important techniques and sensors for the optical 3D measurement of surfaces has been presented. The aim was to highlight the wide range of measurement problems that can be solved by using 3D imaging sensors. A number of examples have been shown, with reference to the experience carried out at our Laboratory in the last ten years.

The overview of the state-of-art on 3D acquisition systems proposed in this paper yields a number of conclusive remarks. The first concerns the cost of the equipment for 3D acquisition. Most of the equipment available is still remarkably expensive, and this still represents an obstacle to a much wider distribution of 3D systems especially inside SMEs. However, we assist to a trend towards a decrease in costs, mainly due to (i) the increase in the number of manufacturers, and hence an increased competition, and (ii) the technology evolution, that offers optical/electronic components at low costs.

The second remark concerns the fact that, for most of the applications of real relevance in industry, the use of 3D acquisition is by no means a trivial task: the systems are still rather complex to use, and skilled personnel is required to operate them. Here again, future trends may consist in an overall simplification of the acquisition procedures, to make the system usage affordable for semi-skilled SME operators.

A third remark, which is crucial from the metrologist's viewpoint, is the need of norms to guarantee the traceability of 3D measurements to recognized standards. Being the 3D acquisition rather new, these norms are not yet mature.

A final remark concerns the fact that 3D systems, in many complex metrological issues, may not represent the solution of the problem when used alone; the concurrent use of combinations of contact and non-contact systems, including 3D systems, may be required for a full metrological solution.

Given the above remarks, the future of 3D systems is indeed promising, since the applications of 3D acquisition are dramatically increasing: 3D imaging is now a fundamental part of automation, robotics, of Rapid Prototyping, and 3D modeling. It is also easy to predict that, if the future of 3D rendering through holography will be as positive as it is expected, the applications will expand even more.

REFERENCES AND NOTES

1. Blais, F. A review of 20 years of range sensors development. *J. Electronic Imaging* **2004**, *13*, 231–240.

2. Jarvis, R.A. A perspective on range finding techniques for computer vision. *IEEE Trans. Pattern Anal. Mach. Intell.* **1983**, *5*, 122–139.

3. Besl, P.J. Active, optical range imaging sensors. *Mach. Vision Appl.* **1988**, *1*, 127–152.

4. Tiziani, H.J. Optical metrology of engineering surfaces-scope and trends. In *Optical Measurement Techniques and Applications*; Rastogi, P.K., Ed.; Artech House: Boston, MA, 1997; pp. 15–50.

5. Chen, F.; Brown, G.M.; Song, M. Overview of three-dimensional shape measurement using optical methods. *Opt. Eng.* **2000**, *39*, 10–22.

6. Beraldin, J.A.; Blais, F.; Cournoyer, L.; Godin, G.; Rioux, M. *Active 3D sensing*; *NRC Publication Number*, Technical Report *44159*; Ottawa, 2001.

7. Nitzan, D.; Brain, A.E.; Duda, R.O. The measurement and use of registered reflectance and range data in scene analysis. Proceedings of the IEEE, New York, February 1977; 65, pp. 206–220.

8. Li, Y.; Gu, P. Free-form surface inspection techniques state of the art review. *Comput. Aided D.* **2004**, *36*, 1395–1417.

9. Chen, L.C. Surface digitization techniques for reverse engineering. 2002. http://www.cc.ntut.edu/coop/atc/aoi/html2/tecedu.html.

10. Cheng, W.L.; Menq, C.H. Integrated laser/CMM system for the dimensional Inspection of objects made on soft material. *Int. J. Adv. Manuf. Tech.* **1995**, *10*, 36–45.

11. Saitoh, K.; Machida, T.; Kiyokawa, K.; Takemura, H. A 2D-3D integrated interface for mobile robot control using omnidirectional images and 3D geometric models. Proc. IEEE/ACM International Symposium on Mixed and Augmented Reality, Santa Barbara, USA, October 2006; pp. 173–176.

12. Abellán, A.; Vilaplana, J.M.; Martinez, J. Application of a long-range Terrestrial Laser Scanner to a detailed rockfall study at Vall de Núria (Eastern Pyrenees, Spain). *Eng. Geol.*2006, *88*, 136–148.

13. Godin, G.; Beraldin, J.A.; Taylor, J.; Cournoyer, L.; Rioux, M.; El-Hakim, S.; Baribeau, R.; Blais, F.; Boulanger, P.; Domey, J.; Picard, M. Active optical 3D imaging for heritage applications. *IEEE Comput. Graph. Appl.* **2002**, *22*, 24–35.

14. Xu, Z.Q.; Ye, S.H.; Fan, G.Z. Color 3D reverse engineering. *J. Mater. Process. Tech.* **2002**, *129*, 495–499.

15. Blais, F.; Beraldin, J.A. Recent Developments in 3D Multi-Model Laser Imaging Applied to Cultural Category. *Mach. Vis. Appl.* **2006**, *17*, 395–409.

16. D'Apuzzo, N.; Mitchell, H. Medical applications. In *Advances in Photogrammetry, Remote Sensing and Spatial Information Sciences: 2008 ISPRS Congress Book*; Li, Chen, Baltsavias, Eds.; Taylor & Francis Group: London, UK, 2008; pp. 425–438.

17. Blais, F.; Rioux, M.; Beraldin, J.A. Practical considerations for the design of a high precision 3D laser scanner system. *Proc. SPIE* **1988**, *959*, 225–246.

18. Rioux, M. Laser rangefinder based on synchronized scanners. *Appl. Opt.* **1984**, *23*, 3837–3844.

19. Rioux, M.; Blais, F. Compact three-dimensional camera for robotics applications. *J. Opt. Soc. Am.* **1986**, *3*, 1518–1521.

20. McIvor, A.M. Calibration of a laser stripe profiler. Proc. Second Int. Conf. 3-D Digital Imaging and Modeling (3DIM '99), Ottawa, Canada; 1999; pp. 92–98.

21. Blais, F.; Rioux, M.; Domey, J. Optical Range Image Acquisition for the Navigation of a Mobile Robot. Proc. 1991 IEEE Int. Conf. Robotics Automation, Sacramento, CA, April 1991; 3, pp. 2574–2580.

22. Trucco, E.; Fisher, R.B.; Fitzgibbon, A.W.; Naidu, D.K. Calibration, data consistency and model acquisition with laser stripes. *Int. J. Comput. Integrated Manuf.* **1998**, *11*, 293–310.

23. Lang, S.; Dorba, L.; Blais, F.; Lecavalier, M. Characterization and testing of the BIRIS range sensor. IMTC/93 Conference Record, Ottawa, May 18-20, 1993; pp. 459–464.

24. Sansoni, G.; Patrioli, A.; Docchio, F. OPL-3D: a novel, portable optical digitiser for fast acquisition of free-form surfaces. *Rev. Scient. Instr.* **2003**, *74*, 2593–2603.

25. Le Moigne, J.; Waxman, A.M. Projected light patterns for short range navigation of autonomous robots. Proc. Int. Conf. on Pattern Recognition, August 1984; 1, pp. 203–206.

26. Le Moigne, J.; Waxman, A.M. Multi-resolution grid patterns for building range maps. *Proc. Vision Conf.* **1985**, *8*, 22–39.

27. Morita, H.; Yajima, K.; Sakata, S. Reconstruction of surfaces of 3-D objects by M-array pattern projection method. Proc. Int. Conf. on Computer Vision, Annapolis, March 1988; pp. 468–473.

28. Maruyama, M.; Abe, S. Range sensing by projecting multiple slits with random cuts. *IEEE Trans. Pattern Anal. Mach. Intell.* **1993**, *15*, 647–651.

29. Boyer, K.L.; Kak, A.C. Color-encoded structured light for rapid active ranging. *IEEE Trans. Pattern Anal. Mach. Intell.* **1987**, *9*, 14–28.

30. Tang, S.; Hung, Y.Y. Fast profilometry for the automatic measurement of 3-D object shape.*Appl. Opt.* **1990**, *29*, 3012–3018.

31. Srinivasan, V.; Liu, H.C.; Halioua, M. Automated phase-measuring profilometry of 3-D diffuse objects. *Appl. Opt.* **1984**, *23*, 3105–3108.

32. Sansoni, G.; Redaelli, E. A 3D vision system based on one-shot projection and phase demodulation for fast profilometry. *Meas. Sci. Technol.* **2005**, *16*, 1109–1118.

33. Sansoni, G.; Trebeschi, M.; Docchio, F. Fast 3D profilometer based upon the projection of a single fringe pattern and absolute calibration. *Meas. Sci. Technol.* **2006**, *17*, 1757–1766.

34. Kwon, H.; Park, J.; Kak, A. A new approach for active stereo camera calibration. IEEE International Conference on Robotics and Automation, Rome, Italy, April 10-14, 2007; pp. 3180–3185.

35. DeSouza, G.; Kak, A. Vision for Mobile Robot Navigation: A Survey. *IEEE T. Pattern. Anal.***2002**, *24*, 237–267.

36. Nitzan, D. Three-Dimensional Vision Structure for Robot Applications. *IEEE T. Pattern. Anal.***1988**, *10*, 291–308.

37. Pavlidis, G.; Koutsoudis, A.; Arnaoutoglou, F.; Tsioukas, V.; Chamzas, C. Methods for 3D digitization of Cultural Heritage. *J. Cult. Herit.* **2007**, *8*, 93–98.

38. Baumberg, A.; Lyons, A.; Taylor, R. *3DS.O.M.-A commercial software solution to 3D scanning, Vision, Video, and Graphics (2003), The Euro-Association 2003. Eurographics Partner Event, Video, and Graphics*; 2003.

39. Remondino, F; El-Hakim, S. Image-based 3D modelling: A review. *Photogramm. Rec.* **2006**, *21*, 269–291.

40. Remondino, F.; El-Hakim, S. Critical overview of image-based 3D modeling. Workshop 3D laser Scanning and Photogrammetry for Building Information Modeling, Trondheim, Norway, September 2008; pp. 340–351.

41. Remondino, F. From point cloud to surface: the modeling and visualization problem. Workshop on Visualization and Animation of Reality based 3D Models, Tarasp-Vulpera, Switzerland, February 24-28, 2003.

42. Remondino, F.; El-Hakim, S.; Gruen, A.; Zhang, L. Turning Images into 3-D Models. *IEEE Signal Proc. Mag.* **2008**, *25*, 55–65.

43. Hartley, R.I.; Mundy, J.L. The relationship between photogrammetry and computer vision. In Integrating Photogrammetry Techniques with Scene Analysis and Machine Vision, SPIE 1944, Orlando, FL, USA, April 11-16, 1993; Barret, E.B, McKeown, M., Eds.; 19, pp. 92–105.

44. El-Hakim, S.F.; Beraldin, J.A.; Blais, F. A comparative Evaluation of the Performance of passive and Active 3-D Vision Systems. SPIE Proc. Conf. Digital Photogrammetry, St. Petersburg, Russia, June 25-30, 1995; 2646, pp. 14–25.

45. Remondino, F.; Guarnieri, A.; Vettore, A. 3D modeling of close-range objects: photogrammetry or laser scanning? Proc. SPIE Videometrics VIII, Istanbul, Turkey, July 12-23, 2004; 5665, pp. 216–225.

46. Ronnholm, P.; Honkavaara, E.; Litkey, P.; Hyyppa, H.; Hyyppa, J. Integration of laser scanning and photogrammetry. *IAPRS* **2007**, *XXXVI part 3/W52*, 355–362.

47. Van Gool, L.; Zeng, G.; Van den Borre, F.; Muller, P. *Photogrammetric Image Analysis*; Stilla, U., Mayer, H., Eds.; Institute of Photogrammetry and Cartography: Munich, Germany; September 19–21; 2007; Volume 36, pp. 209–220.

48. Cornelis, N.; Leibe, B.; Cornelis, K.; Van Gool, L. 3D Urban Scene Modeling Integrating Recognition and Reconstruction. *Int. J. Comput. Vis.* **2008**, *78*, 121–141.

49. Leibe, B.; Schindler, K.; Cornelis, N.; Van Gool, L. Coupled Object Detection and Tracking from Static Cameras and Moving Vehicles. *IEEE Trans. Patt. Anal. Mach. Intell.* **2008**, *30*, 1683–1698.

50. Nielsen, T.; Bormann, F.; Wolbeck, S.; Spiecker, H.; Burrows, M.D.; Andersen, P. Time-of-light analysis of light pulses with a temporal resolution of 100ps. *Rev. Sci. Instrum.* **1996**, *67*, 1721–1724.

51. Beraldin, J.A.; Blais, F.; Cournoyer, L.; Rodella, R.; Bernier, F.; Harrison, N. Digital 3D imaging system for rapid response on remote sites. Proc. Second Int. Conf. on 3-D Digital Imaging and Modeling (3DIM '99), Ottawa, Canada, October 1999; pp. 34–43.

52. Berner, J. *The holography Book*; Avon Books: New York, 1980.

53. Moore, D.T.; Traux, B.E. Phase-locked Moiré fringe analysis for automated contouring of diffuse surfaces. *Appl. Opt.* **1979**, *18*, 91–96.

54. Nayar, S.; Watanabe, M.; Noguchi, M. Real-time focus range sensor. Proc. IEEE Int. Conf. Computer Vision, Cambridge, Ma, June 20-23, 1995; pp. 995–1001.

55. Heekenjann, P.B.; Schmidt, H. New UV optic for submicron laser processing with a frequency quadrupled Nd:YAG laser. SPIE, Laser Materials Processing and Machining, Frankfurt, Germany, June 20-21, 1994; 2246, pp. 6–15.

56. Bouguet, J.Y.; Perona, P. 3D photography on your desk. Proc. Sixth Int. Conf. Computer Vision, Bombay, India, January 4-7, 1998; pp. 43–48.

57. Stevens, K.A. Representing and analyzing surface orientation. In *Artificial Intelligence: an MIT Perspective*; Winston, P.H., Brown, R.H., Eds.; Publisher: The MIT Press: Cambridge; March 20; 1979; Volume 2, pp. 104–125.

58. Horn, B.; Brooks, M.J. *Shape from Shading*; MIT Press: Cambridge, MA, 1989.

59. Dorsch, R.G.; Häusler, G.; Herrmann, J.M. Laser triangulation: fundamental uncertainty in distance measurement. *Appl. Opt.* **1994**, *33*, 1306–1314.

60. Besl, P.J; McKay, N.D. A method for registration of 3-D shapes. *IEEE Trans. Patt. Anal. Mach. Intell.* **1992**, *14*, 239–256.

61. Chen, Y.; Medioni, G. Object modeling by registration of multiple range images. IEEE Int. Conf. Robotics and Automation, Sacramento, California, April 1991; pp. 2724–2729.

62. Chen, Y.; Medioni, G. Object modeling by registration of multiple range images. *Image Vision Comput.* **1992**, *14*, 145–155.

63. Curless, B.; Levoy, M. A volumetric method for building complex models from range images. SIGGRAPH'96, New Orleans, LA, USA, August 4-9, 1996; pp. 303–312.

64. Hoppe, H.; DeRose, T.; Duchamp, T.; McDonald, J.; Stuelzle, W. Surface reconstruction from unorganized points. SIGGRAPH'92, Chicago, July 26-31, 1992; pp. 71–78.

65. Soucy, M.; Laurendeau, D. A general surface approach to the integration of a set of range views. *IEEE Trans. Pattern Anal. Mach. Intell.* **1992**, 348–353.

66. Turk, G.; Levoy, M. Zippered polygon meshes from range images. SIGGRAPH'94, Orlando, Florida, July 24-29, 1994; pp. 311–318.

67. Hilton, A.; Stoddart, A; Illingworth, J.; Windeatt, T. Marching triangles: Range image fusion for complex object modeling. IEEE Int. Conf. Image Processing, Lausanne, Switzerland, September 1996; pp. 381–384.

68. Bernardini, F.; Mittleman, J.; Rushmeier, H.; Silva, C.; Taubin, G. The ball-pivoting algorithm for surface reconstruction. *IEEE T. Vis. Comput. Gr.* **1999**, *5*, 349–359.

69. Bajaj, C.; Bernardini, F.; Xu, G. Automatic reconstruction of surfaces and scalar fields from 3D scans. SIGGRAPH'95, Los Angeles, CA, USA, August 6-11, 1995; pp. 109–118.

70. Sato, Y.; Wheeler, M.; Ikeuchi, K. Object shape and reflectance modeling from observation. SIGGRAPH'97, Los Angeles, August 3-8, 1997; pp. 379–387.

71. Pulli, K.; Cohen, M.; Duchamp, T.; Hoppe, H.; Shapiro, L.; Stuetzle, W. View-based rendering: Visualizing real objects from scanned range and color data. 8th Eurographics Workshop on Rendering, Saint-Etienne, France, June 1997; pp. 23–34.

72. Park, J.; DeSouza, G.N. *Machine Learning and Robot Perception*; Patnaik, S, Jain, L.C., Tzafestas, G., Bannore, V, Eds.; Springer-Verlag: New York, 2005; pp. 203–264.

73. Bernardini, F.; Rusheimer, H. The 3D Model Acquisition Pipeline. *Comp. Graph. F.* **2002**, *21*, 149–172.

74. Salvi, J.; Matabosch, C.; Fofi, D.; Forest, J. A Review of recent range image registration methods with accuracy evaluation. *Image Vision Comput.* **2007**, *25*, 578–596.

75. Wang, S.H.; Tay, C.J.; Quan, C.; Shang, H.M.; Zhou, Z.F. Laser integrated measurement of surface roughness and micro-displacement. *Meas. Sci. Technol.* **2000**, *11*, 454–458.

76. Shiou, F.J.; Cheng, W.Y. Development of an innovative multi-detector triangulation probe. IEEE Int. Conf. Mechatronics, Ontario, Canada, July 24-28, 2005; pp. 318–322.

77. Sansoni, G.; Redaelli, E. A 3D vision system based on one-shot projection and phase demodulation for fast profilometry. *Meas. Sci. Technol.* **2005**, *16*, 1109–1118.

78. Sansoni, G.; Trebeschi, M.; Docchio, F. Fast 3D profilometer based upon the projection of a single fringe pattern and absolute calibration. *Meas. Sci. Technol.* **2006**, *17*, 1757–1766.

79. Dorsch, R.G.; Häusler, G.; Herrmann, J.M. Laser triangulation: fundamental uncertainty in distance measurement. *Appl. Opt.* **1994**, *33*, 1306–1314.

80. Tomassini, P.; Rovati, L.; Sansoni, G.; Docchio, F. Novel optical sensor for the measurement of surface texture. *Rev. Scient. Instr.* **2001**, *72*, 2207–2213.

81. Sansoni, G.; Patrioli, A. Non contact 3D sensing of free-form complex surfaces. SPIE-Videometrics and Optical methods for 3D shape Measurement, San Jose, CA, January 20-26, 2001; 4309, pp. 232–239.

82. Krattenthaler, W.; Mayer, K.J.; Duwe, H.P. 3D-Surface measurement with coded light approach. *Proc. Öesterr. Arbeitsgem. MustererKennung* **1993**, *12*, 103–114.

83. Bidanda, B.; Hosni, Y.A. Reverse engineering and its relevance to industrial engineering: a critical review. *Computers Ind. Eng.* **1994**, *26*, 343–348.

84. L. Chen, L.; Lin, C.; Grier, C. A vision-aided reverse engineering approach to reconstructing free-form surfaces. *Robot. Comp. Integr. Manuf.* **1997**, *13*, 323–336.

85. Motovalli, S.; Suharitdamron, V.; Alrashdan, A. Design model generation for reverse engineering using multi-sensors. *IIE Trans.* **1998**, *30*, 357–366. []

86. Cauchick, M.; King, T.; Davis, J. CMM verification: a survey. *Measurement* **1996**, *17*, 1–16.

87. Carbone, V.; Carocci, M.; Savio, E.; Sansoni, G.; De Chiffre, L. Combination of a vision system and a Coordinate Measuring Machine for the Reverse Engineering of Freeform Surfaces. *Int. J. Adv. Manuf. Tech.* **2001**, *17*, 263–271.

88. Li, L.; Schemenauer, N.; Peng, X.; Zeng, Y.; Gu, P. A reverse engineering system for rapid manufacturing of complex objects. *Robot. Comp. Integr. Manuf.* **2002**, *18*, 53–67.

89. Chow, J.; Xu, T.; Lee, S.M.; Kengskool, K. Development of an Integrated Laser-Based Reverse Engineering and Machining System. *Int. J. Adv. Manuf. Tech.* **2000**, *19*, 186–191.

90. Clark, J. Implementing Non-Contact Digitization Techniques within the Mechanical Design Process. *Sensor Rev.* **2000**, *20*, 195–201.

91. Lee, K.H.; Park, H. Automated Inspection of Free-Form Shape Parts by Laser Scanning.*Robot. Comp. Integr. Manuf.* **2000**, *16*, 201–210.

92. Sansoni, G.; Docchio, F. Three-dimensional optical measurements and reverse engineering for automotive applications. *Robot. Comp. Integr. Manuf.* **2004**, *20*, 359–367.

93. Hemsley, J. *Digital Application for Cultural and Heritage Institutions*; Ashgate Publishing Group: Aldershot, UK, 2005.

94. Guidi, G.; Beraldin, J.-A.; Atzeni, C. High accuracy 3D modeling of Cultural Heritage: the digitizing of Donatello's "Maddalena". *IEEE Trans. Image Proc.* **2004**, *13*, 370–380.

95. Bernardini, F.; Martin, I.; Mittleman, J.; Rusheimer, H.; Taubin, G. Building a digital model of Michelangelo's Florentine Pietà. *IEEE Comput. Graph.* **2002**, *22*, 59–67.

96. Levoy, M; *et al.* The digital Michelangelo project: 3D scanning of large statues. Proc. SIG-GRAPH 00, Computer Graph. Proc., Annu. Conf. Ser., New Orleans, Louisiana, USA; 2000; pp. 131–144.

97. Lambers, K.; Eisenbeiss, H.; Sauerbier, M.; Kupferschmidt, D.; Gaisecker, T.; Sotoodeh, S.; Hanusch, T. Combining photogrammetry and laser scanning for the recording and modeling of the Late Intermediate Period site of Pinchango Alto, Palpa, Peru. *J. Archaeol. Sci.***2007**, *34*, 1702–1712.

98. Balzani, M.; Callieri, M.; Fabbri, M.; Fasano, A.; Montani, C.; Pingi, P.; Santopuoli, N.; Scopigno, R.; Uccelli, F.; Varone, A. Digital representation and multimodal presentation of archeological graffiti ad Pompei. 5th Int. Symp. Virtual Reality Archeology and Cultural Heritage, Eurograhics Symp. Proc., Brussels: Belgium, December 6-10, 2004; Chrysanthou, Y., Cain, K., Silberman, N., Niccolucci, F., Eds.; pp. 93–103.

99. Boulanger, P.; Taylor, J.; El-Hakim, S.F.; Rioux, M. How to virtualize reality: an application to re-creation of world heritage site. Proc. Conf. Virtual Systems and Multimedia, Gifu, Japan, November 18-20, 1998; pp. 18–20.

100. Kampel, M.; Sablatnig, R. Rule based system for archaeological pottery classification. *Patt. Recogn. Lett.* **2007**, *28*, 740–747.

101. Anderson, S.; Levoy, M. Unwrapping and Visualizing Cuneiform Tablets. *IEEE Comput. Graph.* **2002**, *22*, 82–88.

102. Sansoni, G.; Docchio, F. 3-D optical Measurements in the Field of Cultural heritage: The Case of the Vittoria Alata of Brescia. *IEEE Trans. Instr. Meas.* **2005**, *54*, 359–368.

103. Sansoni, G.; Docchio, F.; Trebeschi, M.; Filippi, S.; Motyl, B. Virtual and rapid prototyping by means of 3D optical acquisition and CAD modeling: application to cultural heritage and to the automotive domain. In *Virtual Modelling and Rapid Manufacturing - Advanced Research in Virtual and Rapid Prototyping*; Bártolo, P.J., *et al*, Eds.; Taylor & Francis Group: London, UK, 2005; pp. 251–257.

104. Sansoni, G.; Cavagnini, G.; Modonesi, N.; Piccoli, A.; Marchesini, S. Generazione ed elaborazione di misure mediante sensori non a contatto per l'analisi e l'interpretazione di reperti archeologici. Proc. XXV Congresso Nazionale Associazione GMEE; 2008; pp. 289–290.

105. Jones, P.R.M.; Rioux, M. Three-dimensional surface anthropometry: applications to human body. *Opt. Laser. Eng.* **1997**, *28*, 89–117.

106. Simmons, K.P. Body measurement techniques: a comparison of three-dimensional body scanning and physical anthropometric methods. Ph.D. Thesis, North Carolina State University, Raleigh, NC, 2001.

107. Tukuisis, P.; Meunier, P.; Jubenville, C.E. Human body surface area: measurement and prediction using three dimensional body scans. *Eur. J. Appl. Physiol. Occup. Physiol.* **2001**, *85*, 264–271.

108. Cheah, C.M.; Chua, C.K.; Tan, K.H.; Teo, C.K. Integration of laser surface digitizing with CAD/CAM techniques for developing facial prostheses. Part 1: Design and fabrication of prosthesis replicas. *Int. J. Prosthodont.* **2003**, *16*, 435–441.

109. Remondino, F. 3-D reconstruction of static human body shape from image sequence.*Comput. Vis. Image Understand.* **2004**, *93*, 65–85.

110. D'Apuzzo, N. Surface Measurement and Tracking of Human Body Parts from Multi Station Video Sequences. Ph.D. Thesis, Institute of Geodesy and Photogrammetry, ETH, Zurich, Switzerland, 2003.

111. Thali, M.J.; Braun, M.; Dirnhofer, R. Optical 3D surface digitizing in forensic medicine: 3D documentation of skin and bone injuries. *Forensic Sci. Int.* **2003**, *137*, 203–208.

112. Bruschweiler, W.; Braun, M.; Dirnhofer, R. Analysis of patterned injuries and injury-causing instruments with forensic 3D/CAD supported photogrammetry (FPHG): an instruction manual for the documentation process. *Forensic Sci. Int.* **2003**, *132*, 130–138.

113. Banno, A.; Masuda, T.; Ikeuchi, K. Three dimensional visualization and comparison of impressions on fired bullets. *Forensic Sci. Int.* **2004**, *140*, 233–240.

114. Goos, MI.; Alberink, I.B.; Ruifrok, A.C.C. 2D/3D image (facial) comparison using camera matching. *Nether. Forens. Inst.* **2006**, *163*, 10–17.

115. Park, HK.; Chung, J.W.; Kho, H.S. Use of hand-held laser scanning in the assessment of craniometry. *Forens. Sci. Int.* **2006**, *160*, 200–206.

116. Cavagnini, G.; Scalvenzi, M.; Trebeschi, M.; Sansoni, G. Reverse engineering from 3D optical acquisition: application to Crime Scene Investigation. In *Virtual and Rapid Manufacturing - Advanced Research in Virtual and Rapid Prototyping*; Bártolo, P.J., Ed.; Taylor & Francis Group: London, UK, 2007; pp. 195–201.

117. Sansoni, G.; Docchio, F.; Trebeschi, M.; Scalvenzi, M.; Cavagnini, G. Application of three-dimensional optical acquisition to the documentation and the analysis of crime scenes and legal medicine inspection. Proc. 2nd IEEE Int. Workshop on Advances in Sensors and Interfaces, Bari, Italy, June 26-27, 2007; pp. 1–10.

118. Little, C.; Small, D.; Carlson, J. 3D Imaging and Modeling for Crime Scene Documentation. Proc. ICIP99, Kobe, Japan; 1999; pp. 27–34.

119. Altschuler, B.; Monson, K. Initial progress in the recording of crime scene simulations using 3D laser structured light imagery techniques for law enforcement and forensic applications. Proc. SPIE, San Diego, CA, USA, July 1998; 3240, pp. 230–241.

120. Cavagnini, G.L.; Sansoni, G.; Trebeschi, M. Using 3D range cameras for crime scene documentation and legal medicine. Proc. SPIE, 3D Imaging Metrology; 2009; 3272. in press.

Chapter 9

Virtual Prototyping and Performance Analysis of Two Memory Architectures

Huda S Muhammad and Assim Sagahyroon

[1] Schlumberger Corp., Dubai Internet City, Bldg. 14, Dubai, UAE

[2] Department of Computer Science and Engineering, American University of Sharjah, Sharjah, UAE

ABSTRACT

The gap between CPU and memory speed has always been a critical concern that motivated researchers to study and analyze the performance of memory hierarchical architectures. In the early stages of the design cycle, performance evaluation methodologies can be used to leverage exploration at the architectural level and assist in making early design tradeoffs. In this paper, we use simulation platforms developed using the VisualSim tool to compare the performance of two memory architectures, namely, the Direct Connect architecture of the Opteron, and the Shared Bus of the Xeon multicore processors. Key variations exist between the two memory architectures and both design approaches provide rich platforms that call for the early use of virtual system prototyping and simulation techniques to assess performance at an early stage in the design cycle.

1. INTRODUCTION

Due to the rapid advances in circuit integration technology, and to optimize performance while maintaining acceptable levels of energy efficiency and reliability, multicore technology or Chip-Multiprocessor is becoming the technology of choice for microprocessor designers. Multicore processors provide increased total computational capability on a single chip without requiring a complex microarchitecure. As a result, simple multicore processors have better performance per watt and area characteristics than complex single core processors [1].

A multicore architecture has a single processor package that contains two or more processors. All cores can execute instructions independently and simultaneously. The operating system will treat each of the execution cores as a discrete processor. The design and integration of such processors with transistor counts in the millions poses a challenge to designers given the complexity of the task and the time to market constraints. Hence, early virtual system prototyping and performance analysis provides designers with critical information that can be used to evaluate various architectural approaches, functionality, and processing requirements.

In these emerging multicore architecture, the ability to analyze (at an early stage) the performance of the memory subsystem is of extreme importance to designers. The latency resulting by the access of different levels of memory reduces the processing speeds causing more processor stalls while the data/instruction is being fetched from the main memory. Ways in which multiple cores send and receive data to the main memory greatly affect the access time and thus the processing speed. In multicore processors, two approaches to memory subsystem design have emerged in recent years, namely, the AMD DirectConnect architecture and the Intel Shared Bus architecture [2–5]. In the DirectConnect architecture, a processor is directly connected to a pool of memory using an integrated memory controller. A processor can access the other processors' memory pool via a dedicated processor-to-processor interconnect. On the other hand, in Intel's dual-core designs, a single shared pool of memory is at the heart of the memory subsystem. All processors access the pool via an external front-side bus and a memory controller hub.

In this work, virtual system prototyping is used to study the performance of these alternatives. A virtual systems prototype is a software-simulation-based, timing-accurate, electronic systems level (ESL) model, used first at the architectural level and then as an executable golden reference model throughout the design cycle. Virtual systems prototyping enables developers to accurately and efficiently make the painful tradeoffs between that quarrelling family of design siblings functionality, flexibility, performance, power consumption, quality, cost, and so forth.

Virtual prototyping can be used early in the development process to better understand hardware and software partitioning decisions and determine throughput considerations associated with implementations. Early use of functional models to determine microprocessor hardware configurations and architectures, and the architecture of ASIC in development, can aid in capturing requirements, improving functional performance and expectations [6].

In this work, we explore the performance of the two memory architectures introduced earlier using virtual prototyping models built from parameterized library components which are part of the VisualSim Environment [7]. Essentially, VisualSim is a modeling and simulation CAD tool used to study, analyze, and validate specification and verify implementation at early stages of the design cycle.

This paper is organized as follows: in Section 2 we provide an overview of the two processors and the corresponding memory architectures. Section 3 introduces the VisualSim environment as well as the creation of the platform models for the processors. Simulation Results and the analysis of these results form Section 4 of this paper. Conclusions are summarized in Section 5.

2. OVERVIEW OF PROCESSORS MEMORY ARCHITECTURE

2.1. The AMD Opteron Direct Connect Architecture

The AMD's direct Connect Architecture used in the design of the dual core AMD Opteron consists of three elements:

- an integrated memory controller within each processor, which connects the processor cores to dedicated memory,
- a high-bandwidth Hyper Transport Technology link which goes out the computer's I/O devices, such as PCI controllers,
- coherent Hyper Transport Technology links which allow one processor to access another processor's memory controller and Hyper Transport Technology links.

The Opteron uses an innovative routing switch and a direct connect architecture that allows "glueless" multiprocessing between the two processor cores. Figure 1 shows an Opteron processor along with the system request queue (SRQ) and host bridge, Crossbar, memory controller, DRAM controller, and HyperTransport ports [3, 8].

The Crossbar switch and the SRQ are connected to the cores directly and run at the processor core frequency. After an L1 cache miss, the processor core sends a request to the main memory and the L2 cache in parallel. The main memory request is discarded in case of an L2 cache hit. An L2 cache miss results in the request being sent to the main memory via the SRQ and the Crossbar switch. The SRQ maps the request to the nodes that connect the processor to the destination. The Crossbar switch routes the request/data to the destination node or the HyperTransport port in case of an off chip access.

Each Opteron core has a local on-chip L1 and L2 cache and is then connected to the memory controller via the SRQ and the Crossbar switch. Apart from these external components, the core consists of 3 integer and 3 floating point units along with a load/store unit that executes any load or store microinstructions sent to the core [9]. Direct Connect Architecture can improve overall system performance and efficiency by eliminating traditional bottlenecks inherent in legacy architectures. Legacy front-side buses restrict and interrupt the flow of data. Slower data flow means slower system performance. Interrupted data flow means reduced system scalability. With Direct Connect Architecture, there are no front-side buses. Instead, the processors, memory controller, and I/O are directly connected to the CPU and communicate at CPU speed [10].

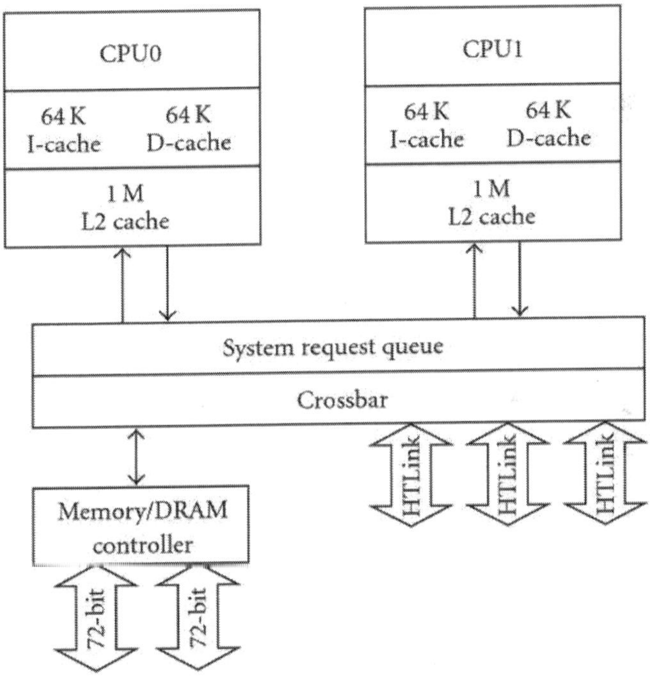

Figure 1. AMD dual core Opteron.

2.2. Intel Xeon Memory Architecture

The Dual-Core Intel Xeon Processor is a 64-bit processor that uses two physical Intel NetBurst microarchitecture cores in one chip [4]. The Intel Xeon dual core processor uses a different memory access technique, by including a Front-Side-Bus (FSB) to the SDRAM and a shared L3 cache instead of having only on-chip caches like the AMD Opteron. The L3 cache and the two cores of the processor are connected to the FSB via the Caching Bus Controller. This controller controls all the accesses to the L3 cache and the SDRAM. Figure 2 below provides an overview of the Intel Dual core Xeon and illustrates the main connections in the processor [5].

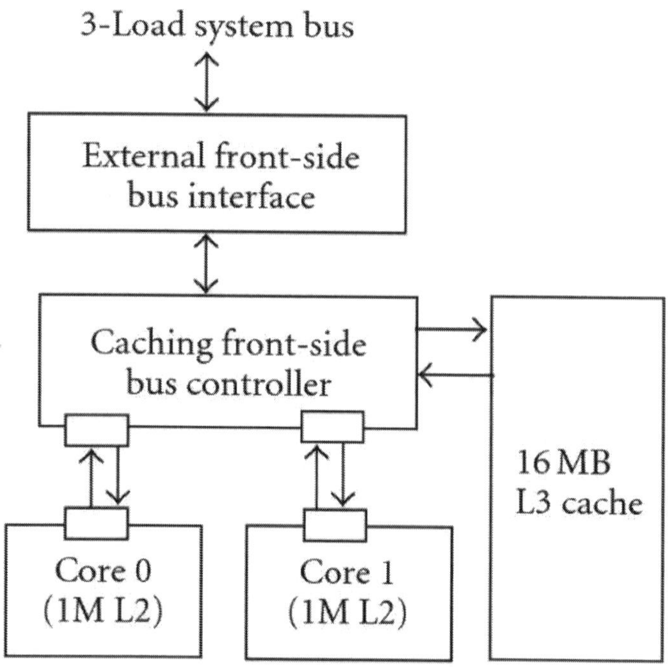

Figure 2. Block diagram of the dual-core Intel Xeon.

Since the L3 cache is shared, each core is able to access almost all of the cache and thus has access to a larger amount of cache memory. The shared L3 cache provides a better efficiency over a split cache since each core can now use more than half of the total cache. It also avoids the coherency traffic between cache in a split approach [11].

3. VISUALSIM SIMULATION ENVIRONMENT

At the heart of the simulation environment is the VisualSim Architect tool. It is a graphical modeling tool that allows the design and analysis of "digital, embedded, software, imaging, protocols, analog, control-systems, and DSP designs". It has features that allow quick debugging with a GUI and a software library that includes various tools to track the inputs/stimuli and enable a graphical and textual view of the results. It is based on a library of parameterized components including processors, memory controllers, DMA, buses, switches, and I/O's. The blocks included in the library reduce the time spent on designing the minute details of a system and instead provide a user friendly interface where these details can be altered by just changing their values and not the connections. Using this library of building blocks, a designer can for example, construct a specification level model of a system containing multiple processors, memories, sensors, and buses [12].

In VisualSim, a platform model consists of behavior, or pure functionality, mapped to architectural elements of the platform model. A block diagram of a platform model is shown in Figure 3.

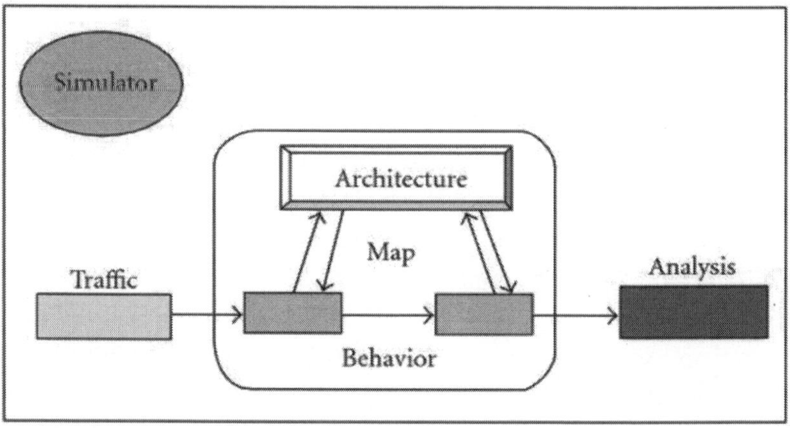

Figure 3. Block diagram of a platform model.

Once a model is constructed, various scenarios can be explored using simulation. Parameters such as inputs, data rates, memory hierarchies, and speed can be varied and by analyzing simulation results engineers can study the various trade-offs until they reach an optimal solution or an optimized design.

The key advantage of the platform model is that the behavior algorithms may be upgraded without affecting the architecture they execute on. In addition, the architecture could be changed to a completely different processor to see the effect on the user's algorithm, simply by changing the mapping of behavior to architecture. The mapping is just a field name (string) in a data structure transiting the model.

Models of computation in VisualSim support block-oriented design. Components called blocks execute and communicate with other blocks in a model. Each block has a well-defined interface. This interface abstracts the internal state and behavior of a block and restricts how a block interacts with its environment. Central to this block-oriented design are the communication channels that pass data from one port to another according to some messaging scheme. The use of channels to mediate communication implies that blocks interact only with the channels they are connected to and not directly with other blocks.

In VisualSim, the simulation flow can be explained as follows: the simulator translates the graphical depiction of the system into a form suitable for simulation execution and executes simulation of the system model, using user specified model parameters for simulation iteration. During simulation, source modules (such as traffic generators) generate data structures. The data structures flow along to various other processing blocks, which may alter the contents of Data Structures and/or modify their path through the block diagram. In VisualSim simulation continues until there are no more data structures in the system or the simulation clock reaches a specified stop time [7]. During a simulation run, VisualSim collects performance data at any point in the model using a variety of prebuilt probes to compute a variety of statistics on performance measures.

This project uses the VisualSim (VS) Architect tool, to carry out all the simulations and run the benchmarks on the modeled architectures. The work presented here utilizes the hardware architecture library of VS that includes the processor cores, which can be configured as per our requirements, as well as bus ports, controllers, and memory blocks.

3.1. Models' Construction (Systems' Setup)

The platform models for the two processors are constructed within the VS environment using the parameters specified in Table 1.

Table 1. Simulation models parameters.

	AMD Opteron	Intel Xeon
Core Speed	2 GHz	2 GHz
$Bus_{(Core\text{-}to\text{-}Cache)}$ Speed	N/A	2 GHz
$Bus_{(Core\text{-}to\text{-}SRQ)}$ Speed	2 GHz	N/A
Crossbar Speed	2 GHz	N/A
FSB Speed	N/A	1066 MHz (Width = 4 B)
$Bus_{(SRQ\text{-}to\text{-}RAM)}$ Speed	2 GHz (Width = 4 B)	N/A
L1 Cache Speed	1 GHz	1 GHz
L2 Cache Speed	1 GHz	1 GHz
RAM Speed	1638.4 MHz	1638.4 MHz
I1 Cache Size	64 kB	64 kB
D1 Cache Size	64 kB	64 kB
L2 Cache Size	4 MB (2 MB per core)	4 MB (shared cache)

3.1.1. The Opteron Model

The basic architecture of the simulated AMD dual core Opteron contains two cores with three integer execution units, three floating point units and two loads/stores, and branch units to the data cache [2]. Moreover, the cores contain 2 cache levels with 64 kB of L1 data cache, 64 kB of L1 instruction cache, and 1 MB of L2 cache.

The constructed platform model for the AMD Opteron is shown in Figure 4.

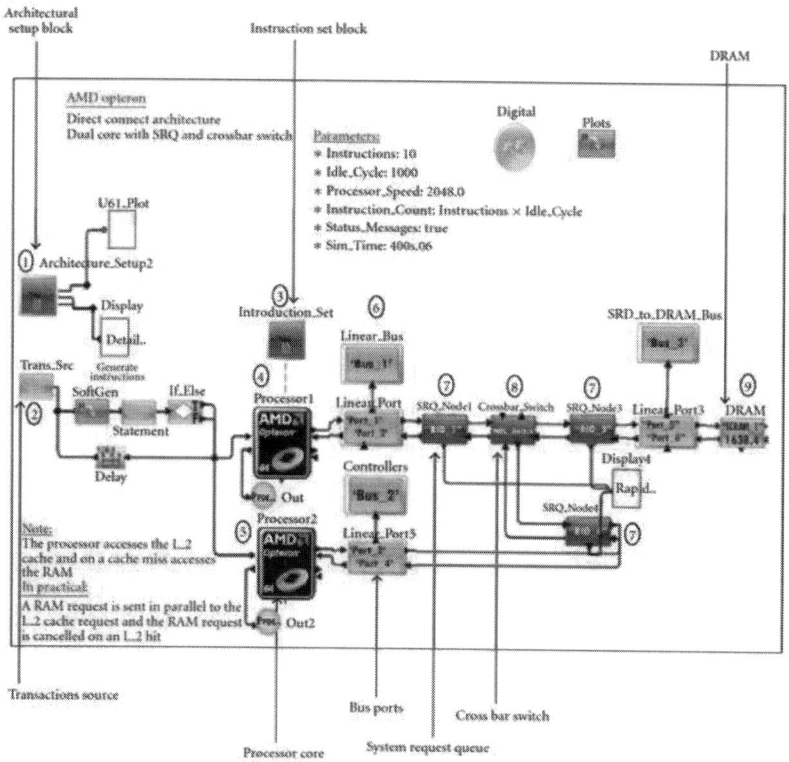

Figure 4. Platform model for the DirectConnect Architecture.

In the above model, the two large blocks numbered 4 and 5, respectively, are the Processor cores connected via bus ports (blocks 6) to the System

Request Queue (block 7), and then to the Crossbar switch (block 8). The Crossbar switch connects the cores to the RAM (block 9) and is programmed to route the incoming data structure to the specified destination and then send the reply back to the requesting core.

On the left block 2 components contain the input task to the two cores. These blocks define software tasks (benchmarks represented as a certain mix of floating point, integer and load/store instructions) that are input to both the processors (Opteron and Xeon) in order to test their memory hierarchy performance. The following subsections give a detailed description of each of the blocks, their functionalities, and any simplifying assumptions made to model the memory architecture.

Architecture Setup

The architecture setup block configures the complete set of blocks linked to a single Architecture_Name parameter found in most blocks. The architecture setup block of the model (block 1) contains the details of the connections between the fields mappings of the Data Structure attributes as well as the routing table that contains any of the virtual connections not wired in the model. The architecture setup also keeps track of all the units that are a part of the model and its name has to be entered into each block that is a part of the model.

Core and Cache

Each core of Opteron implemented in the project using VS is configured to a frequency of 2 GHz and has 128 kB of L1 cache (64 kB data and 64 kB instruction cache), 2 MB of L2 cache, and the floating point, integer, and load/store execution units. This 2 MB of L2 cache per core is compatible with the 4 MB of shared cache used in the Intel Xeon memory architecture. The instruction queue length is set to 6 and instructions are included in the instruction set of both the cores, so as to make the memory access comparison void of all other differences in the architectures. These instructions are defined in the instruction block that is further described in a later section.

Certain simplifications have been made to the core of the Opteron in order to focus the analysis entirely on the memory architecture of the processor. These assumptions include the change of the variable length instructions to fixed length micro-ops [9]. Another assumption made is that any L1 cache miss does not result in a simultaneous request being sent to the L2 cache and the RAM. Instead the requests are sent sequentially, where an L1 cache miss results in an L2 cache access and finally an L2 cache miss results in a DRAM access.

Pipeline

The pipeline of the modeled Opteron consists of four stages, mainly the prefetch, decode, execute, and the store. The prefetch of each instruction begins from the L1 cache and ends in a DRAM access in case of L1 and L2 cache misses. The second stage in the pipeline is the decode stage that is implemented by introducing a delay into the entire process. The decode stage does not actually decode the instruction; instead the time required to decode the instruction is added to the time comprising of the delays from the prefetch stage to the end of the execution stage. The third stage, the execution stage, takes place in the five execution units that are present in the cores, and finally after the execution, the write-back stage writes back the specified data to the memory, mainly the L1 cache. The *Pipeline_Stages* (text box in Figure 5) shows the four pipeline stages that have been defined for both cores. It also contains the configuration of one of the cores of the Opteron along with the number of execution units and the instruction queue length. The lower text window depicts the details and actions of the pipeline stages.

Crossbar Switch and the SRQ Blocks

The Crossbar switch configured in the simulation model, is used to route the data packets to the destination specified by the *"A_Destination"* field of the data structure entering the switch. The main memory is connected to the Crossbar switch via the System Request Queue (SRQ) block both of which are implemented using the virtual machine scripting language available in the VisualSim environment. The SRQ accepts only 8 requests in the queue and does not entertain any further requests until there is an empty space in the queue. Each core and the SDRAM are connected to individual SRQ blocks that are in turn connected to the crossbar switch. Figure 6 shows the crossbar switch as the *NBC_Switch* and the SRQ blocks as the *RIO_IO_Nodes* which are linked to the bus ports connected to the SDRAM and the processor cores. Figure 4 provides a general overview of the crossbar switch and the SRQ nodes in context of the entire model.

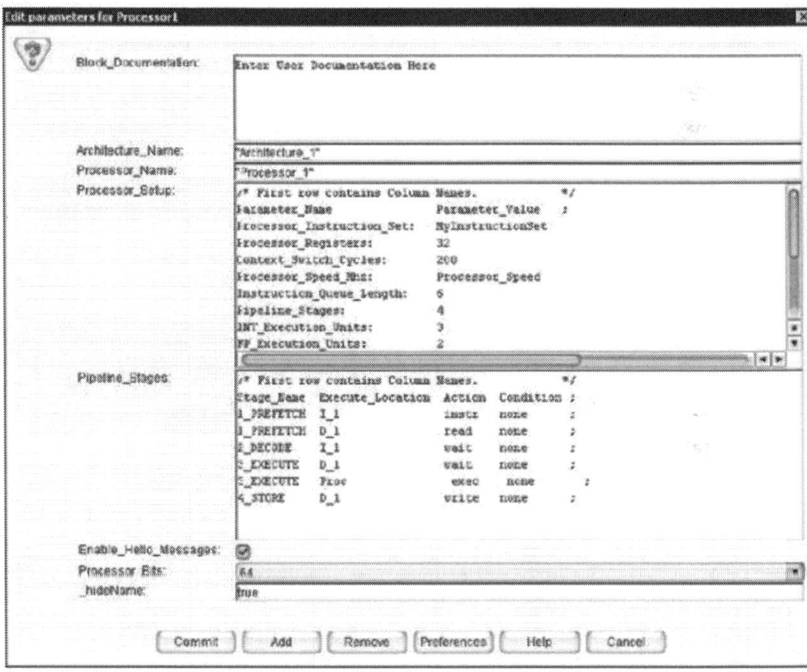

Figure 5. Opteron processor core and pipeline configurations.

Main Memory and the Memory Controller

In the simulation model, the RAM has a capacity of 1 GB and has an in-built memory controller configured to run at a speed of 1638.4 MHz. At this speed and a block width of 4 bytes, the transfer of data from the memory to the cache takes place at a speed of 6.4 GB/s. This rate is commonly used in most of the AMD Opteron processors but can be different depending on the model of the processor. The same rate is also used in the model of the Xeon processor. Each instruction that the RAM executes is translated into delay specified internally by the memory configurations. These configurations are seen in Figure 7 in the*Access_Time* field as the number of clock cycles spent on the corresponding task.

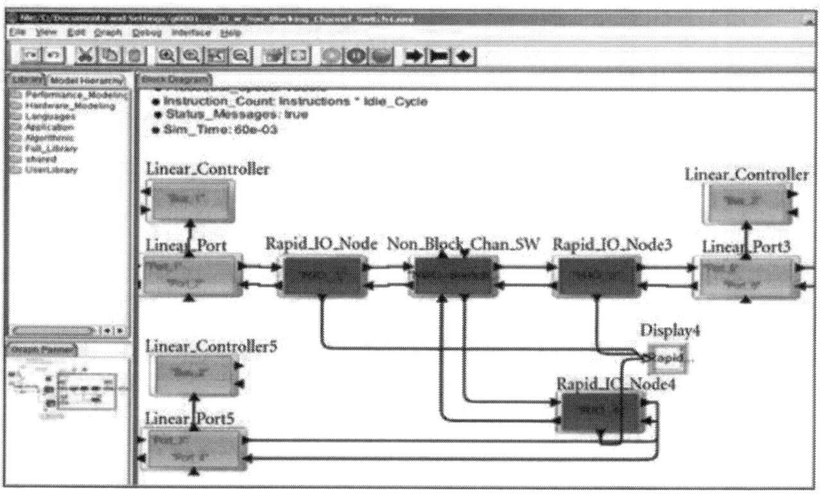

Figure 6. Crossbar switch and SRQ blocks in VisualSim.

The SDRAM connects to the cores via the SRQ blocks and the Crossbar switch which routes the SDRAM requests from both the cores to the main memory block and then sends a response back to the requesting core, in terms of a text reply. This process requires a certain delay that depends on the type of instruction sent to the SDRAM. In case the SRQ block queue is empty, a single DRAM response time depends on whether the instruction is a memory read, write, read/write, or erase instruction. Each of these instructions takes a fixed number of clock cycles to complete and is determined in the SDRAM configuration as determined by the *Access_Time* field seen in Figure 7. To separate the SDRAM access time from the cache access time, a simplification is made such that the SDRAM access request from the core is not sent in parallel to an L2 cache request as in the actual Opteron; instead, the SDRAM request is issued only after an L2 miss has been encountered.

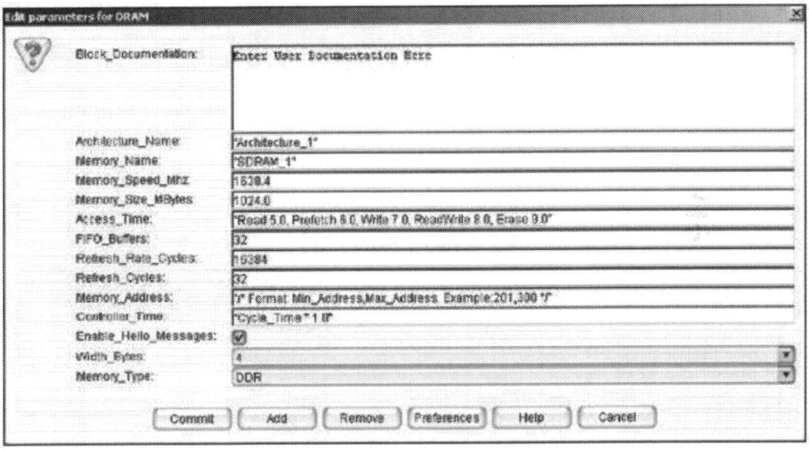

Figure 7. SDRAM and memory controller configurations.

3.1.2. Xeon Model

Basic Architecture

The basic architecture of the Intel Dual Core Xeon is illustrated in Figure 2. The corresponding platform model is depicted in Figure 8. The two cores of the processor are connected to the shared L2 cache and then via the Front-Side-Bus (FSB) interface to the SDRAM. The modeled Intel Xeon processor consists of two cores with three integer execution units, three floating point units, and two loads/stores and branch units to the data cache. The same specifications used to model the Opteron cores in VisualSim are used here as well. Besides, each core is configured with 64 kB of L1 data cache, 64 kB of L1 instruction cache, whereas the L2 cache is a unified cache and is 4 MB in size. The FSB interface, as seen in Figure 8, was constructed using the Virtual Machine block in VS [7] and is connected to the internal bus which links the two cores to the RAM via the FSB. The software generation block (block 2 on the left side of the model) contains the same tasks as the Opteron.

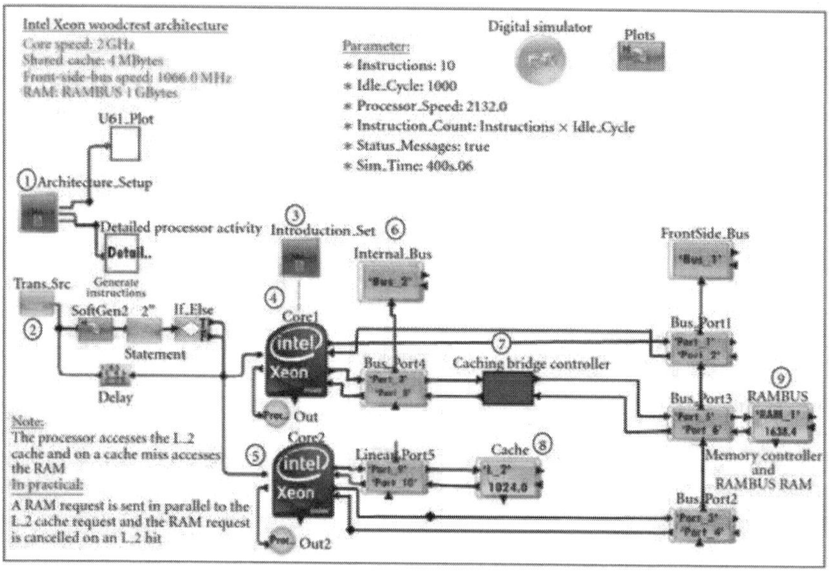

Figure 8. Shared Bus Architecture.

Architecture Setup

The architecture setup block of the model of the Xeon (Figure 8—block 1) is the same as the one implemented in the Opteron and the field mappings of the Data Structure attributes are copied from the Opteron model to ensure that no factors other than the memory architecture affects the results.

Core and Cache

The core implementation of the Xeon is configured using VS to operate at a frequency of 2 GHz and has 128 kB of L1 cache (64 kB data and 64 kB instruction cache), 4 MB of unified and shared L2 cache [5], floating point, integer, and load/store execution units. Here as well, the instruction queue length is set to 6 and instructions are included in the instruction set of both the cores, so as to make the memory access comparison void of all other differences in the architectures. These instructions are defined in the instruction block that is described in a later section.

Certain simplifications have been made to the core of the Xeon in order to focus the analysis entirely to the memory architecture of the processor. The assumption made in accessing the memory is that any L1 cache miss does not result in a simultaneous request being sent to the L2 cache and the RAM. Instead the requests are sent sequentially, where an L1 cache miss results in an L2 cache access and finally an L2 cache miss results in a RAM access.

To simplify the model and the memory access technique, the process of snooping is not implemented in this simulation, and similar to the Opteron, no parallel requests are sent to two memories.

Pipeline

The pipeline of the modeled Xeon consists of four stages (similar to the Opteron model), the prefetch, decode, execute, and the store. The prefetch of each instruction begins from the L1 cache and ends in a RAM access in case of L1 and L2 cache misses. The second stage in the pipeline is the decode stage that is mainly translated into a wait stage. The third stage, the execution stage, takes place in the five execution units that are present in the cores, and finally after the execution, the write-back stage writes back the specified data to the memory, mainly the L1 cache.

Caching Bridge Controller (CBC)

The CBC, block 7 of the model is simply a bridge that connects the L2 shared cache to the FSB [13]. This FSB then continues the link to the RAM (block 9) from which accesses are made and the data/instruction read is sent to the core that requested the data. The CBC model is developed using the VisualSim scripting language and simulates the exact functionality of a typical controller.

Main Memory and the Memory Controller

The dual-core Xeon contains a main memory of type RAMBUS with a speed similar to the memory connected to the Opteron. The size of the RAM is 1 GB and contains a built-in memory controller. This memory controller is configured to run at a speed of 1638.4 MHz. At this speed and a block width of 4 bytes, the transfer of data from the memory to the cache takes place at a speed of 6.4 GB/s. Each instruction that the RAMBUS will carry out implies a certain delay which has been specified internally in the memory configurations. These configurations are seen in Figure 9 in the *Access_Time* field as the number of clock cycles spent executing the corresponding task. The RAM connects to the cores via the CBC and data or instruction requests to the RAM from either core are sent to the main memory block via the FSB. The RAM then sends a response back to the requesting core which can be seen as a text reply on the displays that show the flow of requests and replies. DRAM Access Time is the time taken since a request is made and when the data is made available from the DRAM. It is defined in nanoseconds by the user for each operation like Read, Write, or a Read-Write as an access time parameter in the*Access_Time* field of Figure 9.

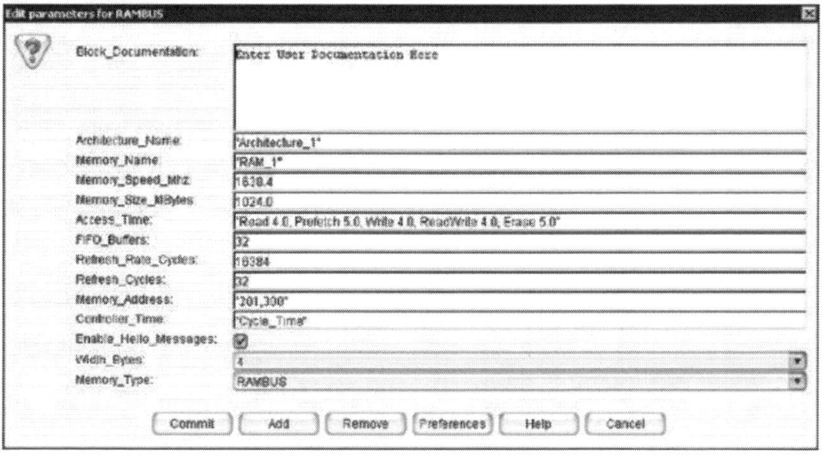

Figure 9. Main memory and controller configurations of the Intel Xeon.

FOLLOWING A SERIES OF 4. RESULTS AND ANALYSIS

Experimental tests and numerical measurements using benchmarking software, published literature [14–16] discusses the performance of the AMD Opteron when compared to the Xeon processor using physical test beds comprised of the two processors. These three references provide the reader with a very informative and detailed comparison of the two processors when subjected to various testing scenarios using representative loads.

In this work, we are trying to make the case for an approach that calls for early performance analysis and architectural exploration (at the system level) before committing to hardware. The memory architectures of the above processors were used as a vehicle. We were tempted to use these architectures by the fact that there were published results that clearly show the benefits of the Opteron memory architecture when compared to the Xeon FSB architecture and this would no doubt provide us with a reference against which we can validate the simulation results obtained using VisualSim.

Additionally, and to the best of our knowledge, we could not identify any published work that discusses the performance of the two memory architectures at the system level using an approach similar to the one facilitated by VisualSim.

Using VisualSim, a model of the system can be constructed in few days. All of the system design aspects can be addressed using validated parametric library components. All of the building blocks, simulation platforms, analysis, and debugging required to construct a system are provided in a single framework.

Synopsys integrated Cossap (dynamic data flow) and SystemC (digital) into System Studio while VisualSim combines SystemC (digital), synchronous data flow (DSP), finite state machine (FSM), and continuous time (analog) domains. Previous system level tools typically supported a single modeling specific domain. Furthermore, relative to prior generations of graphical modeling tools, VisualSim integrates as many as thirty bottom-up components functions into a single system level, easy to use, reusable blocks, or modules.

Finally, it is worth mentioning that results obtained using the VisualSim environment in this work are generally in line with results and conclusions found in the literature [14–16].

In the work reported here, Simulation runs are performed using a Dell GX260 machine with a P4 processor running at 3.06 GHz, and a 1 Gbyte RAM.

For simulation purposes and to test the performance of both architectures, traffic sequences are used to trigger the constructed models. These sequences are defined data structures in VisualSim; a traffic generator emulates application-specific traffic. The *Transaction_Source* block in Figures 4 and 8 is used to generate tasks that are applied to the processors as input stimuli. These tasks are benchmarks consisting of a varied percentage mix of integer, floating-point, load/store, and branch instructions. The different percentages are inserted into the software generator's *Instruction_Mix* file and supplied to the processor cores. Thirty three tasks (Table 2) were generated and used to assess the performance of the DirectConnect and the Shared Bus architectures.

Table 3 shows the "Task Latencies" and "Cycles/Task" measured for both processors. Since the models were constructed by having similar configurations in almost every aspect except the memory architecture, the values obtained are therefore a reflection of the performance of that architecture. Figure 10 is a graph of the "Latency per Task" results for each configuration. This graph is plotted using the total number of clock cycles that were taken by each task. The instructions contained in each of these tasks are defined in the software_generation block. At the end of the execution, a text file is generated by VisualSim that contains the number of cycles that were taken by each of the task, including the stall time and the delays caused by the components linking the RAM to the cores.

Table 2. Benchmark tasks [12].

Model task name	Actual task name
Task_0	DFT
Task_1	DFT
Task_2	DFT
Task_3	CS_Weighting
Task_4	IR
Task_5	Q_Taylor_Weighting
Task_6	CS_Weighting
Task_7	IR
Task_8	Q_Taylor_Weighting
Task_9	CS_Weighting
Task_10	IR
Task_11	Q_Taylor_Weighting
Task_12	CS_Weighting
Task_13	IR
Task_14	Q_Taylor_Weighting
Task_15	CS_Weighting
Task_16	IR
Task_17	Q_Taylor_Weighting
Task_18	CS_Weighting
Task_19	IR
Task_20	DFT
Task_21	DFT
Task_22	DFT
Task_23	DFT
Task_24	DFT
Task_25	DFT
Task_26	DFT
Task_27	DFT
Task_28	DFT
Task_29	DFT
Task_30	DFT
Task_31	DFT
Task_32	DFT

Table 3. Task latencies and Cycles/Task.

Task_Name	$Latency_{(Opteron)}$	$Latency_{(Xeon)}$	$Cycles/Task_{(Opteron)}$	$Cycles/Task_{(Xeon)}$
Task_0	1.21E-7	1.27E-7	247	260
Task_1	7.713E-7	7.99E-7	1579	1636
Task_2	7.235E-7	7.299E-7	1481	1494
Task_3	6.538E-7	6.605E-7	1338	1352
Task_4	8.538E-7	1.027E-6	1748	2103
Task_5	7.358E-7	7.415E-7	1506	1518
Task_6	7.453E-7	7.52E-7	1526	1540
Task_7	8.538E-7	1.0222E-6	1748	2093
Task_8	7.362E-7	7.43E-7	1507	1521
Task_9	6.783E-7	7.051E-7	1389	1444
Task_10	8.538E-7	1.0241E-6	1748	2097
Task_11	6.858E-7	7.09E-7	1404	1452
Task_12	7.1629E-7	7.216E-7	1466	1478
Task_13	8.537E-7	1.0179E-6	1748	2084
Task_14	7.298E-7	7.365E-7	1494	1508
Task_15	7.133E-7	7.196E-7	1460	1473
Task_16	8.537E-7	1.0251E-6	1748	2099
Task_17	7.11299E-7	7.169E-7	1456	1468
Task_18	6.862E-7	6.92E-7	1405	1417
Task_19	1.5795E-6	1.9301E-6	3234	3952
Task_20	7.4229E-7	7.482E-7	1520	1532
Task_21	2.6452E-6	3.3117E-6	5417	6782
Task_22	7.4649E-7	7.769E-7	1528	1591
Task_23	2.6454E-6	3.3002E-6	5417	6758

Task_24	7.4529E-7	7.52E-7	1526	1540
Task_25	2.6451E-6	3.3039E-6	5417	6766
Task_26	7.523E-7	7.58E-7	1540	1552
Task_27	2.645E-6	3.3078E-6	5416	6774
Task_28	7.458E-7	7.524E-7	1527	1540
Task_29	2.6453E-6	3.3313E-6	5417	6822
Task_30	7.9129E-7	7.976E-7	1620	1633
Task_31	2.6453E-6	3.2723E-6	5417	6701
Task_32	7.558E-7	7.6189E-7	1547	1560

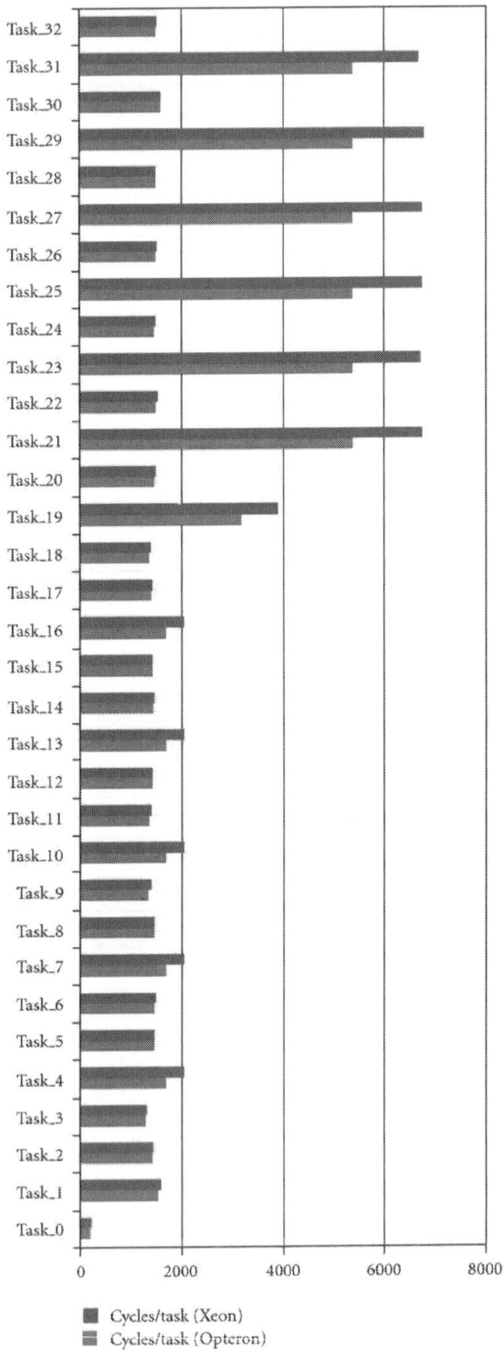

Figure 10. Latency per Task (Cycles per Task).

Cleary, the Xeon has exhibited a higher latency in almost every task. These numbers show that the time taken to execute the same task in the Xeon were more than the Opteron.

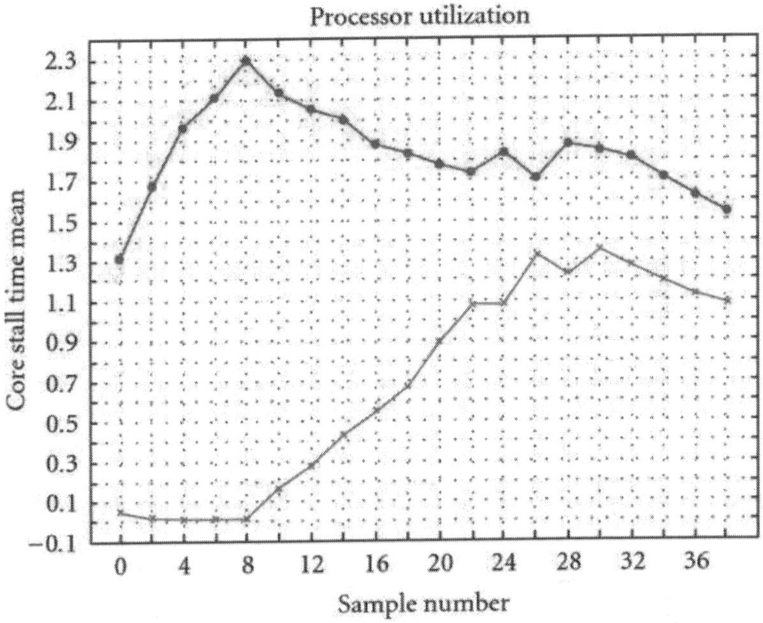

Figure 11. Processor Stall Times (Opteron).

Figures 11 and 12 show a graph of processors' stall times. In both cases, 20 samples are taken during the entire simulation period and the data collected is used in the depicted graphs. During the execution of all the tasks, the maximum time for which the processors stalled was different for each kind of architecture. The maximum stall time for the DirectConnect architecture was 2.3 microseconds whereas for the Shared Bus architecture the maximum stall time was 2.9 microseconds. Due to the shared bus in the Xeon's architecture, delays were greater than the DirectConnect approach of the Opteron, and thus the difference in the stall time.

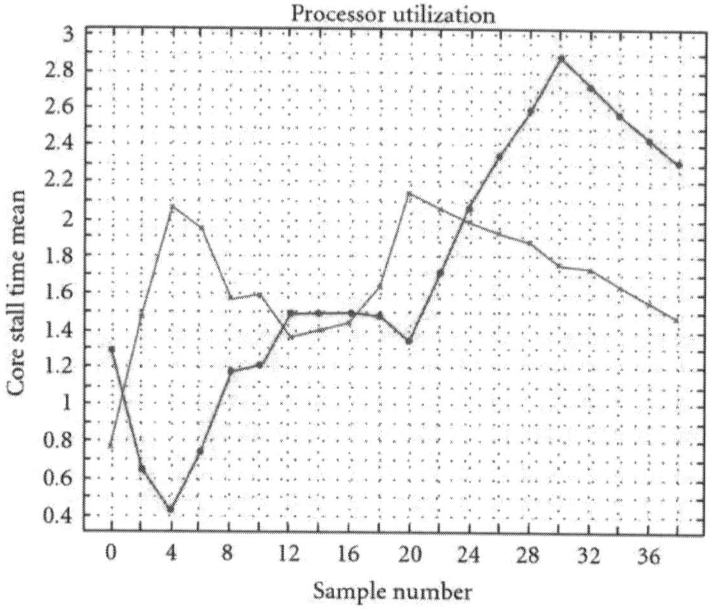

Figure 12. Processor Stall Times (Xeon).

As the models described earlier suggest, the Opteron follows the split cache approach where each core in the processor has its own L1 and L2 cache; thus no part of the cache is shared between the two cores. On the contrary, the Xeon processor employs the shared cached technique and thus both the cores have access to a larger amount of cache than the ones in the Opteron. Whenever one of the cores in the Xeon is not accessing the shared cache, the other core has complete access to the entire cache which results in a higher hit ratio.

Table 4 shows the hit-ratios of both the architecture models. As the values suggest, the hit-ratios of the Xeon/Shared cache are higher than those of the Opteron/split cache, the reason being discussed above. It is worth mentioning that few simplifying assumptions were made to the memory architectures operation of both processors as discussed in Section 3.

Table 4. Hit ratios.

Hit Ratios (%)	Opteron	Xeon
Processor_1_D_1_Hit_Ratio_Mean	97.23	98.37
Processor_1_I_1_Hit_Ratio_Mean	92.13	95.11
Processor_2_D_1_Hit_Ratio_Mean	98.98	99.92
Processor_2_I_1_Hit_Ratio_Mean	95.21	96.14
L_2_Hit_Ratio_Mean	N/A	96.36

5. CONCLUSIONS

In this work, we utilized a system modeling methodology above the detailed chip implementation level that allows one to explore different designs without having to write Verilog, VHDL, SystemC, or simply C/C++ code. This approach contributes to a considerable saving in time and allows for the exploration and assessment of different designs prior to implementation.

Since predictability of performance is critical in microprocessors design, simulation models can be used to evaluate architectural alternatives and assist in making informed decisions. Simulation is an acceptable performance modeling technique that can be used to evaluate architectural alternatives and features. In this work, we used Virtual System Prototyping and simulation to investigate the performance of the memory subsystems of both, the Opeteron, and the Xeon dual core processors.

Simulation results indicate that the Opteron has exhibited better latency than the Xeon for the majority of the tasks. In all cases, it either outperformed the Xeon or at least had similar latency. This demonstrates that using an FSB as the only means of communication between cores and memory has resulted in an increase in stalls and latency. On the other hand, in the DirectConnect Architecture, the cores being directly connected to the RAM, via the crossbar switch and the SRQ which were running at processor speed, had minimal delays. Each RAM request from either of the cores was sent individually to the SRQ blocks and they were routed to the RAM that had its memory controller on-chip and the cores did not have to compete for a shared resource.

REFERENCES

1. Balakrishnan S, Rajwar R, Upton M, Lai K: **The impact of performance asymmetry in emerging multicore architectures.** *Proceedings 32nd International Symposium on Computer Architecture (ISCA '05), June 2005, Madison, Wis, USA* 506-517.
2. Conway P, Hughes B: **The AMD Opteron Northbridge architecture.** *IEEE Micro* 2007,**27**(2):10-21.
3. Keltcher CN, McGrath KJ, Ahmed A, Conway P: **The AMD Opteron processor for multiprocessor servers.***IEEE Micro* 2003,**23**(2):66-76.
4. **Dual-Core Intel® Xeon® Processor 5000 Series Datasheet** May 2006
5. Varada R, Sriram M, Chou K, Guzzo J:**Design and integration methods for a multi-threaded dual core 65nm XeonÂ ® processor.** *Proceedings of IEEE/ACM International Conference on Computer-Aided Design, Digest of Technical Papers (ICCAD '06), November 2006, San Jose, Calif, USA* 607-610.
6. Prowse-Fosler L: **Virtual Systems Prototyping Ensures Reusable Design Platforms.** http://www.vastsystems.com/solutions-technical-papers.html
7. **Mirabilis Design User's Manual** vol. 1, http://www.mirabilisdesign.com/
8. **HyperTransport I/O Link Specification** http://www.hypertransport.org/
9. http://www.chiparchitect.com/
10. http://www.amd.com/us-en/Processors/

11. Rusu S, Tam S, Muljono H, *et al.*:**A 65-nm dual-core multithreaded Xeon® processor with 16-MB L3 cache.***IEEE Journal of Solid-State Circuits* 2007,**42**(1):17-24.

12. Shankar D: **Selecting Memory Controllers for DSP Systems.** DSP DesignLine, May 2007

13. Tarn S, Rusu S, Chang J, Vora S, Cherkauer B, Ayers D:**A 65nm 95W dual-core multi-threaded Xeon ®processor with L3 cache.** *Proceedings of IEEE Asian Solid-State Circuits Conference (ASSCC '06), November 2006, Hangzhou, China* 15-18.

14. Peng L, Peir J-K, Prakash TK, Chen Y-K, Koppelman D: **Memory performance and scalability of Intel's and AMD's dual-core processors: a case study.** *Proceedings of the 27th IEEE International Performance, Computing, and Communications Conference (IPCCC '07), April 2007, New Orleans, La, USA* 55-64.

15. Guiang CS, Milfeld KF, Purkayastha A, Boisseau JR: **Memory performance of dual-processor nodes: comparison of Intel Xeon and AMD Opteron memory subsystem architectures.** *Proceedings for ClusterWorld Conference & Expo, 2003*

16. **Advanced Micro Devices: AMD Opteron vs Intel Xeon Processor Performance Comparison** http://www.veritest.com/

Index